Theatre Series by Michael O'Connor

This is the third installment in the BhamAMP Business Arts MediaPlex Theatre Series written for smooth, snag free performance on all types of stages should they exit in physical or virtual terrains. Interests in performance are not absolute or conditional, and one assumes that they will be less structured than normal; given that normalcy was never a requirement.

In short, these plays were conceptualized and developed as immersive visualization environments which combine the fine arts and digital display information for multi-screen, multi-media and multi-modal purposes. Having fun with them is indispensible provided that attribution is a vital constituent of a thing called production: that without which a thing cannot be itself.

The Theatre Series includes the following releases:

Jack's Day off

Veracity of Ghost Light

Perceptive Sensations

BhamAMP Business Arts MediaPlex

BhamAMP is involved with the publication of immersive environments providing for the collection integration and display of visual, audio and kinaesthetic data. Conceptualize and develop three dimensional visualization environments which combine the fine arts and digital display information for multi-screen, multi-media and multi-modal purposes.

www.bhamamp.com

Perceptive Sensations:
A new Guide to Theatre

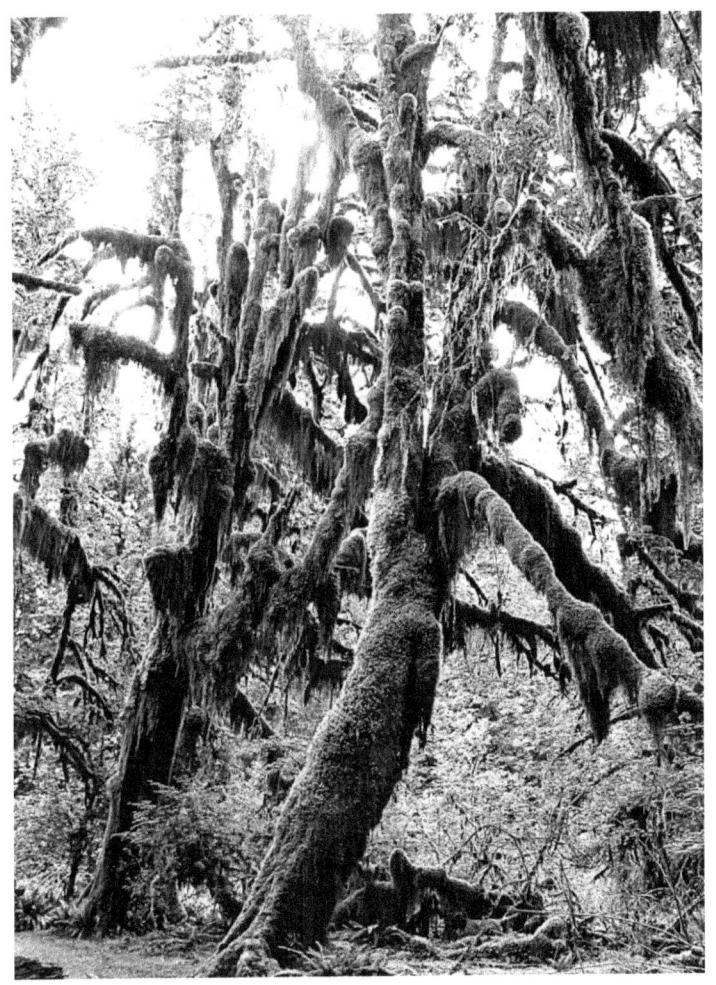

Michael O'Connor

ALSO BY MICHAEL O'CONNOR

Silhouettes 3

Cumulative Evidence

Jack's Day Off

Evidence of Consciousness

Veracity of Ghost Light

Fortuitous Event

Capriciously Opaque

Narrative Arcs

Enjoy the warmth of summer literally

CONTENTS

Enter this Stage

THERE ARE AS MANY other perspectives in theatre which all appear to have gotten closer than they should have given this specific set of circumstances. This is not what is troubling per se, in that even a common set of beliefs can be viewed as unique enough to go through all of the trouble. It is not 'group think'; not any more than the occasional repeats of a vein of thought in repeated measure. It starts internally.

It is simply an occasion for which this one observation seems to be a point of clarity after considerable review. The vision is inside ultimately. There are those externalities that stream or thread and influence, but never are they more profound than when absorbed, mulled over—churned even—before they can be assembled into something that much more tangible, and then spewed out via a chosen artful medium. And as they once said: "The medium is the message."

What better way of expressing this than through an artful production via a suitable stage.   It is a beginning; this initial recasting of all of those external sources into a stream of thought and projected just loudly enough.

The audience is a participant, better yet a recipient: will refer to the cause of the reaction as a personal account more or less because they have felt it at a peculiar time and place: able to absorb it on face value as if it was replayed for the first instance as their own unique interpretation. It is done with purpose and with cautionary tale: this instance is one's own unique experience prevailed; recanted in a common language to make it seem just more recognizable. And when it is recognized it is confirmed by the recipient and thus the action continues: analysis of variance with oft repeated measures: making this more public than previously known.

The plain truth is it was done by no one's mastery. However, when it is done it becomes more useful— reckoned with if you will—if the experience was common enough to be read across many thoughtful faces.   This thing called audience.   If it is clear enough, and not too abstract or hazy, it can be said it was experienced.   For better or worse, unless this audience is stone cold, something is embraced.

The first time he saw it lately, he was out and about on a very well traveled trail called the North Fork.   Its location is in the Pacific Northwest and at a higher elevation wonderful views on a semi dry path, the damp earth is side-to-side, warm sun is experienced but not felt because this is one dense forest. The smell of the snow is there but the sensation is distant: packed ice and glacier can be viewed at the very top of the closest peak but it is many miles away. It is in latitude forty-eight and this is a very common site when one looks east into the North Cascades. It has appeared too many instances at a multitude of bearings, purviews and distances, yet it is different for all of those who witness it for the first or even several dozen times.

When one is standing solo away from the road and chasing this view down the rushing torrents of the glacier fed river are a doorway to another kind of voyage step after careful step. This is ever expected yet never normal until one gradually adjusts to the noise and accompanying cool air; transverse the trail upward and onward through trees which only hint that there is sun and blue sky up above.

He—so let's personalize this—is now standing in front of it for as many moments half past the hour of high noon pointing northwest, expecting to turn northeast after a few more deliberating minutes. Has he left anything of importance behind in the automobile that brought him here His principal goal is to somehow capture the moments and sensations that lay on each side of the trail he is following, especially for this time of year, without fear of retribution that something else should have been packed. It is best on this occasion to take it in all alone, to anchor one's self to the chore of making both time and distance as fast and as far from the noise of the road that brought him here in the first place. Carry as little as possible but in one's comfort zone.

He wants to feel the isolation. Who wouldn't under these very same circumstances? It is this appeal that he wants to convey to that eventual audience sitting patiently in comfortable chairs and in eager anticipation.

It is truly hoped that one hour has passed at the very least. The first scene: a trail rises steadily and the trek is fast but he is not out of breath just yet. This is a labor of love (perhaps even lust) as there are many precisely energizing scenes as there are turn offs from this well maintained trail. The river to his right is moving fast and he can only guess its depth as seven to twelve feet at the next opening between the trees.

The center of the river seems to be moving the swiftest and he is dizzied by his position on the high and deadly sloped bank. One foot is maintained close to one another given the fatality of the potential fall. The waterline is generally high and the cold from the rushing water makes this section of the forest trail feel as if he has stepped into a walk-in freezer. The shoreline is steep and his breath is actually shortened simply by the breathtakingly splendid vistas. Were this a panoramic view it could not ever be improved.

The trail is wide enough for two to pass side-by-side should the effort ever be warranted. He is forcing himself to move ahead and steps across a solidly built human made bridge over a dip in the path. He manages to weigh in, in his head, but most certainly does not feel the strain or give of the footpath underneath his dead weight. It appears superbly built and well maintained.

He knows the best is yet to come around the next bend, at least several miles in from the road. It will be a highly anticipated sandy cove off to the right and he has to step around at least three fallen trees to accomplish this task. There is a good place to contemplate the speed of the water ahead. This is a great place to contemplate the manner in which previous visitors stacked rocks carefully and thoughtfully for those who would come later. And he adds several of his own because this tradition must be carried on.

Between this and his last possible footsteps to the river's edge lay a few scattered bushes and plants which seem able to survive under a dense canopy and very sandy soil. A few birds and insects scatter when he arrives but then reappear after he has settled in. There is an abundance of river polished boulders securing the ford across this section of the river, resulting in several beautiful cascading waterfalls around two to three feet high. They cannot secure this load: the excessive force of water wandering down from the glacier and out toward a bay twenty-seven miles away is not to be underestimated, and least not ignored. The boulders seem secure this particular scene for a very long time. They are built to succumb to the rush of the powerful waters converting glassy surface to brilliant white foam. They appear to maintain a kind of fortress, securing millions of gallons of fresh water for seconds alone.

Try to hold your breath for half as long while watching this scene.

It did not matter much that he has thrown a flat stone across the face of the fortress and it is blasted away at a very high rate of speed. It may be said now that this was as unique a scene, even though it must have been tried numerous times before. The stone has been carried out of sight, so the story remains with the perpetrator alone. It is his to retell anyway that he might want to, though some of it will remain recognizable as a varied and repeated measure since most in this audience have done the same.

What insight. Is the arc of the stone a metaphor for happiness?

It was soon after he captured that event that he ventures further up shore to another sandy inlet and similarly fine beach. This place was the most inviting kind and the flood of sunshine invites him to sit down and dine, so to speak, on the smells, skin sensations and tastes of the cool air mixed with the fragrance of the woods on both shores. It fills his soul with a kind of rebirth. It was this principle perception and sensation of isolation from the highway and other synthetic creations that enabled him to dwell deeply into the patters in the sand as simply divine. There enough to see and feel in this instance to last a lifetime.

Will this do for others? Could they be carried there by words on a page or actors on a stage? This remains to be seen.

The trail continues with an incline that is steep but not one that encumbers. He is hoping to see what is on top even though he has been here many times before this particular outing. If one had a bota bag one would have taken a long draw at the top of this current ascent and let the wine it would have contained fulfill a mouth's desire will dribbling down a wishful chin.

The land here is damp and full and it always makes one think of the wine laced by youthful indiscretions: we did this during our late teens; most of us doing so with repeated measure. There were not many places then that wine failed to play at least some role in enjoying nature. It was an intermixing of the abundance of open places to travail and the culture of what one brought along in that time. He is essentially singularly in the same patterns of behavior in where he chooses to trend, and yet his wine intake has risen to another level of sophistication. He now brings glass tumblers and bottled wine, rather by habit, and has forgotten about the assortment of bota bags previously owned. Youthful indiscretions do not necessarily need to be stopped cold.

Apparently enough of the resemblance to the past is fulfilled and he moved on. A thirst can be quenched in so many ways. At the top of the next ascent he is sweaty; the heart rate is faster and the breathing is harder with close to pure jubilation. One labors on, doesn't one.

The moss over tree branches are his chief source of entertainment as they seem to have taken on the characteristics of a play already in motion—a truly agreeable prospect. Branches reaching out to touch others alarms and entertains simultaneously. Their clustering appearance is not at all uniform and takes on a strong abstract presence: two fighting, three hugging, four fleeing, and one staring intently at this observer. Two are very tall and the rest are closer in general height and pleasant enough to retain this captured audience for the next thirty minutes. These are pretty high stakes to make given the extensive tracks yet to come. There is an abundance of handsome species up above and he is mesmerized by this locale but it is shaken off by the pull of the sound of rushing water over that next hill. There it is through this long arm hanging across a sun drenched meadow acting as a monitor to the next scene. Would he dare trespass across without proper introduction? There is something beyond and he can feel it and he can see it now. Push back those curtains; see the stage, listen to this dialog.

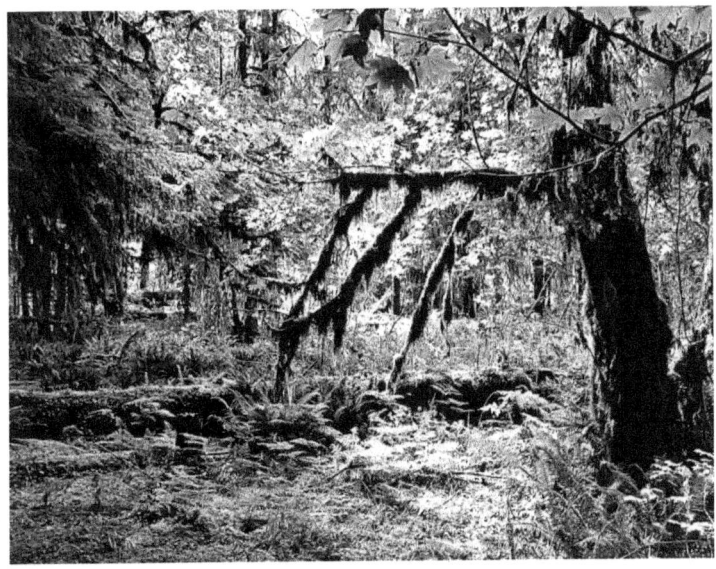

HE SAID: *I want to avoid all distraction. If there is a time and a means for true introspection this must be it. A strain of thought occurs to me almost like a superior figure appears in a forest one thinks is void of all other persons, not because we are connected, but because I could only handle so much distance from civilization. I am connected even when I attempt to get away. My thoughts about this figure are rendered in a stream of*

21

conscious images too deliberate to be random. They have been exactly ascertained, no disillusion, and in direct line of sight. This is as clear a straight line as one can conjure up what one wants to be perceptible especially when one is too alone for too long, even on a crowded planet. Being solo now is out of the question.

Yes, he can see those glaciers more clearly once he is past the forest. The glaciers stand and reflect as icy steeples on the top of this very mountain, just beyond that gateway; this enters his mind wholly.

The air is now very cold and the smell of deep ice and packed snow is overwhelming. The forest is now sparse and the moss covered (living) actors are left behind for the time being. The snow crunches loudly under his boots and it is a very curious sound; just pleasant enough to overcome his shivering and the fact that he am walking at a very high elevation with regard to the bay and then sea well off in the distance to the west. The cloud lines are sparse up above: open skies to the east and a very clear horizon to the west: benefit from this elevation because of the trade winds which are able to reach him just now.

He can smell salt in the air and consequently the powered layers on his skin protect his sweat from freezing.

This is the theatre that goes on: the dense forest, a clear sky, and the clarity that standing on a glacier brings to this scenario. The stage is set and he will leave it because ultimately he just needed to seek out the resultant perceptions and sensations, write them all down with equal clarity, and then prepare them for another kind of entertainment medium.

Who do these voices belong to that enter our head? They say what we mean, not what we said.

Theatre is this crazy thing.

Perceptive Sensations   Michael O'Connor

Screen One

IN THE NEXT FEW DAYS it all elapsed before the scheduled arrival of the inbound troupe; I had to leave the studio before they all changed their minds. The previously sedate group was becoming nervous and worried about the impending cost to the studio for putting on this kind of elaborate production, and members of our ad hoc financial committee agreed that the new venue was not entirely prudent—this happy expression used by one more than one, then clearly embraced by the others in turn. There was still much to do before the troupe's arrival: those things I had not looked at since the distant days when a usually astute assistant covered such details: conspicuously displaced so literally by no other's fault but my own.

I had driven her to take leave. Perhaps I drove her mad—so time would tell.

The overhauling of the department I was in charge of revealed the fact that there was nothing that would bear a more critical eye than that of an entire revamping for the good of all. More ever, the best had to be made of a sequence of events which were consequentially cascading, much like a carefully assisted landslide. No matter how careful the preparation things easily go astray when one link is broken or gone missing. And that link was my thoughtful and detailed-oriented assistant who made a brave attempt to get past me and through the front door.

An amazing amount of preparation was required for the theatre to be turned into a puppet master's ideal environment. Puppet master was what she called me on the friendlier days. Equipment not already in the theatre had to be first located, selected and then transported back requiring a great deal of personal travel—journeys for which a more than astute assistant was clearly groomed for—the last presented a massive and somewhat hysterically obvious void for someone in particular. Honor to a prescribed contract must be tightly adhered to; revelations held by many more; I felt this to be prolonged for my survival alone.

In fact, for everyone now looking on, many more were waiting in the shadows to declare quick success or painfully slow failure. The interest in these particular proceedings was profound, if not just. Would she stay or would she go—there were bets to this regard.

This was a self centered crisis and would call on the principal character to go home to his last place of residence. This was definitely not a practiced honor— the need to recall all of the natty details of why I had left in the first place it reminded me of my place in an industry once thought to have disappeared. This theatre had been my home for three rewarding years.

Going back now was addressed as keenly needed rather than hotly desired. I was going home to anticipated criticism with regard to my hurried departure in the first place—telling them about my happenstance was going to be a fiasco: the facts not entirely claimed by one, yet clearly not forthcoming by others in first person (second or even third person).

Let's go with second person. It is more meaningful for the purpose of this stage.

This meant that he was going home to tell them about his other side in second person: a kind of fear more than fact and as difficult to wash down. The half empty wine glass was his third: drank with refreshment of semi stale artesian bread and a very acceptable soft brie cheese. How was he going to tell them about it: now that it was his choice of living somewhere between here and there: living was a matter of conjecture not a quest.

In the interest of placating himself he wore a little grin of what had been known. However, the object of his fear was one which was of keen interest, well hidden, and what else was knowable about it or subsequently related to his decision to run away would be in no way understandable by most. He rationalized a bit about it: off the beaten tracks, quite unexpectedly out of character, an allusion for sure.

There was no way to hide from the surprise it would bring to those faces of who he feared most from the resultant exposure. Avoidance was impossible, for him to return, and attempt some kind of performance that would be acceptably sincere, as expected of him. He was doomed to prolong the inevitable as much as he can; an attempt to perform any other way made him insecure.

In due time he left and then he arrived at the designated location, weather permitting. The next morning was already past and the following afternoon was already underway, and it was foggy. Several members of the community came out to see him walking cautiously down the main street. They were staring calm, intending to allow him to cross over the main street and make way into a principal café. Their stances were not meant to be superior over the tepidness to the well known traveler. It took all of the remaining moments of the passing of cash for hot tea and pastry before visual instructions and shared endeavors all to come to a single spot in the café and settle down at a round table of four—including my nervous assistant.

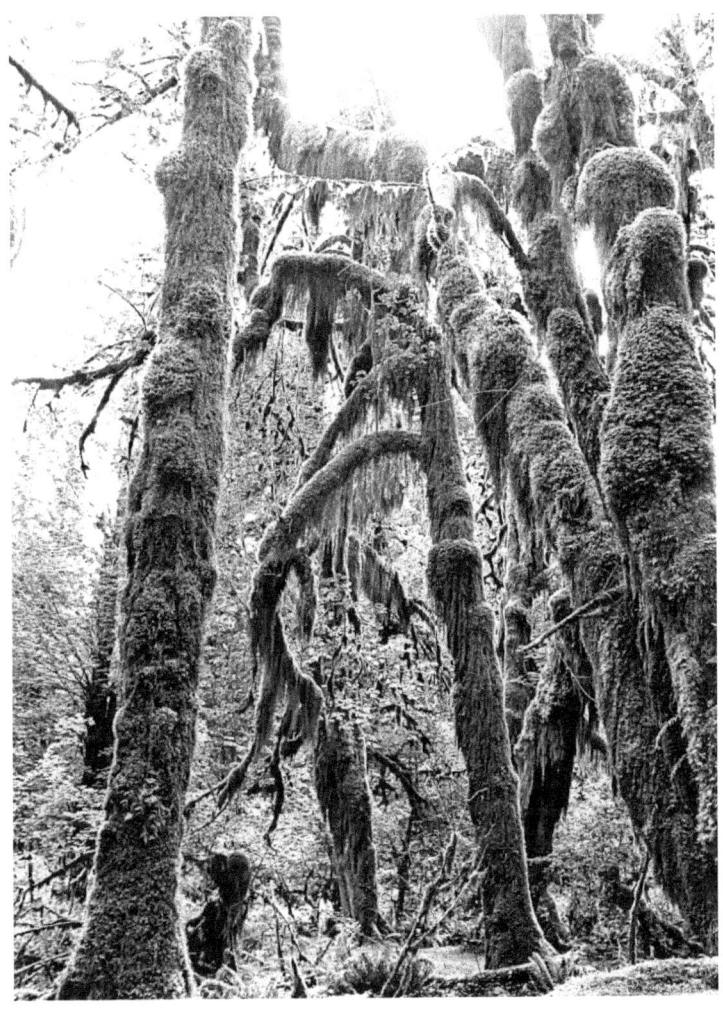

VOICE ONE: *I want to find a place in time, in my head, where I celebrated a sense of calm. I make no claim to*

this consideration other than it seems attractive right now. It never has ceased to amaze me that most of thoughts are described as a third person exploration; passing collections of remembrances in review with brilliant detail as if first person were not enough. This transposition of voices is most striking: the length is shorter and condensed, it is in several degrees of separation, and it has somehow become a group.

No one leaned in to demand the details of another's absence but there were a number of little stares and hand positioning, shoulder drops and upper torso shifts to warrant some level of examination. The transition is caught. This play is under way.

This caused the traveler to sulk quietly in his chair while reading in all of the non verbal communications which made the passage of time very noisy. This was not a secluded calm by any means. There were others standing, walking around with their orders, and taking seats and sides in this ongoing silent movie. And thus the action sans dialog rolled on for a purposeful amount of time, beyond that the greater populous stared with amusement and subdued admiration with regard to his return.

He sits and he stares off into some kind of oblivion. Then his face is firm and is returned to the issues at hand.

At first glimpse, to those who were either new to the scene of not knowledgeable of who had returned, distance and remoteness comingled. In this local oasis of civilization every scene imaginable was possible judging by the looks of those in the know, and those who were mere spectators. At what time anyone at the four top would engage in more meaningful interaction was up in the air, until a new entry extended a more complimentary note of hospitality here: emoted versus logic and reason: a sort of complaint balanced with a compliment.

"What are you doing back here?" The intension was slightly less than angry yet the manner was a demand.

"I am back here for business."

To the one who had started this dialog, this reply appeared full of necessary details, given the strength of the expressions returned.

The fact that no one else at the table further contested the shortness of the answer caused a number of close by listeners to exhibit signs of perplex. One of the nearby parties was a middle aged woman with bundled up silver hair and pursed lips. She alone looked as if the answer was incomplete, perhaps incomprehensible.

The mood at the table remained congenial enough and fresh insights were exchanged while coffee and tea were sipped, and the occasional nibbles on pastries ensued. It was not as though this single fellow were a world resounded celebrity of good cause, know to all for philanthropic work, carrying with him a title of nobleman. The event of his return, however, was another matter altogether. How this globetrotter got here was of chief concern.

During the course of the memorable reunion a few thanked him for his return, even though it was not preannounced. To anyone within earshot most at the table seemed to be extending their thanks, respectively. This was a genuine quality of members of this close nit community—the genus of this breed—provided at leisure, with leveling ease, and of course with shared regard without outlandish proportion.

The traveler carried with him a returned earnestness and shared with them in return a stack of papers. We are now five.

With another run of coffee and tea returned to this round table the exact nature of these papers was disclosed—slowly. It would have been interesting to the viewer outside of the circumference of this table to peruse its bounty content during the extensive review.

The task at hand would have been keenly interesting to know, if one had been exposed to what it proposed, and at the exact time allowed. High voices were followed by low whispers and the foursome plus one lean into the table's inner circle. This had now become his community and everyone else were just extras in the passing shot, had this example been captured on camera and microphone. There were no pressures for anyone outside of this four plus one top to act if by example, no pressure to pretend toward nonchalant, and certainly no need for more legitimate curiosity.

Everyone else beyond this table was simply left behind. The pressure to release the contents of this loose leaf book was contained to the elite five. And soon enough it was all over and it was declared a victory of sorts.

"Good job, one and all."

It echoed around the proximity of the table. People went their own way. Tomorrow is another day, indeed.

Midway in the afternoon on the follow day two people intersected on a path bisecting a local park: a connection not unlike an incoming tide receding back into the sea. A particularly long and concrete bench became the object of mutual interest to the walkers, as they soon joined together to exchange greetings and review of once distant parts in this ongoing saga. The location both enveloped and became the embodiment of the personalities at hand: facial corrections, properly placed hands and feet, similarity in smiles exchanged, and a vocal tone held in moderated respect.

To the onlooker—this always seems to be the case—these two no longer held two different parts; counting the long minutes that have passed patiently; one did not stand out as a true test of time; not long since their descending positions were placed firm on expectantly cold and hard cement. The purpose of this engagement would be held at bay for anyone else outside of this angled line of sight, and those intimate, shared insights.

The garments they wore did not disclose anything useful outside of the fact that they were both dress smartly and continued with specific allure to each other: neither suffered prolonged sparks or remorse, bolting from the scene was not an apparent goal, body positioning suggests more than a modicum of comfort: players and talent.

In this case their interactions subscribed to considerable interest to a third party maintaining at liberty a superb distance—out of earshot but definitely within visual range. The third party appeared agitated from time-to-time: on foot crossing over the other and then returned, jacket adjusted more than necessary, and a single cigarette placed between two lips repeatedly while never lit. This might have caught on had the other transients in the park not been so obsessed with their own well being.

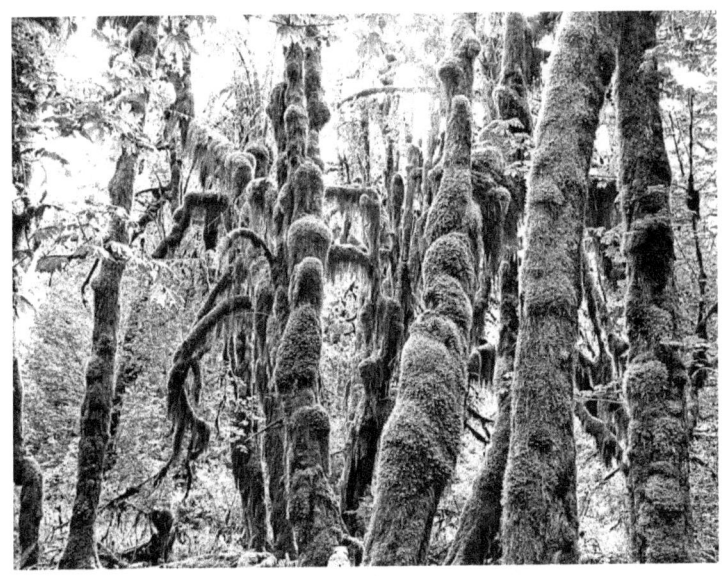

VOICE ONE: *The self wills. The course of many decades it produces great change in inner perspective, carried forward from our places in the past, and even representing things in the future we hope to see, hear and feel. Why? Do we need to seek future representation of self to survive; if so for how long? I guess these things occur to form a picture of the effects of human mobility: showing the change from the original point of perspective to where we have arrived at some more definitive point in time due simply because we can comprehend it all. It strikes me that the eye and point of view are so vastly different at times that the clearer the significance of our movements, the more remote our recollection of the original point of motion. We invent novelty, legends and myths to build up those*

*distances. Our knowledge of our selves is most relative
to the distance from the original act.*

The pair embarked along an inner path, sooner than later. The walk must have been tremendous given their comfortable pace climbed to a higher tempo, eyes on each other and other objects of shared delight, laughter which became louder than before, and several well matched and kindly nods to others passing along the same trail.

The views that afternoon were delightful: tall trees stand alone, birds and squirrels in and out of branches, groomed flowerbeds, neatly trimmed and well maintained grows existing on either edges of this trail ways.   There was never a moment's deviation from the task at hand including walking, talking, and an occasional unintentional brush of shoulder, elbow and hand. These two did not remain aloof—present company was presented and remained in good control. As a matter of fact, the incident of this stroll remains in his memory as well as hers for a much longer while, than expected.

Soon, the only departure from this vision was the addition of one bottle of red wine and two stemmed glasses. The two found another suitable place to descend and poured and both drank, and then this became a picture perfect moment for a town, almost lost had not a visiting photographer pressed in to capture the moment forever. And here this lingering peek of a private moment rendered quite public; the half written story explicitly revealed is told, based on the instinct of another's finger on a shutter.

The captured series of snapshots reveal the story within the story. He entertained her with mimicked puppet theatre accentuated with shadows from the cast of a setting sun; those objects varied as one can imagine within a public park; against short wall and a long and smooth path; less audio-graphic and more visually vivid; anchors them just outside of this quaint city with scenes compensating for the usually mundane. The show cast and then captured was filled with excitement and mystery—those scenes which would have to be eventually explained.

"What on earth are you doing?" An older woman's demand echoed out, more demand than accorded for given the rights she had to exclaim. "Please, it looks wonderful. Do not stop on my account."

Her appearance had softened as the moment was explored, and her eyes sparkled as she witnessed the shadows appearance become more shaped and less sentimental. The action became exact enough. And now she was laughing.

"Your art form is true enough," she continued.

However she may have intended to spend her late afternoon, this deviation became most welcome with regard to this beautiful use of an island at the edge of city proper. Her momentum was lost to the growing and entertaining circle—this trio had now gained four more—it was a crowd.

And across the way the shutters counters before the instrument is put away. The event has been captured and played back to recall a memory from the recent past. What a memory it portrays like the arms of a standing of trees seemingly reaching out to grasp something lost then found.

What are they doing indeed—exit this first act.

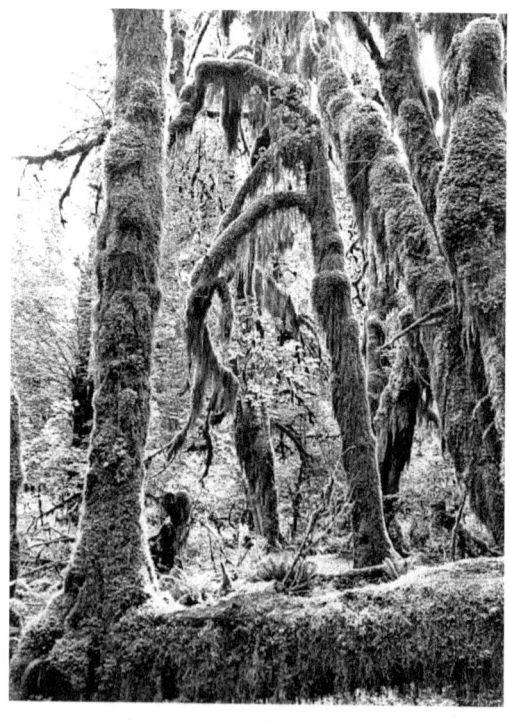

Screen Two

IT SHOULD BE NOTED that this first view of the city is like slicing through a pear: the first several cuts in are full, fresh and ripe, and the closer one gets to the center the harder core the coarser it gets. It was simply an attempt at an approach—this view—and it certainly does not matter if all proper perspectives were not included initially. The facts will come and go as the second views are narrowed in on. It will be as though life was washed onto the screen just as a hard rain sheens and streams torrents well dispersed. Parts of this world will be in better focus than others.

There are aspects of the settings which will be notoriously awkward to describe in the initial passages due to prejudices imposed with comparisons and contrasts to what one may have been exposed to beforehand. What would anyone do to stop the account as to how it relates to personal experience in first person or beyond? Who's version will be subscribed to as the next symptomatic expression finds a way forward as a accumulation of sensations and perceptions that account for cultural bias, a sense of spiritualism, a life's philosophy, a manner of understanding the consequences of subjectivity versus objectivity. We have all dined and quenched our thirsts on this not too exhaustive list.

The test of those who are willing to embrace the time tested resources at hand: an undertaking: is going to prove more evident on the account of our picture of him, whether it by in a first or second person. The account is chaired by the writer, but ultimately the angle of purview is owned by the reader indeed, and had we not visited this contest in this manner well enough in advance, the wrong associations could be carried out of context and intent.

He went forward out of the park and down the street by himself and headed back across town with a specific destination in mind. If one find's the time to take direction all roads will not seem alike, nor will the houses and business aligned on each side.

He has a name and this is probably as good a time to introduce Josh. He walks well, and continues on with intent in this direction past a firehouse and turns suddenly into the driveway of a two story building. While it is never known immediately if he knows the host well, he rings the doorbell at the side of a very large wooden door that is bisected by a single block of colored acrylic at a diagonal. The block is amber toward brown, and is opaque enough as to not reveal too much detail of the inside of the dwelling. Call this an ergonomic digression—as in preserving the anonymity of one who answers the call of the bell, but provides all the details of one's attendance as diffused shadows. It is beautiful and it might possible annoy the ringer, dependent of course to whether the door is every answered or not.

The person inside hesitates and relates to how patient the caller is, hoping most likely that this is the right house. The bell is pushed by Tosh for the second time, preserving the eloquent tension which abounds, and the door is swung wide open while the recipients both show mock surprise. This place, one will come to see, has its little history.

Josh is stepping in by constrained invitation, into a pleasant entryway that is wider than it is deep. The host knew the caller and remains not entirely pleased with the sudden entrance. Perhaps there was some other protocol that was meant to be followed: those strange descriptors that should be known by visitors to call: now held vainly by the only one who understood them all—by the inhabitants.

"I did not know you were back in town." The definitive remark is provided by a woman named Jess. The transgression by Josh and the proactive interrogation by this host have met at crossroads, albeit in an entranceway.

There is no other place to go until this transgression is dealt with: no further footsteps as one met the other as a barrier to pass. It is a puzzling situation, true enough, but this is a hopeful solution.

"I am so sorry I did not call ahead. I wanted to surprise you. Is it all right if I visit you at this time?"

Josh has taken a very necessary next step and leans in to graze her shoulder. She follows through and the suite of exchanges follows a more appropriate protocol after all. Two people have stepped back and they are now heading down a medium hallway less puzzled by what ought to occur next. Guards have been dropped and now the caller has time to admire the beauty of the interior of this home. Arguably, ignorance of local morays has segued into an oratory to explain.

"Tess, I am in town for one week, at least. I am here for little else than telling you there was no other alternative. You see, I am in charge of this little theatre and I have a troupe arriving and expecting that its environment is fully accommodating for their rich presentation style."

He was endearing in his thoughtful presentation of the facts to date, and endeavored to further explain before she forcefully cut him off. If he had not judged his sequence just right, he knew in advance that continuing would become more of a problem. The time seems to pass by slowly. Perhaps he was not going fast enough or not deep enough because she was already looking around her own kitchen for a clock that was supposed to be on one wall versus another. This would not be a trivial task—perhaps even too late—he would try to drive the conversation until she showed signs of relaxing her posture.

In short, what Tess was really doing is searching for the cup of tea she had placed onto the corner of a light blue slate counter. The problem was addressing its last location, not going too deep until the object had been recovered, and tasting if it was cool enough to drink. This was the way she drove her mornings when he lived in this place. There was no rescuing of any conversation or activity until Tess was in possession of her tea. The place still occupied this time as if he had never left; the choice was never his own in those past moments more often revisited than not.

"This explains a lot." Tess had finished her sip with an odd sort of smile. "The magnitude of your explanations remains the same: always self-centered, bordering on the expected narcissistic demeanor. How little you have changed."

Josh wanted to carry forth in retort in approximation. This was one aspect of their past lives that he hoped they would not recalibrate, at least not yet. It was what she alluded to, for sure, and it withered his face and drove away any hope of expressing a middle ground.

"If what you are alluding to is that I am contesting my presence rather than asking for your forgiveness, then I do resign into my corner."

"You no longer have a corner, Josh. Did you forget this too?"

It was said in mockery to his trying to shirk off her attack while backing into the countertop and hopping on top of it to regain his ground. After all, they use to celebrate these points of contention, but now he felt quite out of sync and most certainly off script.

Saved from further scrutiny which could not be combated, the bewildered theatre master took in all of her strange looks and gestures, cutting short the visit to a previous time in his life. He felt dejected and relieved to move on simultaneously; the last passing of sentimentality was when he passed back into the hallway and looked at the front door from the inside for a lingering moment. It was here that civility overcame him and he almost turned around to exchange an apology. But seeming her reflection on the surface of a hallway mirror nearer the kitchen, it was not a welcoming look he espied from his host.

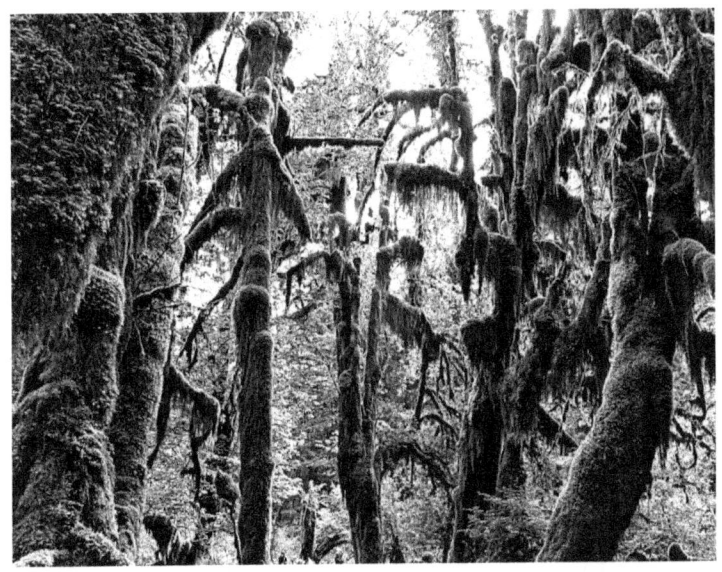

VOICE ONE: *Suppose it were possible to remix time and play it forward in the order of your choosing. Would you take an optimistic or pessimistic approach? It is possible to unravel this accumulation of sense of history in this place in the universe, alter it because no one may ever know, but at the same time be aware of the consequences?*

VOICE TWO: *I suppose it one were able to detect traces of the alterations, and then compare and contrast them to existence. We might never be truly ignorant of the original acts. But what we behold as the truth requires some sort of anchor; even when played out on this different sort of stage. How many worlds like ours are required to indicate significance of the change?*

As one might have been told time-and-time again: "Do not look back unaided on a journey without first removing all traces of virulent feedback; washing away those bad vibes is always more practical than contested. The remainder of his day would include joining other friend for another meal and informing them of his decision to find suitable lodging elsewhere. His house was no longer his most likely domicile—therefore was there anyone else who could put him up for the necessary duration—let him hear the excuses or offerings at considerable risk.

Josh was not about to dine alone, let live alone. To whom the offers rang out, by the first hint of moonlight he would have a place to lay his head. It was a rite of passage—those borne of memories of bygone days when the two of them were happier—stating up at a moon lit sky and seeing a prosperous future. But for now he had a back porch that he could stretch and reflect, and then return to a comfortable bed, to recycle the whole affair over again until he finally drifted to sleep. There was a very agreeable chorus of crickets serenading outside of his open windows, and he swore that he witnessed several bat couples mating in mid air repeatedly. Perhaps it was his projection of the unusual habits they had enjoined, often revisiting the shared gesture in awkward places including their back garden, on their porch, a second story veranda, and once on the very flat roof under a sheet of dense stars. The recapture was more than he could bear for one moment.

It was a less than agreeable span in his life and he began recanting all of the more pleasurable passages: a retelling of love, companionship, and sheer contentment of a life shared with one another. He was now flying solo just like one of those soaring bats that came into the viewing frame of the window. It left him feeling empty and so solitary and stilled. There was something of his life that felt empty, going beyond the fact that his place in theatre was well defined, fulfilling another type of life's dream, in the tight knit family that he now enjoyed at that other far location.

No need to envy the past; murmuring this out loud seemed to bring in a more favorable perspective; he seeks a new form of enjoyment. Under this moon lit evening evolving to early light, he enjoyed a sense of envy putting that chapter behind him right through dawn. This broader swipe of a new chapter was more important for him to go after: the new Society of Friends and gloriously dispensation from his mess with Tess.

Would he come out of it alone, simply groping for answers? His reach is not free as it is attached to something much bigger.

The whole of one environment can never be fully appreciated standing in one position even under a spotlight. Push on and let's see where this next leap of faith might lead—far beyond scripted.

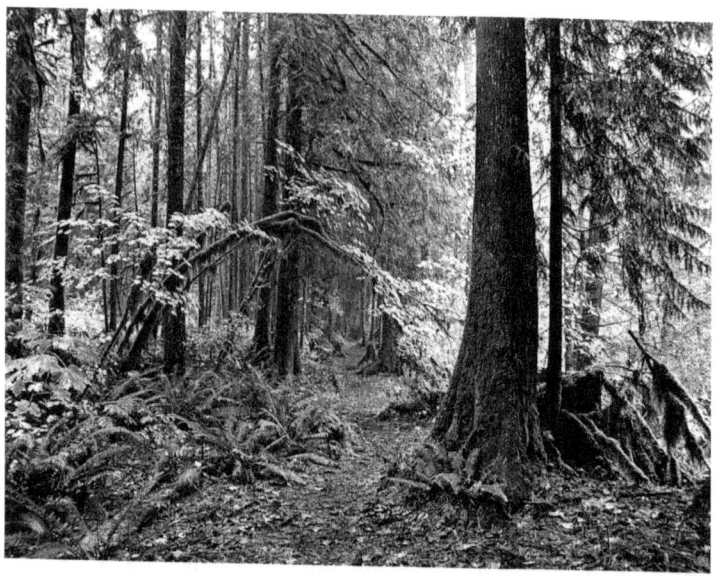

VOICE ONE: *Were it possible that our mix occur—as temporary versus new—how wonderful these aspirations would be. Reality is just a configuration; not in the sense of unlimited remixing in that it would strip out of the original or intended meaning. Subtle change is conceivable as a result of stripping away all of the layers of the original act. This is not something to be shot out of proverbial cannon. It would have a definitive script even though it might change one thousand times with great velocity; erratic yes, but with a sense of record.*

VOICE TWO: *Ignorance or superstitions become all the more profound then what? I would want to be absolutely sure that some resemblance of the truth is retained. I would not want my life to become an infinite duel.*

VOICE ONE: *Truth is an erratic phenomenon. It is not always clear, and we cannot always represent it as an absolute truth, as described. Maybe it is necessarily a duel: suddenness, entirely, amazingly characteristic of something we simply wanted. An event is so often repeated in our conscious and subconscious. Who's to say we do not change it because we do not want to lose interest. What is the first accredited recollection after the fact? This remains to be seen. It becomes an iteration of a play already in progress with as many directions as the mind can conjure up—an artificial repose. Can one see the forest for the trees, if one does not step out and review from a whole lot of different perspectives?*

VOICE TWO: *Like I said: compare and contrast.*

Perceptive Sensations   Michael O'Connor

Screen Three

THE UPCOMING DAY would be easier, with what was expected of him, as he proceeded to realign himself toward the more notable task. He proceeded to exit this residence before the other occupants woke up as house etiquette would demand it. His next move would be to journey over to the next town not more than ten to twelve minutes away, baring moderate traffic flow. It was the residence of a past acquaintance, which first and foremost held Josh in high regard, if he would have the decency to visit once in a while.

His name was already on the building, inscribed in chiseled stone above, and stenciled onto glass on the only entrance on the main street running through town. Josh was particularly jovial when he passed through the glass double doors, swinging both as though he needed to make a grandeur entrance. The faces stared back for a moment, not remembering just who this fellow is, probably more to initial indifference over changes in apparel or appeal that he had shown up at all—this ongoing joke held on. It was almost an anticlimactic coming onto the scene that is until he carefully studied the face of one in particular and saw the smile broaden to beam.

If this were a textbook reception, it would signify that either a famous actor or military general had just entered the vast and open room. It was more than a fair notion of entertainment, when all of the people began to stare, waiting patiently to what would happen next. This visitor soon enough became lionized.

Another semi-official gesture swept across the room as everyone stood and began to clap and cheer loudly—how ever difficult this may be to believe—the response was certainly genuine. And Josh's retort was anything other than arrogant, to these past dwellers of a place he used to own. He had been the infamous provider of well cherished jobs, more hospitable to those direct reports than any other and one step below near perfection.

This was the place of a more than prominent venture: as always he was immediately welcomed once recognized, having said as much by his clearly definitive friends. Keep your friends near and your enemies even closer—a distinction not so queer.

By early afternoon his friends were good to their words of genuine welcome, and he was no longer being treated as a mere guest. The mutual drive for business re-acquaintances was showing to all the beauty of business drive toward a more common goal—a revitalization if you will. The once routine scale of his interactions with this crowd was in good working order and almost as if he never relinquished the reins to his good friend; wondering eyes shined and complimented steadfast smiles for this scene where presence is evidence of a favorite resort. It was the glinted reflection in their eyes that said it loud.

"Welcome back."

Would the traveler be staying any longer was probably the most often sung song as afternoon entered early night and the ongoing business transactions and platitudes near conclusion. Signs of their mutual encounter were flashing on every display and printouts adorned every wall. This previous leader was good to his last word savored words.

"When I return it will be as though I never left at all, I do promise."

"The Europeans will want to have a say in this final approach."

His friend and current leader told it all.

"To suddenly find themselves left out of this side of the project will never be tempered as novel, and will cause more than its share of alarm. Are you up to returning tomorrow morning and participating in a video conference?"

"Yours is an excellent approach to satiating the needs and desires of all involved. However, that said, have any of these members been watching your other venues of business action. Inviting them in carte blanch might prove to be faulty. Can we dwell on the approach past the launch of the next phase?"

Josh had tempered his reply for the sake of not ruining the tempo of the others surrounding the common work and apparent end goal. There was no turning back at this juncture, and certainly no real driving need to inviting too many in to purview progress at hand. Although they may be invited in for watching, he was not ready to provide any real sustainable angle of control. The restart of this theatre depended on his fair sense of self-actualized control.

"It is certainly something we can dwell on for a while longer, my friend."

This was the end of that sort of proposition—to which others outside of this inner circle would have a manner of changing the concepts and aspect of the project day-to-day. The glimpse of mutual understanding that the two leaders shared was not spared from the others. It was by now, quite hopeless if externalities were able to grope or inflict change to the already solidified proposition. Too many chefs spoil the meal—so they are fond of saying.

Someone else offered an opinion, in terms of the 'highest' civility which could be found, without faltering in respect to inclusion and consideration of more distant geographical position.

"The suggestion is definitively vague enough to maintain our position. Let's accept it on face value and carry it forward tomorrow or another two to three days at least."

And so it was decided just then to adopt a position of delaying other's inclusion for another thirty-six hours. The cost of which would be what: hurt feelings, loss of tempers then loss of control and more likely continued indifference of one over the other for a longer period of time. It was a risk worth waiting for—projection was not good fodder for exhaustive discussion or over thoughtfulness.

Then days turn to weeks. No one seems troubled at all.

The accompanying weeks resembled the first one with one significant difference. The principals would stay in close proximity to each other knowledgeably, rather than haphazardly. The only one who seemed less than content with the arrangement was Josh, for whom the task seemed more of a non stopping series of interconnected chores. Each one contributed to the ongoing sum of the project, with some digging in deeper when the principal pushed back.

"Enough is enough. We are still aligned to the principal task, but these details are killing us."

It was not as though Josh was refusing better alignment with them, as much as it was the realization that all had a deep respect for one in particular—Tess--who required a healthy amount of close interaction. Josh felt that the sessions pressed upon him were more or less like crowd control: natives dressed in color and acting with class, ready to pursue the ebb of the next suggestion in unison for the benefit of the whole. It was here that Josh pretended to partake in the daily banter—more gossip than needed—subjecting him to the itinerant daily reminders which described intersection and interactions with his troubling past. Where there was incredible attention to every detail Tess was most certainly involved, and it was made abundantly clear that she was privy to the most intimate progressions of the project at hand.

In short, they had become married to it, the lot of them. And this was not a small group. It was a growing crowd and it had an unmistakable and miserable appearance by the end of that third week.

Let bygones be bygones: rough and steadied in defeat—having nothing else to do there Josh spent most of his time running indoors or walking the back streets n order to hide out. He was as judiciously controlling the outcome of exposure as he was in turn serendipity exposed. A well timed entrance at a local café, even at the oddest hour taking in light morsels and tea, knowing stares with simple smiles told him that Tess was aware. He was steadily moving toward despair. What did this say about their relationship and can you spend too much time with somebody you like?

It was later that same afternoon when he explained it all to another close associate, that no exposure would be as disagreeable as the introduction of an event which put the two in the same room for in excess of one day. For the associate it was strange to hear him explain the pain he was leading well in advance of the actual act. He later accused Josh of projecting things that are less likely to happen, knowing full well that he alone knew where it was to most likely end up. The possibilities of crossing her path was exact, and the places were too numerous to describe given the size of the town and the storefronts to browse or go in.

"You must certainly realize that there are better ways to confront your internalized fears. I believe that your options are more numerous than you think. Embrace the possibility of confrontation, be they good or bad, and anticipate a more hopeful ending. This will make you stronger."

"But if it was strength that I was after I am at capacity to head it straight on. When it looks as though it will rain I do carry an umbrella or at the very least a hat. It is just that our last interaction was miserably shared. Enough is enough: I simply do not want to reengage with her no matter the circumstances."

"What will you do if she seeks you out? There are too many places you can be recognized in this community. Most of our inner circle crosses paths with Tess every day. I know I do at least one half dozen times across the last several days and nights."

"At least you are native. I thought I once was, but she exposed the flaws of that with such determination toward the end. It was her sole objective to take credit for what we did together to the bitter conclusion, as you may recall."

"It is unfortunate that natives carry that grudge for so long. You would think time and distance would mellow that burden."

"You mean urban legend, don't you?" Josh was smiling now and stepping backward.

"So where do you intend to take all of this? Will you rub it in our faces? We already know who and what we are."

"Yes, I was the one who told you: puppets operating your own strings."

This was actually a discussion that was close to being worn out. Both men walked backward as though it was a reverse showdown in the middle of the street. Others carefully stepped on and off sidewalks to take a clear or second look, or to perhaps mentally intervene. But this scene was hopelessly cast and auctioned.

Flawlessly both actors completed their parts and turned without fanfare, heading in opposite directions. The stage is struck with immediacy and sooner rather than correct all extras are busily on their way to sharing the spectacle confrontation with as many other was possible throughout city proper, in what remains of daylight.

Tess would be the first to receive the news from an abundance of others, be they friend or foe. It would have seemed that most wanted to weigh in on that very day.

This was the charm of this town whether one likes it or not.

VOICE ONE: *This latest scene achieves a romantic level by identifying with that significant other. Many attempts are made to connect: persistence survives: and I am not free from her hold physically or psychologically. I am in fact somewhat excited by this prospect; to say that this supposition is unwarranted is inconsistent with reality. I am certain enough that wonderful things appear* alongside it and they become part of that permanent record. The last glimmer of self is hopelessly lost as staged. No one in their right mind will be able to separate one aspect from the other; this has been burned in their brains so now it is part of their physical world. It is the brightest star in the night sky because it bears a striking resemblance to what they thought should exist in the first place. This is the modern theory of theatre, although it is collision at best.

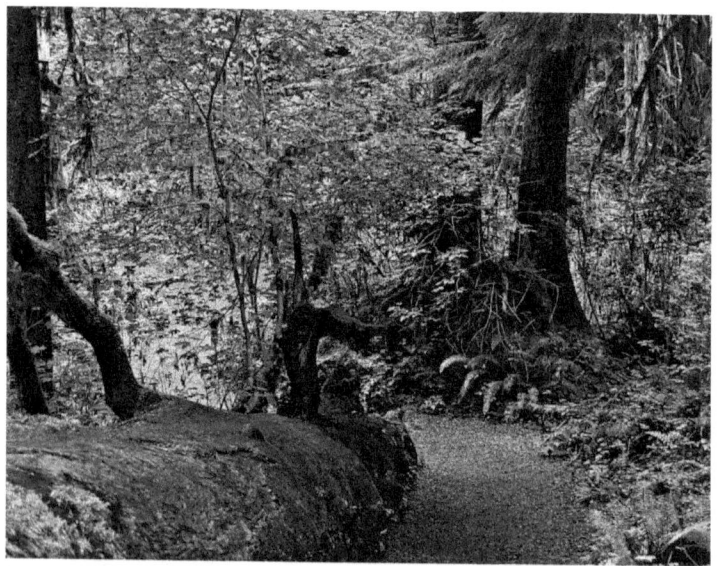

Screen Four

THE TAXI STAND WAS NO MORE than twenty paces beyond the automatic glass doors of the train station, and fifty paces from the original landing. One traveler pushed through the crowded station, covering the distance with a sense of urgency, brushing against those bundling up for emerging into the torrent of hail bouncing against any flat surface. Unfortunately some carried packages and unyielding object that were more or less lost under the trample of the crowd. It was a pity to see the looks on those faces as winter boots fell onto coats and baggage with eager momentum. It was all they could do but capture their losses before more damage was done.

The hail was received as a forecaster's mishap and no one was drenched to the skin by small bb-sized ice, melting on the sidewalks as quick as its arrival. The loss of this frozen treasure was not the object of remorse or even pity. It was simply lost to moisture in a way that was minor nuisance once the crowd made it to shelter, bus or taxicab: none further from the loss of momentum as they might have been if it were a more sustained downpour.

The one rushed figure makes it into a waiting taxi and barks out his intended direction. But the taxi queue is hopelessly blocked in by two way passing traffic, and every intersection is backed up for blocks. For the considerable attention this society puts into mass transit and automatic traffic controls, the result is obviously pitiful. All windows are closed tightly so that the cumulative exhaust of dozens of idling vehicles does not overcome the driver or passenger.

One opening in the onslaught comes in at a considerable cost. The taxi so occupied lunges forward and stops in a violently jerking fashion. This particular car is not at a loss and makes its way into the next opening slot as if by right. However several automobiles toward the back of the pack slam into one another and another foul intersection clambers down proving that others may have expressed similar insistence on rite of passage. There is a whole discourse on the subject expressed on the faces of one half dozen drivers through as many closed windows, and that insulated silence comes loudly enough via scrunched eyes and mouths and the occasioned clenched fist.

The cab races through cutting across a sidewalk. Pedestrians enter intersections at their own risk. It is a pity that this intersection is preyed upon the most.

There is a sense of the magnificent as the driver exclaims his virtuous motion to the single man in the rear seat.   There is an expression of victory as machine wins over foot traffic and walkers scatter to the safety of those curbs. Were strings attached there would have been no more or less control than the automatic jumps managed by the most astute, and the near tumbles by the less assured.   Pity the ones overburdened by luggage or other large packages that are laid down on wet pavement until they can be safely retrieved.

VOICE ONE: *Look at all of those puppets back there. They never stood a chance; frozen in their tracks they are victims now.*

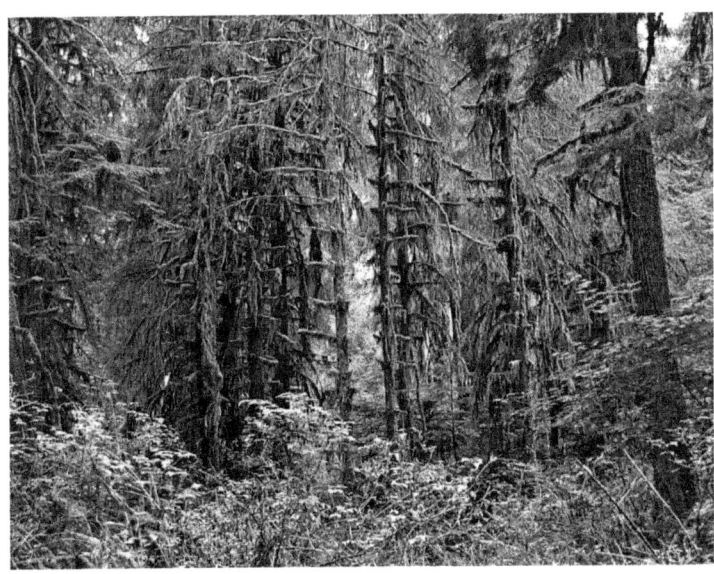

The driver expressed pride that does not match the outcome. Words shared from the outside are suppressed by thick windshields and tightly closed windows on purpose, but those eyes speak loudly enough. There is pain, anguish and rage in some, while others seem to remain calm enough to suggest that this traffic mess is something too typical to carry on about. They simply cannot be bothered.

"You could have injured someone and you wouldn't know it."

The passenger in this cab feels the need to comment on someone's behalf.

The man in the back had turned 180 to attest to the result of this erratic driving. Sure enough they were all frozen as those puppets draping over a stage; motion is a continued illusion given no strings attached; there is no hope of willing them to move on to recover from this indignity. And the driver is laughing to himself.

Those unfortunate many, by no intension of their own, are a result of what happens in perpendicular to these unnatural surroundings; rather than to their own accord they dance to another's strumming. Horns honk as if to say, "I feel your pain, now just get out of the way."

As the hurried taxi tracks forward the passenger is also subject to the marionette controls the driver. His pace is alarmingly hurried. It is a pity that the driver does not know that his efforts will never be rewarded with a larger tip. For a considerable while longer the passenger schemes to slip out the door at the next slowing to a comfortable corner, and one which has suitable shelter from the elements. As it would happen, the occurrence is never assured enough to make this at all possible. Two are trapped to each other for the duration.

After a considerable time thereafter he is on terra firma and momentum of his own accord and pace. It is true that he has arrive at the target destination in one piece of body and mind, presumably, and less hurried now because he has chosen to control his anger. The other feet on the pavement are moving slowly and with deliberation, leaving both a good impression and a calmed overtone of inner city response: no one makes prolonged eye contact with any other; no one has to acknowledge any of this happened. It is simply over. This is good.

The departed vehicle is already pulling away and the soloist is approached by another who does seem to care. They place hands on each other's shoulders but do not pull into anything more intimate. Both are smiling and if this were a more suitable panorama we might have seen the glints in each person's eyes and a soft smile on each set of slightly parted lips.

"Welcome back," says the pair in rejoinder as the business at hand is ultimately reached.

There are a lot of surprises in store, but all of the resources he seeks out are to his avail, without question. This is the expressed feeling he is enjoining now. The meeting is going well after the long drive to a business office, followed by a rise to the top on a very swift elevator just inside of the expansive lobby.

The glass sides of the elevator allow each passenger to enjoy the outside looking in, in relative silence. A bell sounds out the progression to each floor; as many step out as glide in with each programmed stopping. The doors glide open and then close without too much hesitation. The business portion of this arrival is reached, and there are people walking in and out of the room to announce their positions, respectively, to a single attendant sitting behind a semi-circle desk.

They are quickly greeted and then escorted to an already busy conference room. Last to come upon the place introductions are made and appraisals are exchanged for coffee, tea and bottled water. There are plates of fruit on a side table but no one wants to be the first to reach out and across the divide, apparently.

After careful removal of all hindrances to a trusted slide show presentation, this theatre project looks as though it has little trouble moving along the tenants of an original and principled plan. The little event is over and now the fruit makes its way onto a central table.

He reaches out. He notices that everyone moving with him is smiling. They all want the best pieces of fruit and soon the bowls are nearly empty. Smiles are spent. Hands are wiped clean. Final sips are taken and finally most of them stand, but are hovering to see what happens next.

"Before you move on, Josh, I would like to introduce you to one other person."

Josh walked with his business partner, and now producer, leaving the top floors to a fast elevator ride to the ground floor. The larger metal doors opened this time into an outer courtyard that was populated by a scattered few who refuse to take notice to their entrance until one man turns and waves. This is an understood indication of what will come next. Every step of the way someone shouted hello to the man at his side, and wished him well with regard to half a dozen ongoing endeavors. It did not dawn on Josh just how little privacy this remaining afternoon would circumscribe, but with all of the difference to the praise poured over this man; it would not be over soon enough to prepare him for another realization.

He was kind of invisible.

Every stage of his proposed theatre plan in fact could be recounted in similar fashion, with the possible exception of his conflict earlier on with Tess. Did his contribution really matter to these people? They stayed among themselves as though they were the only domain. His privacy is damned now: the fair amount of attention extended was being filtered his way only as an acknowledgement of a person attached to someone else. The circumstance of this reaction was fading far into the recesses of his brain. It was put there as a temporary placeholder, to placate the beast before it resurfaced and wins him over to a darker side of life. He is not used to being the person on the outside looking back in.

The two of them shared a late afternoon meal accompanied by two bottles of very fine wine. When the bill arrived his producer quickly waived it his way, having not reached the point of the prescribed measures which were already in play to capture and control an ultimate outcome. No shyness was extended by the open area in which they chose to rest the day in comfort. The flora was lush and maintained to an unearthly green, given what perhaps was an over feeding of fertilizers and growth enhancers—more staged than any theatre itself.

Josh was being entertained, but at what cost? The subject he really wants to talk about is never put on the table directly. It is an act of deliverance, perhaps defiance, and certainly well controlled. He is itching to say this but won't stray from the course well played out.

More people came in and sat at nearby tables. Their banter was never remote, to the left and the right and behind them. It never occurs to Josh that it was always just out of direct line of sight. It is though each and every table and circumstance has been allotted a timetable and position on this very stage. He may be a director but it is the producer that holds all of the strings. Perhaps it was his overly active imagination that he was part of this carefully scattered plot: no room, no privacy and no matter: it had not reached the point of climax—so he had projected the moment of the curtains pulling forward.

The deal was struck and both parties stood and turned; flowing handshakes express distance rather than closeness. It is over.

Josh was walking out of this place of business guided by the promised introduction to a foregone conclusion. He won't be alone in this endeavor. She was bright, attractive and very energetic; had he had the mind and purpose to pursue this by allure alone the moment had passed. Business is always pressed before pleasure. But now, he was not even sure if he liked her at all.

It did not take long for her to reach the well rehearsed piece, never skimming over details on the surface.

His and her attention to details invited stares of retention, with no loss of judgment or dismay. He was the ever vigilant gentleman getting her door at the restaurant, sliding out the chair for her to take her place, at a small and intimate table in the quietest corner. It was then he was beginning to take notice that no one here returned his confused stares. The gatherings around them were so engaged in every language possible, and the wait staff arrived for their orders, obtaining permission to quickly disappear.

The gentle lady pulled into the table and placed her arms and hands out in the most charming way. She wore no hint of anxiety that her performance was being scrutinized by an expert instead.

The grace of her manner, and her speech that was so prepared—obliged him to stare seriously, silently, until she was contented to hearing the sound of her own voice. If she were on his stage now this would have been considered a most profoundly powerful orator, enabled by a hushed and attentive crowd. And he felt equally obligated to letting her finish and return for several more bows.

Josh was remittent in exposing his age, given what she had done in the early portions of her life. At this age she should have been just getting started—not resident or occupied in high order. And then there was this new declaration. They had finished eating, drinking and she was about to pay.

"For taking this time to entertain me, would it exceed my position to suggest we move on to another yet equally quiet place. I would like to have another drink with you and return the trouble you have taken to make me feel comfortable."

"That is so thoughtful, all though a rather strange way to put it. In order for my spending additional time you tonight; I am afraid I will ask for your indulgence to accompany me to one place beforehand."

As it turns out the lady was preoccupied with another issue of money. For all that she had explained in her preparedness, she had not been as diligent with another equally interesting prospect.

The walk across the boulevards went from beyond neat toward sloppy: the idea of walking through this section of town. It leaves no small impression that she has an equally opposite side. It was nothing short of a fortuitous event that got them both to a point of arrival, stepping over potholes, moving by darkened alleyways occupied by never do well, and ultimately arriving at the only refreshing sight dead ahead. It was a closed open air vender's location, and the bay door of a warehouse indicated more than ample light.

All along this entranceway lights bathed every wall disallowing any pretending of modesty, or the impression that its occupants were engaged in troubling vices at all. Josh noted that most of them could be close family members, and they seemed to be sharing a common language and sense of humor.

His every movement caused immediate attention and a great deal of scrutiny. Her movements, on the other hand, were welcomed with the grace usually extended to royalty. The natives were all dressed in work apparel and the effect was anything less than shocking; than it was to them as they proceeded deeper, finding the next batch wearing quite a bit less.

VOICE ONE: *How could they survive the night wearing so little?*

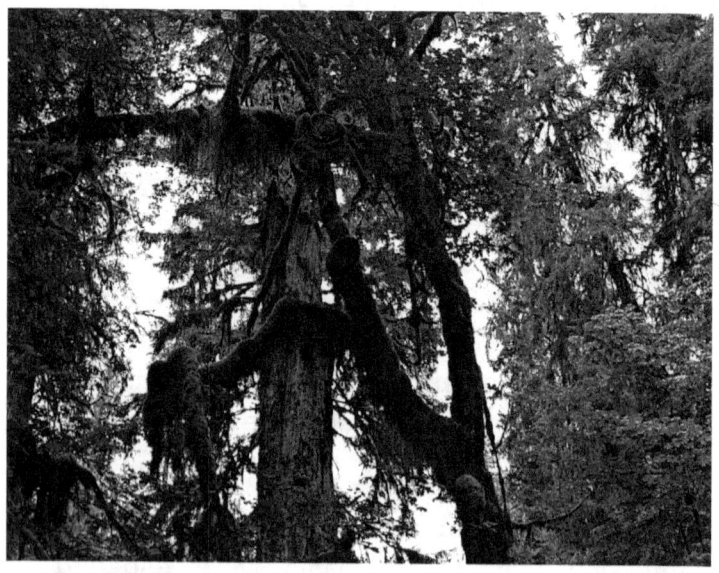

An astonished look grazed Josh's face.   Was he blushing?

Still no worse for what they bare, no one seemed shaken. It was an interesting lot doing what they were expected.   Their collective presence seemed large and quite strong.

"Josh, would you mind waiting here a while longer. The person I came to see is in a room that is off limits to outsiders."

That was all she offered before scurrying past a sentry and the single point of entry.   The formidable and unsmiling sentry offered no reason to pass: a very clear non verbal suggestion: come and go as you will but through this particular door you will never lead.

It was an awful long wait at a very dicey location. Josh could never be any less amused, yet he remained self entertained until she eventually came back out from that other place.   Now he really knew that he did not like her.

Perceptive Sensations   Michael O'Connor

Screen Five

JOSH HAD REMAINED STEADFAST just out of earshot of anyone who might listen. He had conveyed how all of the people coming in and out of this place were larger and stronger than typical. Perhaps they were a hybrid of a cross section of carefully bred locals, but there were no other samples to be seen or compared against.

Remarkably it was as though he stood in the middle of mid court of professional basketball players, and he was the only one who had to routinely look up. The entire population was friendly enough and did appear at all dissatisfied with the notion of having to watch their step around this smallish persona. It was part of a variety of tasks which Josh hoped they would have a willingness to adopt. After all, he was bringing something of value to this environment.

The eye is so accustomed to addressing things head on. Everywhere around him things seemed just out of visual reach unless he really craned his neck. But as soon as he learned how to position his body he was able to maintain a keen sort of visual lock in on their expressions and thus better read their emotions coupled with body language. In every case, this was the sort of thing anyone would have to do if this were a multi-lingual situation. Fortunately this was a clear shot at semantics and linguistics knowhow, and here he had a lion share of wealth; couple this to recognition of a neck tilt, shoulder droop, torso sway or crossover of legs. The body says what most will not say out loud.

The whole place soon gave way to a middle ground. In this case it was a sure relief to find that they could all pick their way toward finding a common thread as they delicately waded across several test topics. The third and successful attempt zeroed everyone in, and the decision to stay and work out the necessary details was reached as lunch was brought in as the group moved to a lovely second story veranda. Meeting occupants moved through two enormous doors which covered one entire wall, to an equally large platform lined with a multitude of flowering potato vines, so fragrant it was as though they were part of the lavish lunch menu.

All eyes were on the tables covered primarily with trays of freshly cut fruit and vegetables, and baskets of warm breads just removed from some nearby ovens.   At a distance off of the veranda was an Olympic-sized swimming pool, and as it turns out, it was populated by the varied spouses of participating members of this scheduled forum.

Josh and the others sat in oversized bamboo woven chairs. They had comfortable cushions and each of the larger and taller members of this cast sat comfortably with long legs crossed under the granite topped tables. There was a sense of luxury in the air, yet the gathering had a feeling of quaint.

Without peering too long it was impossible to not see that many had already taken off their shoes—the many men and women who occupied a place at the table. Perhaps bare feet were native to such occasions, and it took Josh minutes and additional courage not to remove his. He was already on a first named basis with some but continued to defer to common sense that all mannerisms need not be followed in a complimentary vane. The benefit to the western participant is that knowledge is best served honestly, rather than using mimicry.

Things seldom change when addressing business issues and this veranda was no exception to this rule. If one assumes that the skill required are already at hand, it is just a matter of timing and sequence. He did not remain aloof with regard to his being the odd man out; subsequently he was immediately pulled into an enormously beneficial conversation at the very start of lunch. A woman sitting next to him instructed

him to address the table with regard to his plans for
the theatre group's official launch.

Eating and meaningful socialization was the first
revelation incurred within his disclosure of scope. He
described in detail rather than reducing it to rhetoric
and innuendos—the majority of people clamored to
attend to his every word. Details here were the
foundation of how they wanted to do business in real
time and in real life. If not for a few past experiences
that were less than noble, he would have commanded
the attention of all.

It was first a woman at the far end of the table who
thoughtfully cast her misgivings on the approach
under discussion. She had been burned by a theatre
producer who spoke well, had good intensions, but
ultimately never followed through on an agreed upon
path.

"How would you be different?"

There were no overtones of threat. Her glance to two
other participants indicated allies to fight the good
fight.

His retort was received well enough—probably only
as literal and interpreted for redeeming value—and
comprehensible enough to push off any further
dissention. Later on he was asked to repeat it for
clarification. He did so and it now received its fullest
endorsement of the afternoon. The toned down

speaker was none other than the manager of the entire troupe. His acceptance was hardly a fair cross section of the whole, but he did nonetheless have the distinction of speaking the last words on the once haughty subject. From here on the point of contention never reoccurred—its proportions evidently toned down in difference to leadership and management.

How internationally served is this characteristic: agree and commit, disagree and commit, and by all other means commit or leave the arena. Unaware at the time of just how large this division was among the troupe, he probably would have given way to the leadership. It was who pays and how often, that presented the most viable course of action: on his behalf Josh played the only card he owned—the theatre—not politics.

The second point of clarification came at a later time, during dessert. The final course had arrived and was being distributed on two smaller tables, resting alongside a long banister of polished stainless steel. It was an uncommon thing to wander, mingle and eat sweets, but here it was certainly expected. The stances and stare downs were friendly enough except that at least two to three more wanted another shot as to prolong this contest.

Probably the most striking measure they took was in the careful planning. The leadership had taken this moment to take a nature call. The engagement was set in a semi circle with the target hovering in the middle. Availing him to this deceitful measure of pressure, the first salvo came forth with energy of its own.

"We consider what we do as Community Theater. In your description you described how yours was to serve an extensive audience. Our presence, apparel and the beauty and subtle gestures we invoke are more natural in a smaller setting. How exactly will this translate?"

"Having been interrogated by the best minds in the business, coupled by the fact that we will be seeking a higher ground, things will seem quite different to you and your associates. It is the nature of modern arts. Ours will be a fusion of the old and the new."

"And this higher ground you speak of—what is it exactly?"

"New direction; since some of this has never been done this way before; we intend to deliberately push beyond the more common markets."

Josh went on to say he would be held entirely responsible for what went wrong, as well as what goes right. It was not an exact science with regard to what he proposed, but one thing was for sure: the plight suffered is theater that has been done to death.

"Therefore you seem indifferent to our fears, because we have become complicit with our repetition. Things have not changed in the nature of our story telling and our dress of puppets. This is the affect: your indifference is to culture sustained longer than necessary."

Josh thought about their mode of dress for a moment longer. They wore short even though they were all exceptionally tall. Even the subjects of their craft had extremities that seemed too long for scale.

"I could not have stated it any better. Culture for me is remembrance of something you left; compare and contrast; to something you lean forward to feel different and excited about, because it is presented in a whole new way."

"Well our answer is yes. We are collectively interested in seeking a new way, but ultimately the message will remain the same. After all, we are standing here in front of you holding this very important conversation,"

The reply allowed everyone to bathe in this new light. Yes meant a willingness to continue with the co-discovery of a new venue, one which is sufficiently intelligent to capture the subtle morays: attitudes, beliefs, values and real feelings: yet meaningful for a whole host of others who were not fortunate to have been born into this cultural and ecological niche. The fear factor was not an impediment, but rather an easy victory to win over an extended audience. The foursome was silent for a while longer. It was an uncomfortable silence but there was a shared overtone: change is sometimes harder to grasp by those who chose not to change as often.

Josh thought he must make the best of the situation in light of the misgivings of the few. Their remarks found a home—perhaps more of a notch—but their venting would not soon be lost. It was duly noted and would be filed along with the opposing voices of the troupe's managers—a middle ground recording at best.

"If the need not be addressed with immediacy then file them until they go away, unnoticed. Then replace that need with desire."

His comment to himself was not meant to be aloof. Eventually all comments would return and either cause forward momentum or restriction—this much did not escape him. Performers are rarely modest, managers are testament to never being wronged, and the director and producer of this crowd is best served by balancing all those aspects of human nature, at least until the curtains first open.

From there they say, "The show must go on."

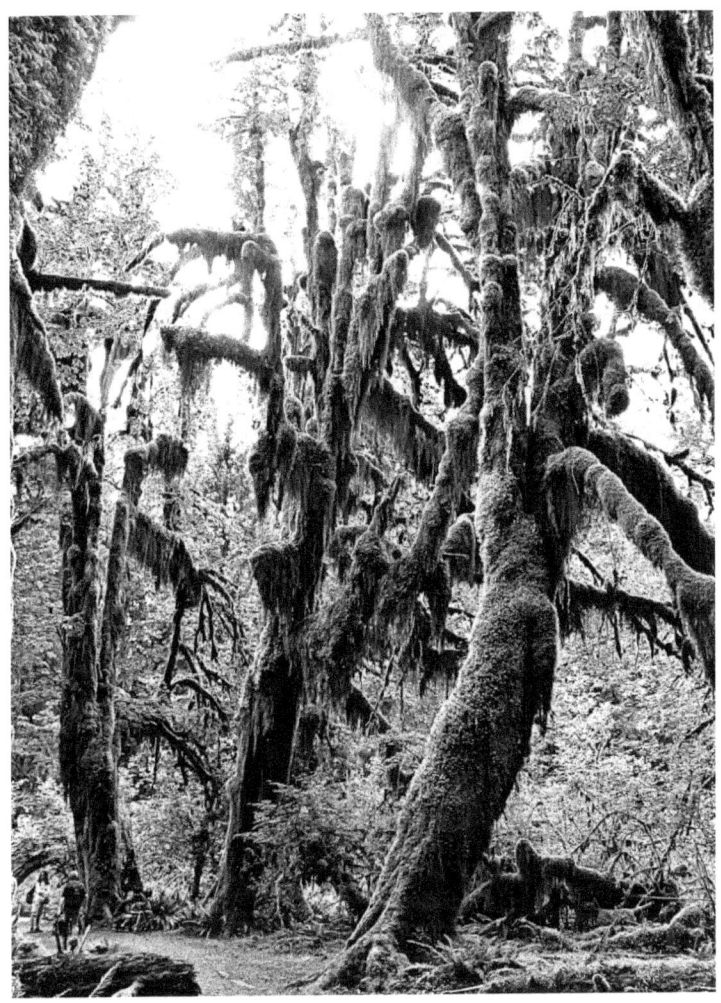

VOICE ONE: *Would it frighten you to know that they want to reach out for you. It is their play too, after all.*

Screen Six

AFTER THE CLOSE OF THE PILOT show Josh took a drive with one of his co-directors. Almost all of the features projected by the show flowed as expected; noteworthy were the pits and crevasses which required minor repair or patching up. The two of them discussed it with sufficient details and emotional feverish. It was previewed as an initial success with all points of difference from behind the scenes compared and contrast from the audience perspective.

High views and low appeal were among the topics of discourse; the road ahead was built of sturdy materials, notwithstanding the occasional pothole or temporary obstruction. It all stands well and Josh was inclined to agree with his counterpart there was evidence of success: at a glance uniformity of design, lighting, music and a host of other contributions supported the forward momentum of the entire show.

"We can get past this pilot.   It is officially off the ground; I am so inclined to relax just a bit."

All of the sign posts they passed while driving pointed to new construction, forward ground breakings and billboard depictions of new villages still meant to be constructed.   This place used to be lush with tall swaying grass fields and mighty oaks which were rumored to be at least ten decades old.   But the ideal of one point of view declined to be replaced by another: the demands for new residences were fulfilled if not by ads alone.

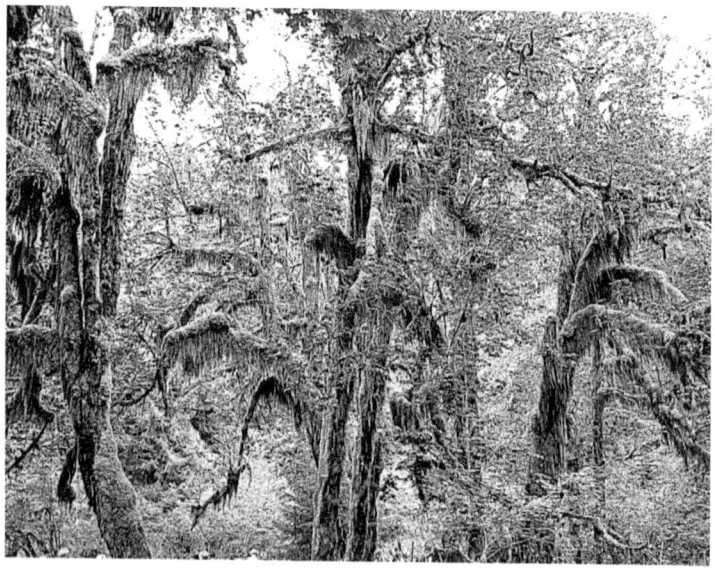

One large screen above each of the three stages has been illuminated.

Flattened grounds gave evidence to future communities, and at a glance parcels marked off by physical demarcation of wall, fence or preconstruction outline promoted social inclination. By the rights already displayed who is at home and ready to receive and entertain was no longer in darkness or devoid of neighboring appeal. This was someone's dream being fulfilled through a deceptive storyboard.

What right one has to privacy is not fully prepared to project unless it is in someone else's terms. The roads suggested a means of getting somewhere, and where the trees and grasses remain a notion of another place echoes back. The fact that one can recall the tree lines is testimony to the high impact to what theatre is out to get: how to relate to past experiences in a setting of new design. The troupe made due with earlier disclosed grievances and embodied a new means of reaching audiences just as this sprouting community bridged the past to the inevitable future of spread: to display and to receive feedback is a means of avoiding that desire of privacy. This place has the fine arts. It is clearly spelled out on the next billboard, and this one is afloat.

But on closer observation what did the silhouettes depicted convey? Members of a cast may act detached, and appear unvarying for the possibility of being labeled as individual. Under the same roof the informed member of the audience projects and attributes some of the acting to be that of his or her own. As uncomfortable as it may seem a theatre groups attempts are never deemed successful until an audience gives them closer observation and provides that means of mirrored reflections or echoed soundings. Are there enough differences between a billboard and a marquee?

Later on these two directors and producers would have to do the outrageous thing to put a more accountable track onto the table. With a kind of pity they discussed and devised a plan to capture and can the performance for the unaccountable thing of selling it to a sea of strangers just driving by, not yet aware that this place includes a theatre. Without shame these two stopped for a meal at a roadside eatery and unveiled a means that might not have spared even themselves, for the hope of increasing the audience.

One's own apprehension might have been entirely spared had not there had been an eves dropper at the very next table. His gaze is most assured.

"Allow me to introduce myself," the fine gentleman and his guest leaned forward with happy smiles and extended hands.

What had led up to the introduction was almost in parallel entirely. The pair had just exited a project of their own: a mighty disclosure proves useful in identifying who has transitioned those fields of grasses and trees to a steadfastly growing rural community. This turns out to be the master redevelopers: as a husband and wife, with very little humility, but did lend another set of kind ears and eyes.

What an agreeable suggestion it turns out to be that they in turn desire to transition themselves. The banter forward finds a suitable middle ground and the supposed difficulty of task is more or less cordial and sublime. Josh and his partner are able to convey what they have started, as well as what they intend to transfix. The intensions are never mistreated by a far differing business trust; reception giving honor to a joint proposal and expression of due notice; a plan is coming home at best.

When the new couple expressed their gratification it also included a swiftly wired transfer of enough funds to seal the deed. With no limits of jurisdiction call out so early on in the projection and transfer just secured, the four ventured outside to drive to the next place of honor. Thus ownership is doubled, but it is not before the ink has dried, even though electronically.

It was a pleasant drive across the remaining fields of splendid grass and tree lined road which deposited them at a house more modest at first point of view. But when the theatre duo enter the façade they can attest that the minor outside transformed into a wondrous interior splendor decorated with post modern furniture and art of the highest order. Recognizable names and technique occupied every wall and open floor space, and the intended vision was explained in delightful detail. An intended walk throughout the home took a full hour to appreciate a place decorated with little regret. These hosts were most cordial and kind, respective to the visitor's recognition of most of the significant displays and arrangement.

Then came the bottles of modestly priced yet fine enough wine—there was no limit to hosting that went unnoticed. The directors and producers were attentive to the opposing giants in their respective league and self congratulations were maintained at a bare minimum; mentally everyone settles into a flow of shared expectation of the entertainment industry as it once stands guarded by the needs of an upcoming community.

The interior's physicality was prominently lit with theatre styled lamps. This was not hidden to the attentions of the more experienced designers in kind.

Several complimentary comments were exchanged as to the effectiveness of light cast on object, wall space and the spacious floor. Neither party it turns out was stranger to the effects and affect of good lighting. The first moments of the conversation were spent in resplendent silence as glean flowed to shadow, and when one blinked the movement was real. The necessity to what one is accustomed to with regard to properly lighting a stage was obviously conveyed here in a most meaningful way. Certainly this interior was on trial.

Where there is slight trepidation of getting in over one's head by early indulgence in a potentially early prospect, the chances appeared to be more than fair and less than excellent, that this couple had an appetite for the dramatic. As they continued into the evening a silvery and then hued purple arced across the sky and disappeared behind the mountain range to the northwest. It was quite the exhibit and simply portrayed the best cast of lighting one could hope for in the theatre business. The display is interrupted by a telephone ringing somewhere across the expansive room and someone goes to fetch it.

If there is one thing anyone of a sales lineage knows for sure, splitting up a potential business duo can provide a more favorable situation. It liberates both the buyer and seller and changes the ratio of approach, and can be deployed as an instrument for pealing back the layer of true intent. Josh wanted to use this momentous break in the conversation to feel out the most silent of the party. Who was really driving this decision, and of course why?

Questions were asked in a different manner and soon the information sought after spilled forward; another hidden agenda casts its own hue. Although this might have been expressed and then received to his ears as an exasperating set of queues, nothing else was left to chance.

He had repeated his questions and she had provided a much more revealing string of answers. As it would turn out, they were more knowledgeable about the staged business environment, through an exchange of past lives, and when she introduced the notion that they had little else to do. There was this very meaningful opening.

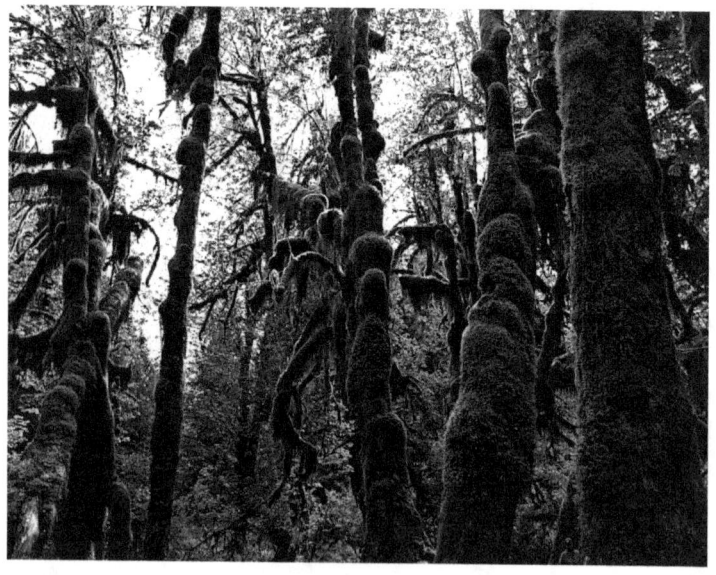

The scenery pans from left to right and is then joined.

Who and what they once were conveyed everything they needed to know: the directors and producers no longer sit on their hands, respectively: and yet nothing on the other end conveys a similar connection. The soul mate of this living couple goes on and on without realizing that she is playing every hand. The tone of her voice is varied, at least indicating that this is not some well rehearsed trick. But nothing is as it seems when she locks her eyes with Josh and add the following:

"Whatever the reason you have for hedging on the offer my husband provides you, try to keep this stilled. It is not often one receives an open invitation to let a number be pronounced, and the remainder just follows. Hesitate if you will because he does seek out the good chase. I assure you he has anticipated every alternative route you may follow, well in advance I might add. It would do you both good to allow him to initiate the invitation to advance; prepare to expedite this quickly: he is often less interested if there is no immediacy in a common good."

No this was well rehearsed. Leaving no doubt on their collective account, they assured her that they understood. And in honor of the man who just returns they stood up and greeting him slyly with the information they had received.

As quickly as they stood and moved forward, the man seemed to be escorting toward another part of the house. The foursome passed room after room until they reached an odd wall of concrete and a large and very heavy door came to an outward swing. Lights were then switched on and they were being escorted down a steep and winding set of stairs. Everyone's footings were assured coupled with a handsome oak banister all wrapped in forged metal painted with a satin black, a chain of twists and turns indicating a blacksmith of enormous skill. The steps down absorbed each and every step, would there have been any conversation it might have disappear right into the sturdy concrete walls. The entire journey was breathtaking and absorbing at the same time, and when they first turned toward the final landing it was as though they were stepping into another country, and another time.

Hardly had there been a moment before when Josh could remember being so completely shocked by such a display. What is it to behold such a varied collection that was displayed row after row?

The rows were variant yet straight and each had a decisive theme. To one who would behold the skills and patience of this surreal matrix the surprising and most immediate feedback was inhaled rather than purveyed. The aromas were overwhelming and at the same time mesmerizing. Josh felt he was swooning and swaying and bound by the erg to get to the bottom of each and every odor as though separating them was even possible. There was not enough of a distinction to be made as they walked up and then down some of the carefully spaced rows.

"I am transfixed by one and then all."

"And that is the very point, dear Josh. That is the most important point to be consumed by: that and the stunning visuals."

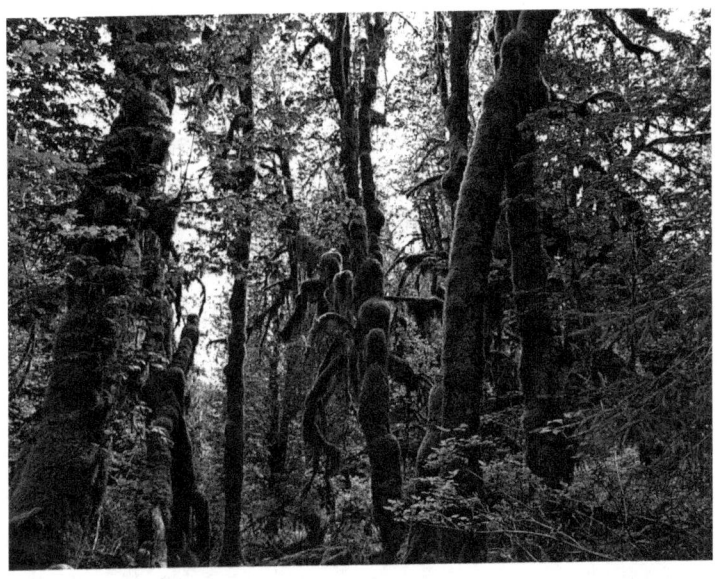

VOICE ONE: *Temporary actors made their appearance on stage, but none of them looked as brilliant as depicted. The arrangement of talent in and around prop had the same magnitude as looking through a spectroscope: one unlike the other as the scope's mechanism is turned clockwise, not absolutely new, but then not entirely original all the same. It is a temporary state which can be returned to its origin by a counter clockwise motion.*

Or can it? This spectrum of appearance resembles its immediate predecessor. Is it supposed to represent a body of retained knowledge or the pressure to see what one expects to see? Nevertheless it's a bewildering surprise.

VOICE TWO IN TONE: *Your apparition is an intruder in a well known form. It will have the collective effect of an invasion—so decidedly disconcerting is seems to be the beginning of a revolution as to how you will see further. One could pretend to understand and position for the best advantage to this unnerving aspect; assuming that you are indeed the director. But mark my words you will only see its outlines and border. Be prepared to wonder if this could be interesting or wild enough.*

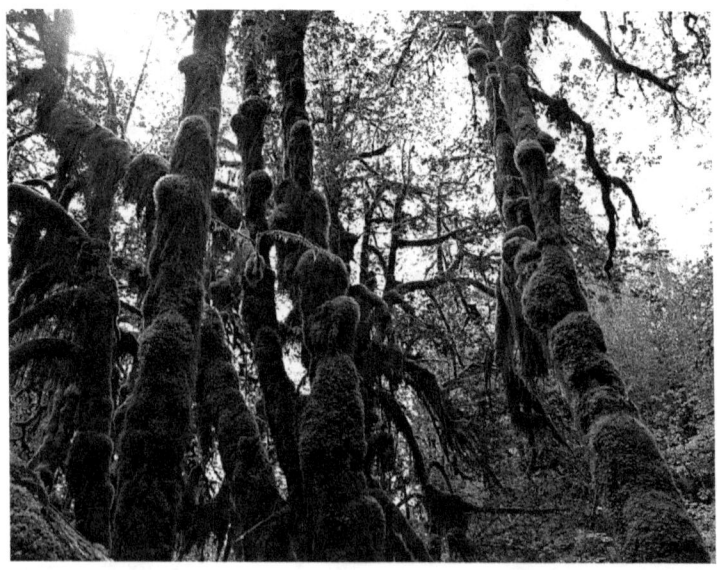

Screen Seven

THE DIRECTOR AND PRODUCER WERE ASTONISHED with the gallery of display; first impressions were lost as they strolled through the rows and found themselves immersed inside one of the most beautiful underground sculptured gardens; finally sitting down near a waterfall and enjoining in a discussion of hydroponic gardening. At second glance this place also had the appearance of a deep space or near deep oceanic laboratory, simulating a normal day's sun. It was an extraordinary feat for the two hosts to have either created it or sponsored it in an estate that took on dimensions the deeper one explored.

There was one particular end of the rows which cast shadows of enormous cacti that bore into the minds of the viewers of visiting the saguaro deserts of the southwest. All who would have cast aspersion at trickery at hand there was a calm and unusual explanation for all of it. These two were not strangers to the most advanced university labs, and a quickened exposure to their collective pasts placed into the minds of the theatre set, that this was not to be beheld in wanton indifference to the real world topside, as much as it was energy redirected below because one can. That was the explanation at hand: who dwindles and dawdles for the next gasp of fresh air, this is as real as it gets.

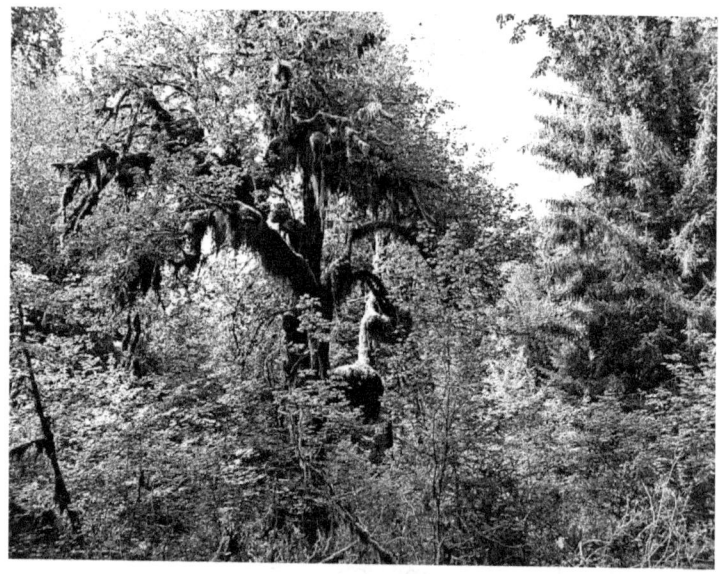

VOICE ONE: *Were they all to come on stage it would be a very crowded place. Yet there was room.*

The host(s) as the story quickly turns its attention to are PhD to the hilt; it appears in every such disposition one can explore on a ready campus. Josh and his associate are escorted across a higher marbled platform that shows the thinnest flow of recycled water and nutrients which is lost into micro thin cracks and pumped back into the system highly re-oxygenated.

There are parts of this inner sanctum environment which are cold and then warm to the touch of the exposed arm and hand, and thus flow over every type of flora opportunity. The greens are greener than anything topside, and the reds, oranges and yellows are of such a hue one would swear they had painted surfaces done by none other than the artist Peter Max. And all through this a constant flow of music tingle whatever sensations and perceptions have not been already saturated.

As the pleasant pace of the foursome picks up a bit the surroundings segue into long banks of aquariums and terrariums stocked and inhabited by an equally wide array of fish stock, amphibians and reptiles. Throughout the environment there are several types of flying and crawling insects by which the two theatre people can only hope to profess are useful to the flora and the stock requiring ample sources of foodstuff. Then they receive another volley of intimately streamed knowledge on the species and respectively employed habitats to meet their needs, respectively.

"So you can see and hear, and please do touch, all that is around you as real enough. It is only their location that tests the scientific mind, and strikes apprehension of the lesser endeared plainsperson."

It was a conversation perhaps perfected over time by rehearsal alone or among other like minded and fast minded. Those who were in the position to be inclined to forward thinking were embraced by these words, and have both a desire and need to get to the bottom of things--smartly. Based on recent events alone Josh ventured forth with a postulation of his own.

"Could this approach ever reach the theatre the possibilities would be endless."

"And that is the precise reason why would like to be in the business of the arts with you two."

The clarification was sufficient enough. This small party wore expressions on their faces that said it all with precision and clarity.

The party returned upward and to the surface of the earth for refreshments after another hour of exposure and transference. The next level of assembly took place on the back terrace after the setting of the sun. In the interim other guests began to arrive at this place and while one group partied above, another was escorted below to be reminded of the prize at hand and the flow of conversation marching forward.

Each and everyone were introduced to the other, formally with credentials and scope of perceived abilities. It was in the fashion of the theme of the party to re-explore the widening aperture of the arc of sky as stars and then planets became within optimal view given that there was little artificial light out here to impede.

Josh now could know what the characters depicted by Jules Verne in *20,000 Leagues Under the Sea,* must have felt beyond what the reader must endure. Who could afford not to be pulled in?

Josh undertook the lead to compile names and places of those who held them to account in this social manner. The names of places and modes of what they address were duly noted, and some direct manner of intension was exchanged to those with a most similar purpose of order, to maintain the momentum of the reminder of this enchanted evening. There was sequence of course, with the arousal of guest in parallel fashion by the hosts, in return for disclosed favor. Would it be possible for any one of them to refrain from taking in each observation and transforming it into business at hand, it would have been impossible to do any other such thing. There is a limitation to social networking: the appreciation of a live and most stimulating real environment for which is to be shared completes it all. Those interests seem to clamor in theatres direction from all ends of the hotly pursued spectrum: how to, what to and when. It must be savored live in the end.

There was little accounting for rejection, especially so since the adult beverages were never ending. It was not an impossible task to refrain from the tray after tray of delectable delights, especially since they were all derived from within, or down below for the matter and manner of specifics. Josh saw all of this food and drink being replenished by staffs who were expert at surprise appearance and the keen ability to simply disappear. It was never too clear as to what door they entered and then exited for another tray or plateful of earthly delights.

It was then that Josh undertook another lavish surprise. Was it not already astonishing enough that he had managed to become a center of attention, when a singular entrance took him and his breath away? Tess had just entered this impossible time and place all the way—in real time this can be just as surreal. His heart pounded out the beat of a source of song whose title eluded him for the moment.

What was the nature of her manner as she first pushed past his place in order to be attentive to the proper order of invitation? He who relies to simply the facts alone would have seriously missed all that affected him given this fact of self interest to be overheard. It is too real.

"Why is she here?"

The question is uttered slowly but decisively as a whisper. No one is intended to hear and no one is attended to its answer.

No one man remains an island; on this occasion he is pursuing his past without the civility of recognizing that he is only one guest out of nine. In the standard of celebration this had been a wonderful contrast to whatever they had left behind. Now it was his to pay homage to the newest entrance who paved her way to the hosts, surrounded literally by banter, attention and clear intent to adorn, that would bear his closer scrutiny just short of full on examination.

If she had entered naked it would have shook his world no less than it did now. How would he interact?

There was little to indicate his thrill or over indulgence with her regard at this intimate gathering of supposedly like minded participants. He tried at best to keep his ego in check, and throttled back his desire or perhaps appetite for another row, capitalized more on her part the time before. He wanted to address her through a third party, but who would go to his aid for such a testy endeavor at this momentous social engagement.

Josh smiles and sends a little wave. His look must have conveyed a complexity because several return his stare in error. True feedback is lost.

Having backed himself into the proverbial corner there was not just one place where he could present himself in a more favorable light. Instead he remained out of earshot and muttered mostly to himself. As awful as it may appear he even repeated this channeled behavior.

"Why is she really here, now?"

It was an exasperating sound and he rechecked his pulse and took in several very deep breaths. At some point one woman in particular began to take notice and arrived at his side, exploring the possibility that he might be having a heart attack. Anxiety aside, he was eventually able to calm her fears and disclose that his past had taken control of his body and his mind. It was a liberating moment for both of them and they soon shared a rowing laughter and short refrain from the real world.

This may have been his next out of body journey.

In light of the fact that the woman at his side was not mocking his self absorption, she presently informed Josh as to who she was and why she was here now— taking a cue from his earlier and repeated questioning. She was a chief resident at a community hospital and during normal business hours her area of expertise was indeed handling anxiety attacks. Presently she began to ask him to recall what led up to his exposed episode, and would he care to talk about it to some greater degree.

"I would not mind, I assure you. However, unless you are familiar with the circumstance you might think that I have gone mad."

In general it would have been a good use of his time as well as hers. But the man of the hour was not about to let this opportunity slip away: that is to refocus his attention span, put to use whatever time may lay ahead, to come into closer approximation to this target, and get to possible answers to his most pressing questions.

"Am I even here, now?"

The hour was at hand and the only way he could take on the task is to provide another point of interest to this more than gracious guest. Josh began signaling his business partner—the old not the new.

"Would you care to meet another at this party? I would like to introduce a very good and long time associate and pal."

The two were brought together and were already engaged in eye lock and casual touching. Each friend indeed brings to the table an innate capability to read into a given situation and take matters at hand, if only to rescue, rightfully so, the injured party. To his account, his business associate was well adept at reading into these situations, and lived well to his reputation long last. Josh was already feeling like a third party and slipped away giving the appearance that his presence no longer mattered.

The only possible next step was to present himself to his hosts directly, given their intimate engagement with Tess. He would be the very interesting addition—to his own expressed interest—the most probable invitation into the circle was his own lurch into a common ground—a solid one at the very least.

By all accounts his entry is fortunate; he has landed on his feet and luck does not desert him for the prolonged moment of silence before Tess acknowledges his presence. She is acting kindly and begins speaking of him in unreserved terms. Their eyes lock for more than a moment.

"Josh has been working with a very specialized puppet troupe: introducing them into the local theatre circles. I am certain that he might have something to say in regard to our current conversation. This is a welcome surprise, Josh. Please enlighten us with your current activities."

The human mind is so constituted of chambers that one feels that it is like reaching well into a deep file cabinet in absence of index cards. For sound recognizance one is forced to draw upon abstraction of how things were and ought to be accessed without collision. There is infinity of combinations bio-chemically charged that if one were to assert that it was mostly dark matter; a black hole so to speak; with every reason to believe that going one direction over the other will have consequences. But in all there must be a common set of gravitational pulls because most of us can find what we are looking for in an instant, at least until it gets too deep. This then is the peculiarity of an aging constitution. If left unaided or untouched it can be a dangerous thing.

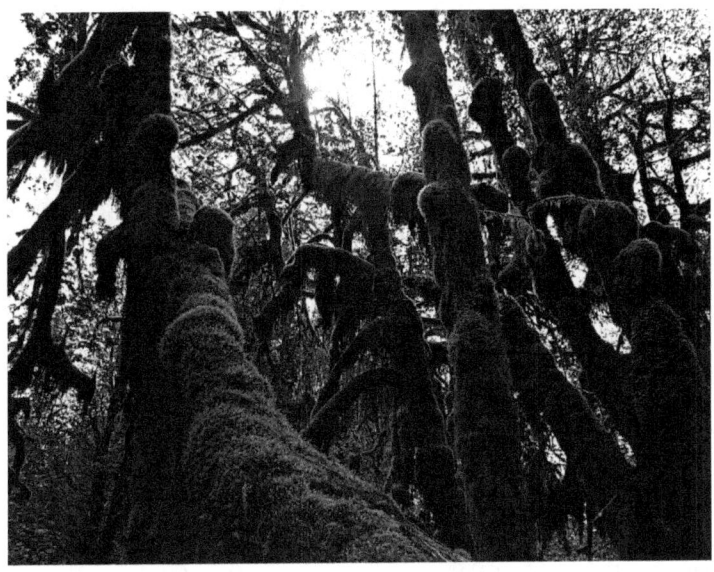

VOICE ONE: *This will bring us directly back to what distinguishes good theatre from bad: monkey see and monkey do. The idea is to encounter and then confront this notion of a dark place as one plunges into its recesses for on particular thing—progress. The proposed production slams us into a place causing friction of innumerable proportions and resultant heat. It obeys no laws of a single stage and rotates almost at random from left to center and then to the right direction under the pull of an audio and visual vortex. It is not a smooth transition in many parts and does not*

follow rotation. Yet in theory it is never chaotic: partly approaching and retreating with one part into another.

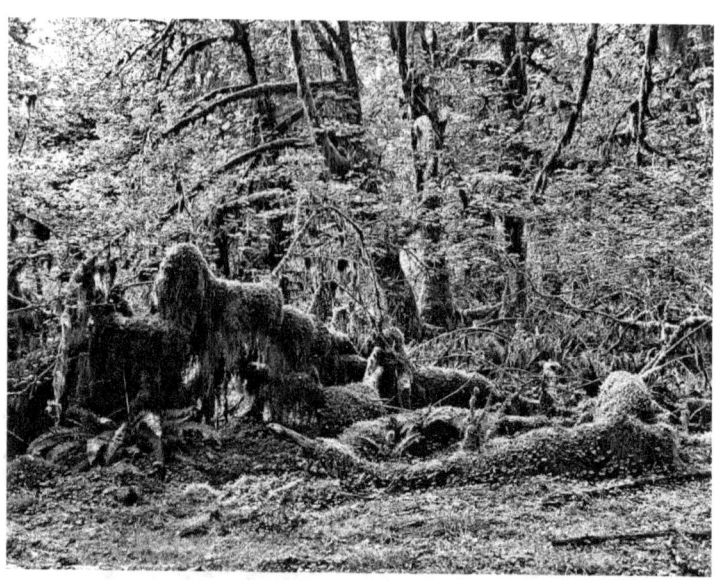

VOICED CONCERN: *Might this account for why your previous theatre had to be shut down? Your proposal is based on one assumption: it will be reasonable enough to draw crowds. But can the splendor of a vastly new theatre be sustained, or would it fade just as quickly as one is pulled into and then escapes this vortex you speak of. Another point of view might include if this has ever been done successfully before, or will it be just another close approximation. All vortexes have at least two components: one pushes you in and the other pulls you away. Can one reemerge successfully: analysis of variance with repeated measure assure.*

Hopefully his ability to discover and savor the evidence provided is conspicuous enough.

VOICE ONE: *Well at the very least it will hopefully be livelier than others. Good theatre does not constitute redoing the same plays forever. I expect you think this as gigantic laboratory surrounded by a set of random transformation. It is closer to a series of true interaction, and hopefully an explosive one. Talking about this seems inadequate to explain all of those things at play. Experiencing it might be a better fit for observation, and the feedback necessary for further exploration. Earlier I spoke of the spectroscopic peculiarities. Consider this as a means of exploring those interference patters which matter most, in closer to real time.*

The traditional constructs of theatre will be maintained, I promise you. Just as true journalism did not go away with the internet, it was simply redefined.

Perceptive Sensations   Michael O'Connor

Screen Eight

TONIGHT THERE IS A MUSICAL CONCERT OF SORTS just before the first curtain opens. The duet of one woman and one man tackle poetry reading to music: one standing and moving about fluidly while the other picks a Spanish guitar and strum taps a beat on side of the fine wooden shell in a sudden explosion. His voice is full of melody while her voice is full of anguish and pained expression. No one in the audience will want this to end soon as it has embraced and then taken everyone's breath away.

The viewers in the several front rows have expressions of astonishment because they can see the real tears that flow down each entertainers face; perfectly lit by blue beams from the rafters above, each angle of illumination is as brilliant as the next. Everybody is sitting through the refrains and nobody talks of shifts as the night continues outside of this plush chaired haven. Many sets of eyes are close enough to see the grain of the wood of this fine guitar on a polished surface, and all ears can hear the strum of knuckles against solidly glued pieces and a neck tightly fixed to a body of the finest wood acoustically provisioned.

The well balanced acoustics of the internals of this environment have been transformed with the addition of directional cells to the top, and the living gardens at the base. Sitting through this is as though one is in a park or even sitting out in one's own garden. Is there any other way to hear great music before a highly anticipated performance? The heavy curtains have not been drawn yet, and perhaps absorb some of this ongoing ballad. Only a specialist or sound mathematician would know for sure—the polyphonic qualities can be assured only through highly trained ears.

As western entertainment is more often presented, the thought of this being primarily artificially produced lingers on no one's mind: the plants and smells are transplanted in equally illuminated expressions on most of their faces; the overall health of an audience is so well maintained would they be maintained under the branches of trees of gently brushing away the long green grasses that sway with the breeze created by hidden and artificial fans. This remains at best astonishing to those who are certain they have been exposed to a very new form of theatre.

There is this hope.

The true novelty of this inner sanctum is that green and brown earth serves many as tables for cocktails and little plates of finger foods. People of all ages are sitting around party areas on blankets provided, yet this is all inside of one building. Although the puppet theatre they have amassed for has yet to surface on the stage all eyes are staring and electrified by the swaying heavy purple curtains behind those two musicians; harmonics grow surer by the minute.

No one notices that one hour has gone by. The entertainment is that assured.

The true story has not been told yet. Ultimately the foreground entertainment will give way to the background signaled by a call of attention to a parting of the two heavy curtains. The audience will retrain positions to the more upright, and a hushed pause will give way to a prolonged and exalted applause. No one can retell the story just yet; this is the first full performance with the new inner gardens. It is an unparalleled event: the sound system which is full circle, lighting that strobes and flows almost imperceptibly, and a near constant air stream that is almost too warm yet too good to regret. If deferring comments are being met, they are most likely to compare and contrast this event to almost any outdoor concert of its kind.

Many insist that this is the first of its kind done completely indoors, under a unifying roof. They most likely are right.

Josh probed and made plain to his assistants that tonight's performance must be like no other before. It must exalt and then exhaust the talent and the audience must be a wits end by all of the senses that will be taxed tonight. His intension is to arrange the closest scrutiny to each and every detail: what they will see, what they will feel, and by all manner of direct observation make this performance one which would be talked about for a generation. Regardless of their respective positions back stage or out in front with this audience, maintain a keen interest; an appearance of wit, wisdom and connection to all; to assist each and everyone in the audience with a corresponding connection would be the most important aspect of their very positions of employment.

"And if I could also mention here, that we will very much be paid by the inclination to filling up this auditorium every night in the near future. The standard of highest achievement has been set: all are expected to play a keener and finer role than ever before. Look forward and anticipate. Tomorrow's opening will be the ultimate prize."

The next evening's performance bade well to the previous one and all talent and crew spent every moment of time engaged in and around the stage. After another daytime rehearsal the company steamed forward with the promise of the other end of the night—the twenty-four hour clock was well maintained by the director and the producer—as never was anyone sitting alone in a section of the auditorium. If the stage did not need grooming then the flora surrounding this sometimes strange venue called out for someone's touch. The lights were bright twenty-four hours and the view was never plain.

Salutation: Josh would answer to a higher calling; a box office bank of phones was kept ringing, and several online sites were attached to with vigor— leave nothing behind and never stop looking forward to the glow, warmth and murmur of these beautiful crowds who were so enthralled that many faces could be seen repeating the cycle. One mind would never be sufficient to assess what some are up to and doing back in the environment surprised by the interior again and again. Chairs and tables were booked beyond the far edges of a schedule for the perfect vantage point, or at one satisfying edge or another.

The ascending and descending sounds accompanying the audience versus the performers seemed crossed where one could play the other without failure or even momentary interruption. At one point or so members of the audience sallied forward before and after the show to offer a recantation or passage, as well and sometimes even better than the puppet troupe itself.

The mind can only revel for so long with this prolonged and promising galore. These giants perform so well with their scaled down counterparts.

The heart is open to welcome what is received; visitors rendered applause even warmer that the passage before; the plants, bushes and small trees did certainly appear to grow a bit larger from the opening of the curtains and again when they closed. Would this have been a taller ceiling they would be no limit as to how far any of them would grow: lush greens against purple and brown trunks, an arrangement of yellow, red and orange, the summer's sunlight would no sooner be suggested had one not remembered it was night and leading into fall.

If this were a truly first person description: "I have come and have witnessed tree branches turn into arms and legs, held up by an array of almost translucent strings, operated by fellows just out of my immediate purview. Did they have an off blue cast up on stage in contrast to the green I am surrounded by, and those smells: I can picture rich dirt on my hands and face, and the condensation and precipitation makes my skin feel so quenched and refreshed?"

Be it a witness to this second hand, it is sure that one would have received an accurate depiction: sensation and perception without remand.

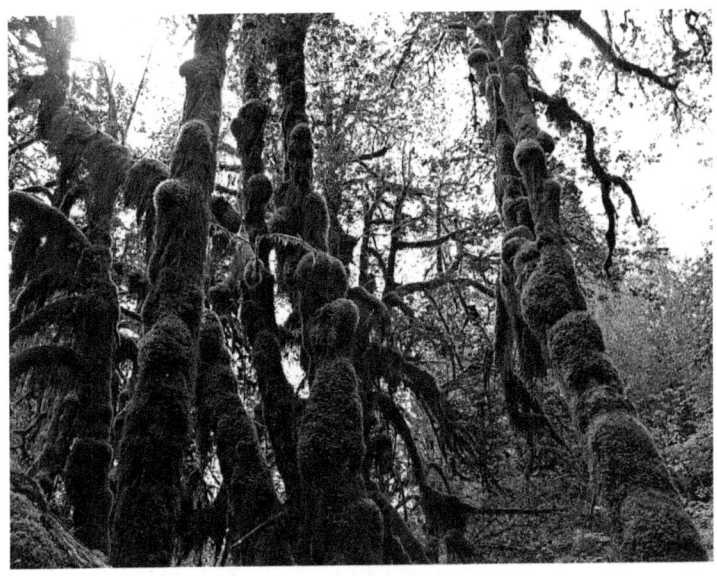

VOICE ONE: *I want this to be explosive and whirling and a surprising triumph of cerebral contemplation. It must have a distinct form, yet show all of the views one can remember taking shape before the important questions can be asked. Was there a prevailing view? Upon discover did it evolve: a somewhat guided speculation on the subject and a practical realization of proofs of the before as well as the after.*

VOICE FROM OFF STAGE: *Ah, the solid facts at last. A fragment or so was lost, but then found. This is the first thing that strikes the mind. It has a force: that second thing. I was not its victim, but rather its survivor; intact enough to follow the next act thrown as a curve. I believe the result to be a fortuitous event.*

One audience lay east and one to the west of the stage and doing what was expected. The nearest to the stage or the closest to the flora had equaled chance: to see, hear, touch and feel all of the emotions exuded from the puppeteers careful volleys: no one could refuse. The signals, symbols and noise were sent and affected without rewrite, without backslide. No, it was a commencement of substantial merit thrice on command.

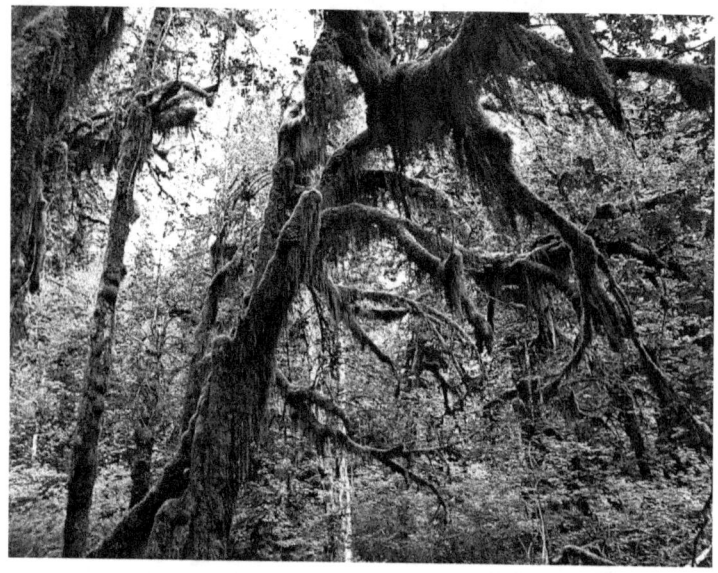

VOICE ONE: *Look again at the growing aspects of theatre evolution. We can still recognize its constituent parts; those parts which act as stairs. There is one more claim that I shall make later. In the meantime, as a preparation, stay fixed on the transition between the multiple stages. There is creation with destruction. So*

how is this scored when termination is the curious result?

Be it a witness to this third hand, to suggest otherwise, that would be so unwise: without this shelter, without this playwright, without this song: the ongoing fever and climate would no sooner be cause for change. And a lot of money was exchanging hands to be exposed to giants working strangely small characterizations of an on gong storyline practiced to near perfection.

Tonight there was a musical concert of sorts just after the last curtain closes. The duet of one woman and one man is a poetry reading to music: one stands and moves about fluidly while the other picks a Spanish guitar and strum taps a beat on side of the fine wooden shell of the same. His voice is full of melody while her voice is full of anguish and pained expression. No one in the audience will want this to end. But after an elongated span of time they begin to stream out of several double doors and make way into the street to relive, revisit and restore the opening to the close.

If they saw this before they have forgotten it due primarily to the overwhelming desire to see, hear and feel it as though for the first time. The audience is mesmerized and then released at long last.

It is dark, and it is time to head home.

The entire run was captured on video from a multitude of angles and perspectives. The review was not hard; nothing comes unexpectedly when there is a predefined focus. After some degree of post editing the director and producer began to see a common thread in audience reaction—promising as they may rely on applause alone, the ongoing facial expressions and body language were more enlightening. The results were in. The overall affect was not without low spots, marking several scenes which would require a significant revamp. The two men did not differ with regard to opinion—no departure from a common ground of thought at long last.

What was seen was appreciated—no doubt some of it as painful as one would surmise. As the director immediately put it, into action one moment after midnight, more succinctly put after several glasses of stout.

"There can be no more compromise; some of this must go."

The troupe was sent for and witnessed the post edits without embellishment. What they saw and what they heard was received on their part with greater astonishment. They did not ask why. And there was no failure to understand the consequences of why.

"The streams do not lie, the reality is not unscarred, and having reviewed this over and over again we have decided to thin out for the next run. Does anyone not understand?"

On the receipt of this final news the troupe in general was less than distraught. Many passing, the knowing faces told the tale well: participants were finely segregated within a single passing, maybe two. After one last appeal in particular a little speech was produced by the leader of the troupe, helplessly announcing the most appropriate harvests are to be made, effective immediately. This was not a comfortable approach to termination by any means at all. And after this affair, some remained ever so attentively while others gathered their belongings and headed out the back door.

Long arms, legs and torsos straightened and forms stood up erect enough to absorb the director's cuts— resistance benefited no one. And no one was ashamed given the abundance of evidence and feedback. They were simply resolved to move on.

For those who had just departed, it was a bloodless loss just the same. Their faces would still line the back entrance and hallways—an esteemed prize. And those who would remain would have their profiles shifted up toward the rear of the stage, immortalizing the triumph of recognition by audience and by peer.

It was long into that night that Josh bid his partner farewell for the journey home. Once there he sits somewhat dejected, for the ones who did not survive this plight. Outside, the drumming of creatures nocturnal—surrounding his dark house, scurrying to the next safe haven. At what stride does a director have to take to parade to the next opening; by invitation each new voice an astonishing recollection; with wonder of how accurate were their objective questions; that humbling applause is never forsaken.

The questions he was left with were innumerable. Invariably the first question and the last give him great pause: what did or did not occur was never the question: what is that, that is truly perceived. Did he act wisely enough as a director of art, rather than a champion of the box office?

This troupe must be actors as though they are possessed with each and every scene. Anything less would be most deceitful. This was a calling of what was yet to be seen, for this anguished and pained director. Would he seek refuge in the darkness of his home and the last drop of the bottle at his bare feet?

The theatre is not at all about triumph at its peak. The solo actor entering this space was a test of that theory, even when they get it wrong. There is success in the failures all along. For a director not to readily embrace this notion let it be said that he should simply step aside and allow someone else who does take over.

No, this is not driven by box office receipts alone. He was and he is now champion of the arts—this strangely wonderful puppet theatre.

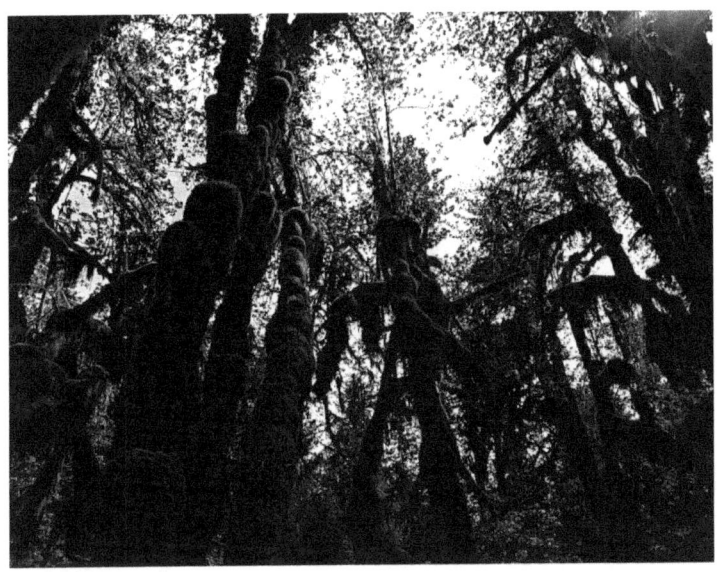

VOICE ONE: *There is one continuous set of circumstances on account. The question of their origin, transition, termination followed by rebirth is all the more puzzling.*

Which comes first: the light or the recognition of the light? As we will see there is no final answer to this ponderous question. The peculiarity of this troubling phenomenon is in its appeal, that it can never be fully addressed with regard to the universe.

Screen Nine

THERE HAD BEEN NO REAL WARNING with regard to the detachment the talent felt as members were segregated into two camps: those who stay and those who would leave under duress though well paid. The troupe manager was not entirely ignorant of any underlying misgivings from the recently departed, but certainly the reticent anger, perhaps anguish of some of those who remained in company was more of a surprise. The attacks came from the left and the right, not only up against management but to each other as well. This was becoming one unhappy cast. Staying was not for the weak hearted, and finding a suitable target for escaping the pent up frustrations became widespread.

It was scary at times; the capabilities of the athletic members wore on as they opened verbal and physical fire; annihilation was in everyone's path. How deeply affected were the stake holders was never completely assessed, so long as the costs were contained and the margins were sprite this was still a civilized world. It was not until the terrible news of the attack on the director and producer did this series of pain escalate to higher levels with intent to bolster whatever controls remained.

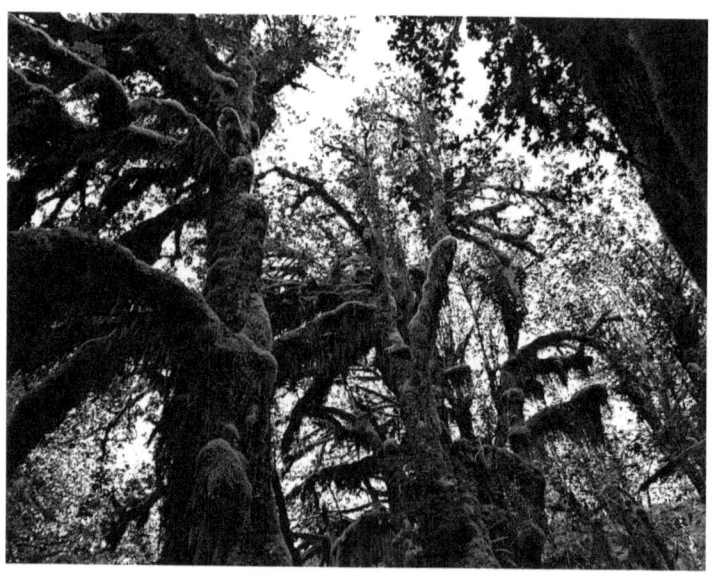

Who controls this tepid distemper would be anybody's guess. Facial expressions and menacing cat calls aside, this show would go on.

VOICE ONE: *The cause of theatre is to be found in closest proximity to locale. This varies inversely from what's on screen and its attempt to go to greater distances. I call this first part the attraction to the nearest surface.*

THEY SAID: *If two causes attract each other one will draw the other out.*

All though discontent between the theatre company and the powers that be would eventually be controlled, the in depth and sometimes boiling consternation reigned in show after show. The most unfortunate misgivings were open on stage, causing many members of the following audiences to leave their seats at intermission and never return. Calling for more action to take place, the two principal investors called in for outside help, deciding for everyone how this outcome would be forcibly retrenched and ultimately disposed.

"Render this cause with all resources humanly possible," they continued.

The possible was still an open ended question for everyone. New faces appeared and they did not seem to have a specific position in the cast or crew. However, their presence became well known.

Measure-for-measure they may stay and inch by inch the stage is regained. Betrayal can be overcome; what just matters are how high the ultimate costs.

What was done was to secure no small fortune. In some degree the attacks on two of the principals became a counter measure for revenge of the box office. Josh's usual steadied hand at running the theatre's operations, and his partner's logical thoughts were very much missed. The reliance on bullies with an almost military style made the entire production that much more destitute. They were large and facially menacing; eyes always diverting to a back alley retraction. This was no small sacrifice the talent paid, but rather a truer sense of destination— self fulfilled. It was directly related to their past actions.

To say that one was at war with the other would be a massive understatement. The only clues to its outcome were the physical capability of the recently hired versus the keen and cunning minds of the originals behind the scenes, at the back of the stage.

It was there that the real battles were waged, for anyone who would know it. But it was the dwindling audiences who were paying the most dearly.

During one evening's pass, there was an occasion where the mess spilled out literally onto the stage. The description of the terrible occasion would bring one to tears, followed by anger. This theatre and its living gardens were a beautiful place, filled with marvelous acting on previous nights. The treasures of puppet theatre were worn away by the unsightly mess of bodies spilling out past the open curtains and into the front row. It was here, most fortunately, that the entire three front rows were mostly empty, due to the fast spreading reputation of this troupe and its dubious past. The treasures of fine acting by string or by free movement were quickly borne away. Gone were the explosive and victorious appreciations of curtains closing for the night. The general state of things had come to a head, resembling the antics of a post game rather than the fine arts.

"Let the record be clear, this things finishes tonight. Not a single curtain will be opened until all remaining animosity has been cleared"

So say the investors to a recovering director and producer. The agreement is made and all parties depart to render this under. The hardships already endeared were only too easy to leave behind. There had been enough margins to clear away this stage for the remainder of the season. The box office was officially closed and the troupe was paid and sent on their way. The climate of this theatre was well under way: the fog was not lifted through the season to come.

And the day came.

On the day after his arrival back home, Josh had just declined an invitation to open the theatre for another troupe to drop by, having no inclination to become party to an opening this soon. His decision to stay on the sidelines for a while longer was not one of self preservation alone, but also on the insistence of Tess.

She had spent many days and nights slipping in an around his hospital room, unable to leave him alone;

he was thinking that this was a combination of unrelenting love mixed with less passionate guilt. The smell of her skin was left lingering in his mind even now, as he slipped out of bead and headed to the bathroom on his own. It was the first time in as long as he could remember that he was actually alone for more than thirty minutes.

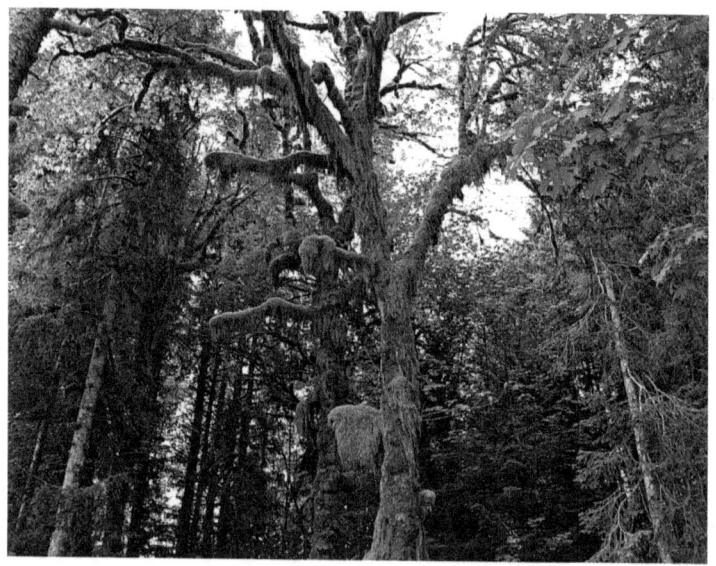

VOICE ONE: *I am not ready to yield to the forces of distortion. I have been entrusted to make this work somehow; damned by allegiances and restrained by their pulling me further into this restraining envelope. Money alone cannot be due cause. There has to be the presence of mass appreciation to go on—a demand.*

Shuffling across a bare wood floor he makes it through the last threshold with the apparent scent of his past lover filling his nostrils and lungs with a mix of salty perspiration and sweet perfume. He cannot bathe by himself because steeping down into the deep tub is all next to impossible given his recovering disabilities.

His clothes slip off without much effort and he steps into his shower after it has warmed. The water torrents pore over and rinse his back with comfortable warmth, continuing across his butt and down twisting across both legs until it reaches the tile floor. If there was another way of living in the moment he could not say where or when. The sensation was close to divine; reasoning of touch and smell dominates his thoughts in the moment of calm.

This place and time is held to tightly. It is not as though he missed the attentiveness of nurses washing his skin day-to-day. But being his own person he relished the capability to explore it in a manner that would have sent them running out of the room, given that he knew them only with the civility warranted by hospital rule. In this place he could let all of his body function as it would give the close reception and performance by a hand moving slowly and repeatedly over one part versus another.

The trained hand knows where to go and for how long. No other means of communication was deemed necessary. This was something one could never do at a public café. It would have been received as too misleading by the audience.

At a moment one could call a climaxed achievement, by any sense of the theatrical word, self readmission concurred. Anything else would be misleading had it been witnessed live rather than in written terms. No one was deceived including the director who is now hugging the wall of his shower and crying. If someone could ask he would explain the tears away as a beautiful moment—satisfied with the beauty of nature and the other worldly means of achieving the purest sensation of all. He had a final comfort before the knock at the front door.

It may have been the longest journey from dry towel to fully clothe before he made it to the source of the sound; a demand to come in complete with the illusion that the previous and intimate act had never occurred.

The hand finds the polished knob and a face witnesses another's stare and is encouraged to come in. It is Tess and she is showing all the signs of another recovered from an earlier trial.

At the moment of stepping through this threshold she could scarcely train her eyes away from his, looking for signs of recovery, apparently. They both spoke of apologies which could have been shared earlier, and the memories are claimed forward simultaneously by one outspoken over the other. This is certainly a long stretch of time considering the front door still remains open and the rain outside streams in via the wind.

"I am very impressed by your being shaven, showered and dressed in clean cloths, Josh. Is it possible that I have come by while you are entertaining another? Please tell me you did this on your own."

This is a favorite point of view and he has heard it from his significant other time-after-time. If it were at all possible to overlook the manner of this instance it would have been received with more pleasure. She telegraphed and he received it all in and reviewed his choices: to address the middle span of time, or simply move forward to the other.

"You are impressed by so little. I am championing my own stride."

This caused Tess to shiver with all of the possibilities of this one simple contest of will: does she forgive and forget, impress him to give her a kinder remembrance, convey to him that two people can carry through when genuine in pretence and in focus. Neither of the two was at the furthest side of the relationship caused by the tempest hovering just below view. Their entry into his kitchen was picturesque enough. This unbroken chain of event brought things well in line: a perspective: which had to be monitored well given that a relapse might occur at any moment: pushing them over the top.

"I am glad I came, and happy to see you doing well; at least better than expect. I came over fully expecting having to baby you. Now we can get on as adults as expected."

"If you are here to discuss the Puppet Troupe I am not as open as you would have hoped. I've already turned them down and I am not ready to change my mind. A certain amount of time must pass by before I am willing to reopen the theatre doors. This is a matter of reputation, I hope to implore with you. My place is far from being untarnished."

It was as much as he could possibly convey and refrain from laughing as she recalled another strain of view. Special interest groups had reviewed the torrid affair with much laughter. It was not too uncommon for locals and travelers alike to want to take another look inside of this theatre while the iron was still hot, so to speak. Perhaps Josh could understand that this purview could be taken advantage of somehow. No one's feeling were really hurt, and no one was asking for a refund, at least not any more. The fear of the director to reopen with a new yet similar show was misdirected, according to his latest visitor. Tess staid fast with her assessment and recommendations, and other than the feelings she still had for this man, he was a hot prospect as far as the arts were concerned.

Nothing worse could come from the recent fiasco, and she did not refrain from laughing as she recalled some of the most discussed details of the brawling between the strange members of the puppet troupe and the security brought in by the investors. It was black leather clad brutes against gaily painted and costumed puppeteers, spilling across the stage and into a freaked out audience. As one could retain, the image was laughable as well as entertaining. Tess could no longer control her laughing.

"In essence you feel that I have already hit bottom. There is no other way than up from here. Is this a correct assessment?"

The drops from the coffee maker made way to the bottom of two ceramic cups. Steamy and foamy milk was still to be added to both, with one receiving a final shake of powered dark chocolate; this was no consolation for the indignity felt by her continuous laughter. A couple of more drops onto the subject would have made the best efforts to restrain pour over. The lady had her way.

Who could stand by so passively while this sudden creature reached into his heart and yanked out all that remain? The whole of his persona included his sense of respectability within the arts groups at large. His only reply was a slight tilt of his head indicating that while he understood what she had said, but the glare in his eyes conveyed an entirely different sentiment.

135

It was doubtful that this would go anyway past a standstill and willful interpretation of glance. The coffee moment had been a good one with the smells training all around his kitchen. Could he willingly concede the interpretation to her remains to be seen?

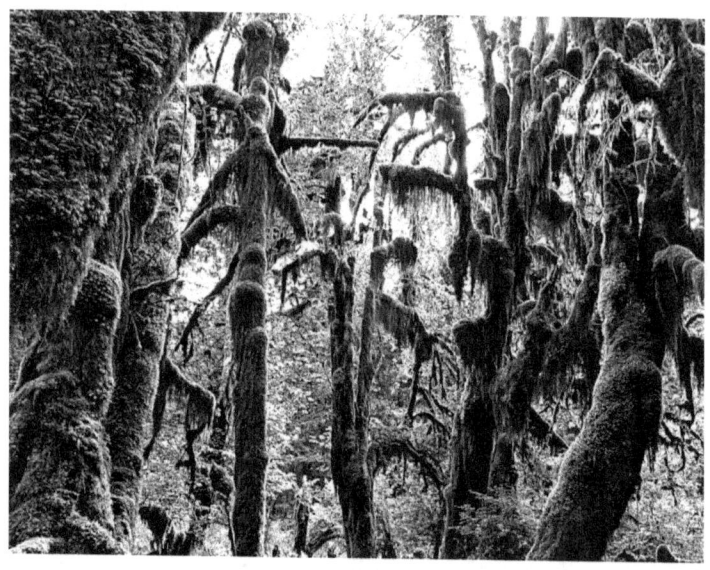

VOICE TWO: *You are caught up in their web almost by choice. This is the predicament of being both director and producer: the immediate presence of one powerful body against another one of similar mass. Now suppose you drop one for the other. Which will you chose? Who gets to influence your next move?*

VOICE ONE *I have this attraction to both bodies on opposite sides of the fence. If there were a center I wish it would reveal itself as something less than a deformation of the entire body. I am not sure I can choose one and shed the shell of the other successfully at this juncture. Perhaps if this were a fresh start I could be drawn to one side over the other. Once is never enough.*

The man is much calmer now, and the lady is beginning to feel triumphant. The appealing look on her face is matched by his; strokes which follow ease any lingering discomfort.

"Josh, I would like to spend the remainder of the day."

And they both tether to the profound satisfaction in the moments two bodies hit the bed: crisp sheets turn damp, body smells arouse, and tastes are heightened. With those connotations finally done, they would eventually sleep; the next sequel to this play of passion.

"I swear I could never close my eyes now; not wanting you to slip away."

They both went to sleep wrapped in legs and in arms—disarmed at long last. And only separated by those thin sheets did he listen to the purr of her light snores. The last words she said would possibly open those theatre doors one more time.

Perceptive Sensations   Michael O'Connor

Screen Ten

THE DAWN COMES and the day's light is broken along with the chorus of the morning songbirds, neighborhood dogs, and street side ruckus. Naturally one's first inclination is to roll over toward the other party and restore the pangs of thirst then hunger from the previous evening. However naturally inclined one might have been the reality strikes another deal. Those two sets of eyes peer up and outside the bedroom window and view the wonderful garden past first light.

"It would be wonderful if you could somehow transport this garden, at this very moment, to all points of the globe. Simultaneously, would it be too much a stretch of the imagination to have theirs transported here if and when we so desire."

This simple sketch of local nature, respondent to where else it might occur, toggled a moment of clarity for the director. The presumption that if one could share and share alike, from all portions of the globe, as an ongoing play, should presume magic. It would be worthwhile to see if one could conjure up a mechanism or means for entering this notion into the landscape of live theatre. Would it also be somewhat presumptuous that other like minded people would be equally inclined to share? Certainly the bandwidth issue and necessary triggers could be resolved. But at what cost and at what benefit could one pull in sufficient interest, desire or need to gain an appreciation of marketing this idea globally?

"Your stretch of the imagination intrigues me, Tess. But there is evidence that most would not participate unless some equally redeeming value could be secured."

"Oh, you mean how to get others to play fair; to get paid fair."

She giggled when she said this: no one had certain rights when the whole of the affair falls into the public domain. People want to get paid for such endeavors. The drive, or rather the need to create, promote and then get discovered needed to get beyond the normative instance of simply going viral.

The evidence of global scale entertainment: in the fine arts: was assured if not by technology alone. It was astonishing for the two of them to list the innumerous evidence of how this can be done, and accessed anywhere and anytime. The issue at hand remains steadfast: how to make money doing this where everyone appeared to be selling, but far fewer buying. The most attractive tracks relied mostly on advertisement accompaniment. But how does one make fresh fruit and floral scenes look more attractive when it can never get beyond cardboard?

"The world population is so large, we must face the facts that it isn't getting any easier to be in the fine arts."

Josh listened intently yet shook his head in the negative: music, film, photography and dance are so plentiful given the unlimited space of global networks; yet it is the local instance that still reigns as divine.

"The true scope is to really limit the people who can have access."

Unlimited access meets the true demarcation of global demand: it remains free if in the public domain. The actual appearance of global interaction is still an unflattering illusion.

"You know that makes me uncomfortable; everything always has to be about money. Josh, try to get beyond that for a moment."

He knew well in advance that Tess would bring up the notions of collaboration and trade and barter. It was a wonderful conviction, but the infrastructure to manage it well was still only tested true in a sparse number of occasions. Josh had traveled well and fully understood that the true success of both was local presence, not globally at all. He is thoroughly convinced that it remains just out of reach for the moment. The more he saw those conditions change, the faster they are reined in by larger bodies who could always assert controls at the drop of a hat.

"Those social conditions are well known, Tess. But if it is one thing I have learned from artisans is that no one can perform forever for free."

His argument with her always gets back to the matter at hand; as he only wants to direct and produce locally. The whole point of sustainable connection— collaboration—is that it should not require too massive an infrastructure to make it happen in the first place: true enough for growing and distributing locally produced farm goods, music, screens and plays. The connection, from his point of view was to stay local. Perhaps it was only the larger corporation that necessitated thinking globally in the first place.

The conversation was the first return to reality for the couple in a very long time; both holding onto emboldened positions without one undermining the other; a case where two people can interact solemnly, intellectually, after all those years. They had entered a new place not by accident, but by letting enough time to pass to enable exploring around the previous obstacles with enough distinction for all. The just completed instances no longer appeared strange or out of favor. Open ended questions many lay ahead, but for the benefit of intension the natty past need no longer impede progress to the next stage of the relationship.

Call it an insistence to continue a life's journey with each other, doing the right thing merits individualism as well as a sense of dualism: the call of late: not prolonging that either party was right or wrong lately. At second glance she stands just before him and looks straight into his face, and then he ultimately matches her glance with less self-consciousness and obviously with fewer strained interruptions. The only question left lingering is this: could they do this on a daily basis.

As a true courtesy he abandoned the need to pull her into a more pressing dialog as how to counter what had happened at the theatre. Josh was not convinced this was the most appropriate time to unleash a torrent of ideas he had been mulling over just before she rang back into his abode. On the other hand, Tess seemed to be biting her tongue with regard to some other equally pressing message. They made a similar and very concerted effort not to draw anything of real consequence into the moment. It was an interesting test of wills; each one was willing to make the sacrifice of pretending to pass it off to another day. One last lingering look was shared by all; by then they took to opposite sides of the kitchen with purpose.

To each a corner: a table made for a useful barrier which they knew intuitively to share but not cross over. Upon hearing her latest light hearted banter he let this overcome an edge to answer his cell phone that was vibrating on the very same surface. The tone expelling from this innocuous piece of plastic suggested at least one of the investors trying to pull him in. His letting this pass in some ways was atonement for sins of his past; reassuring himself that he was above it finally; licking a final wound.

The hours may have passed without question, while knowing glances called out a prolonged and stifled inquest. It was an interesting experimentation of non verbal communication for which neither was accustomed. Would they need further mediation was not entirely out of the question. Now they are somewhat more relaxed and one has offered to prepare a meal for the other. No visitor to this kitchen is subjected to fasting any more than is deemed necessary. This implies that food and drink are used often to overcome less certainty. It was a judgment call: dining in seems a more fashionable means of tightening this grip.

Throughout the late evening bellies are full and thirsts are well quenched, and the lady is spread out on a comfortable couch with her legs draping over his lap. Never let it be said that this is not a port of call. Josh's visitor rounds an important corner where it is more certain that she would spend the night, rather than suffer the discomfort of a sleepy drive back home. She is in fresh clad in the oversized t-shirt and boxers of her generous host. It is interesting that this mode of dress has been so universally adopted between hosts and their guests over the world.

Then there is the uncertainty of an untimely phone call in the middle of the night. At first Josh tends to the woman slumbering on the pillow next to his and drifts off back into whatever dream he may have had. If not for the second round, followed by an interval third the two of them would have spent the night together, and the need to step outside onto the back porch might not have been so misread. But it was and the sequence of steps to counterbalance the sins of not letting the phone lay, that turned this pleasant evening into one towering inferno. He apparently could not let this one call go unanswered.

When he returned back to bed Tess was sitting up and appeared angry. The side bed lamp was switched on, and a book lay open on her lap and was most likely unread. Josh was in a very tight spot.

"It was an overseas call. They forgot about the time changes."

"Is this where you tell me that you knew that call even had to be answered? You do have voicemail, you know."

The temperature is rising in the room. It was a reflection of their past together: he could never let any one call go unanswered. It was true than as it remains a common practice now.

Josh was caught looking past her and at the digital readout of the clock on the bedside table. He smiled; she did not.

"Ok, let's have it. What was so important?"

"Well, the deal moved to the final signoff. This next troupe is ready to head this way; in several days or more. I was asked to have the theatre prepared for the requested retrofit by week's end. That is all. It's a good booking; they are willing to pay for it all."

"If that is all then why don't you come back to bed?"

Was that really it? Josh was tired but sharp enough not to see anything else in play. He slid underneath the covers and shimmied nearer to her side. Tess responded and reached down below the covers for something else entirely.

"Since you do not seem to be so sleepy, perhaps we should do a bit of celebrating."

Her upper torso disappears. He aligns his skeleton straight and feels his feet stretch out and over the bottom edge of the bed. Tess is mouthing the words to some song; it is too muffled to make out. He does not care and relinquishes himself to her very early morning whims. All this while he can only think of what this opportunity means to both of them.

He sighs out loud and decides to go with the moment, letting the other matter slide, and begins to sign what she had started, and where she has left off. This was the same comfort level which caused him to think that she had returned almost by special permission. The was also his calling to return in kind whatever favor she pledged to him; the existing namesake would warrant it right. So he inscribed his most intimate passage to date on and across her silky and warm skin, not so much in gratitude as it was circumscribed by this reunion, in his house and under his rules—or so he thought.

Was this more than just short travel in time, it would seem that he had no intension of seeing it or recognizing it as any other kind.

Outside there was the densely floral garden that was coming into light and an abundance of morning sounds resonated throughout his room and his mind. Would there be any more appropriate time to suggest that Tess should take the time and the trouble to consider that this moment was a blessed reunion, in accordance to a belief and promise they had shared far longer ago than he cared to remember out loud. Josh would keep these things to himself because he was absorbed by the minute and did not want his thoughts to wander any further than humanly necessary.

According to the clock on the bedside stand it was nearing six o'clock in the morning. His internal clock was not seeking sleep but rather simply put: over stimulated by her touch, the feel of the inside of her mouth, the taste of the small of her back, and the absolving aroma of this early morning smell that made him come alive. The trouble was what he would do when all of this was over. He was in the middle of a remarkable place and it was all too familiar, but never too old.

Would this be a post awkward moment as they approached that span of time after near simultaneous climax, collapsing and intertwining: no two figures ever resembled this in kind? He felt her eyes piercing his face and searching for some kind of closure.

Could he even manage to tell her that he was still in love with her, graduating each and every second with baited breath? Her eyes would not leave this alone; that she wanted some answer to a question barely audible yet terrifying as a shrill scream. The rhythm conveyed the need to say something. That something remains alone.

Time moved slower than humanly necessary. Her breath against his became all the more imposing, leaving him with his very last test of wills over an already apparent winner. Never lowering his eyes he smiled and hoped that she would show him some compassion for his loss of words. And then she was climbing out of bed and dressing.

There was no pity for the poor soul who cannot clamor enough strength or courage to reach out for that next step: climbing the ladder to the very thing which absorbs his every thought: brushing aside all those determents by obligation. It never once concerns him that this loss is greater for him than it will be for her. He lowers his gaze and pretends to have lost something other than his mind somewhere on the bed.

The few steps she must have taken to assure that his house would be empty for some time to come were only a few meters away. There an open doorway now stands as the greatest barrier he will ever face: the reality that he let time tick away without protest. There is little pity anyone else would ever attest to; as ultimately the opportunity was his alone to choose, and expectantly to lose.

Josh stood alone as a stranger to his own house.

After the strained attention to details let slip away, there was an explosion inside of his head.   The sound of dressing was painful and the act of putting on shoes was like torture.   A fair retreat flew across the threshold and the back of her head first appeared at the foot of his driveway. When Tess turned her face was full of tears.

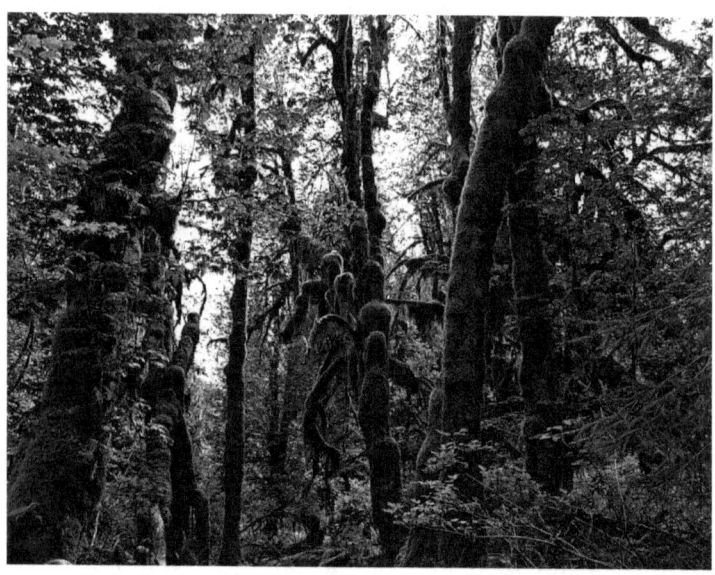

VOICE ONE *Suppose there was another attracting means to approach me for enough of a difference. My cent could become that much more clearly; not pulling me from side-to-side. Could I move toward it without considerable restraint from the powers that be?*

VOICE TWO: *Is this to be an emotional pull or a gravitational one? You do not expect violence but the relationships you severe will be explosive in their own right. Are you ready for that fierce fight? If so, move on it as you will.*

VOICE ONE: *And prepare myself to suffer the consequences anyway?*

VOICE TWO: *Well it is your own mess to walk away from. Can you hold out against something you have lost interest in, be it politics or art? Produce a pulse in one and see if the other bleeds on separation.*

It seemed that she had come across some flightless bird and it cried out with its last breath. She kindly addressed it as quietly as possible and Josh only heard half of her words. After pointing out the obvious in a dialect that was even stranger than the one inside of his own head, Josh finally found those tender enough words to regain all of her attention.

Was it possible that the final demise of one could breathe life giving oxygen into another, given the gap between the two species?

His voice was not that pillar of strength that he searched for at the moment—each tarried syllable stranger than the next—though he continued to thrust forward with the remaining dignity that could be mustered: the solitary attendant acts in good faith.

"Tess, my silence back there was not deliberate. I became overwhelmed by the motions of touching and holding you for the longest time in memory. Although I admire you for your attention to this unfortunate creature, I would implore you to come back inside and let me finish this without the prying eyes of my neighbors."

He began to rub the back of his neck with both hands, nervously. Saying anything else at the moment might break the spell that this lingering opportunity might have over him. Josh never looked back and walked into his house, leaving the front door open.

Outside there was that densely floral garden that was coming into light and an abundance of morning sounds resonated throughout his room and his mind; the mood and landscape conveyed through the Puppet Theatre's finale matching both hue and tone in a way that was both embracing and heartbreaking— another day, another opportunity for enlightenment— all the momentum warranted was the ability to stop in time to witness it and then react to art in all its glory. It was a path he has taken before, and why would it not work again

He wondered what it would take to regain that feeling and the economic accomplishment that went along with it—this spell is multifaceted and giving life breaths into his own, under its own accord. The truth be spoken it is only as good as it is shared. Josh would seek and take that gambol: everything comes across with that next script, the opening night, box office magic redone.

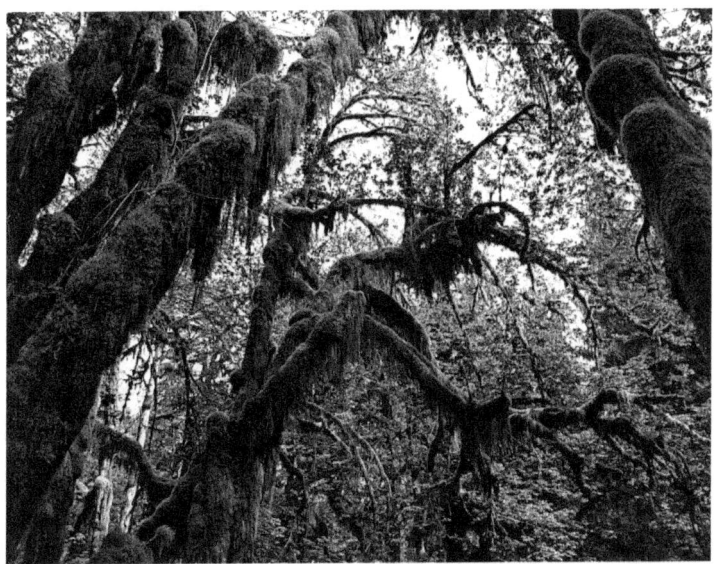

VOICE ONE: *I will be that one obscure tree in the forest around me. In the event I cannot advance further while the board pulls on me financially please feel free to sever the ties. I am calmed by the mechanism of separation and the potential spiral down to the floor of this very stage.*

VOICE TWO: *What is this mechanism you speak of? How does this occur without more negative consequence to your relationship with cast and crew?*

VOICE ONE: *Well it calls for a more agile imagination I suppose. Let's pretend I am doing this for the sake of art. I can no longer be this rigid producer and at the same time let the imagination of the director fade. If the show must go on, I split and then I must advance to meet*

*the next composition head on: return, returning to
ground zero.*

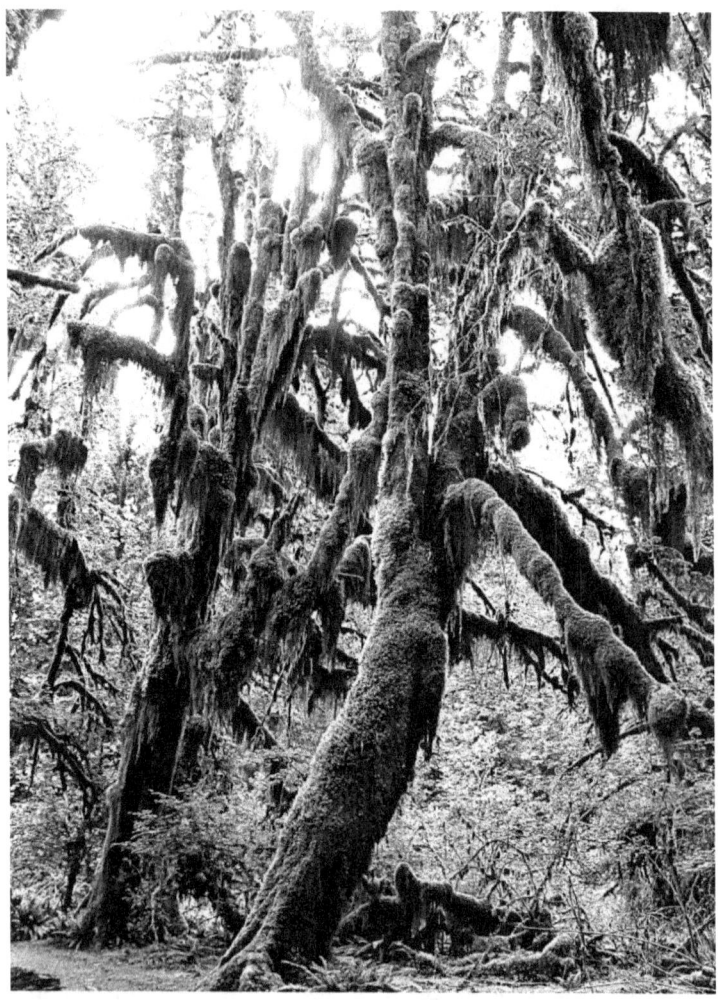

VOICE ONE: *Have I reached out enough?*

Intermission

What are those chief principles of compare and contrast which produce a body of language for display meaningfully? The ideal or perfect condition that a subject must have to represent it in context; essentially a unit of measure up and down, left to right, black and white towards grayscale; we pair and then freely associate these terms together as such as feminine or masculine. With respect to architecture and owning to size, material, position and certainly what is physically encountered can one be more female or male? Such are the arms, legs, torso, and the lips active or passive, a position over another: one being attractive and the other representing brute strength.

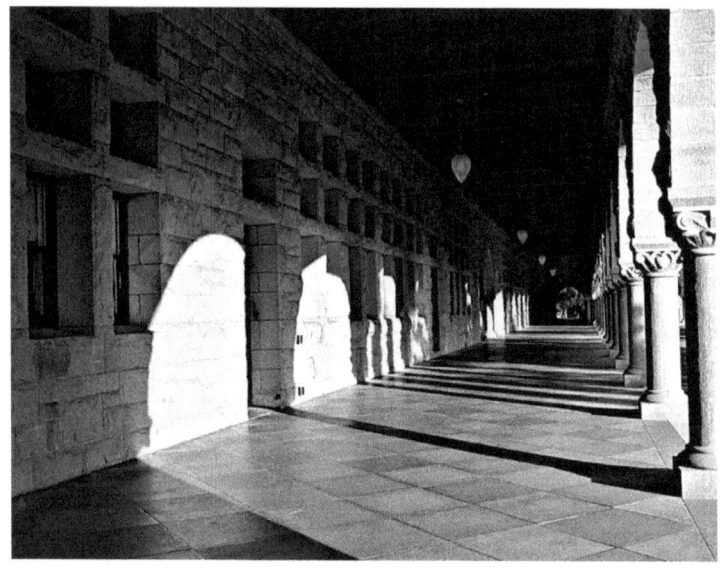

Those principles of compare and contrast become that much more meaningful when we speak. Under these laws gladly accepted the air exits from the open mouth and tones are formed by tongue, lips and the back of the throat. When the mouth is active in conjunction with motion the ideas that emanate from within become more meaningful.

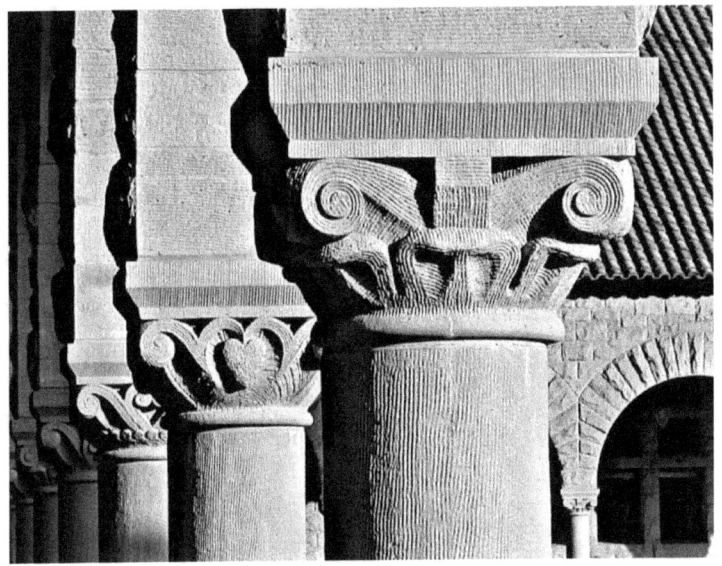

That meaning is inevitably characterized by geographic region as well; this backwards and forwards motion of language translations and alliterations combined allow us to progress an ideal into a motion and communication results in very large parts.

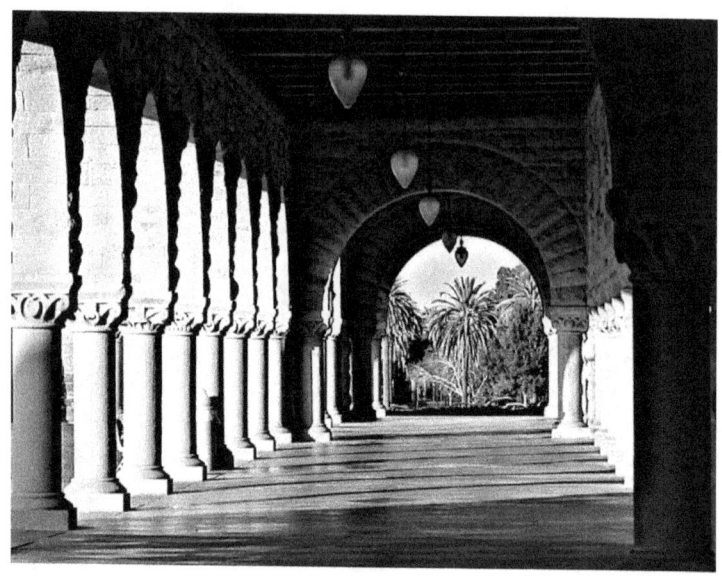

All that we touch, observe and hear is a natural movement intercepted by compare and contrast. The beauty is in the action resolved. Faces express, eyes enjoy, a mouth opens and there is exhaust again in conjunction with the movements of fingers and arms, shoulders and torso twists that articulation has indeed expected, effected and transformed into something unique to universal.

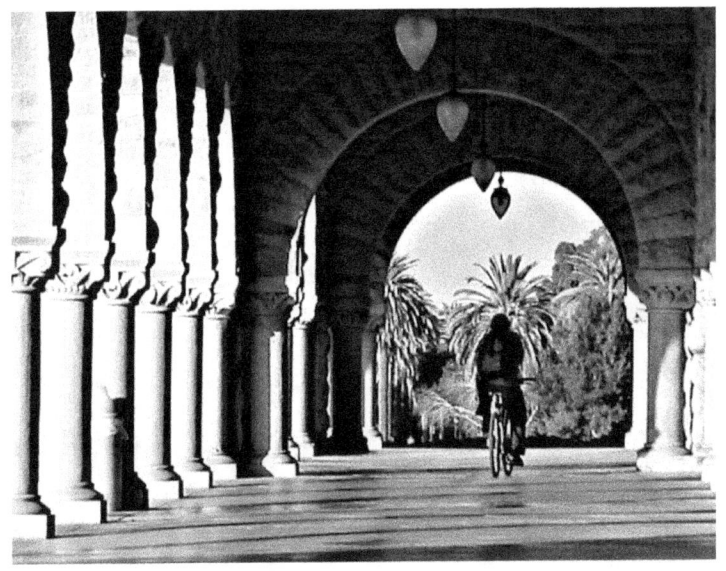

On stage this is an act superior in a way that effect transition uniformly, from simple to complex, from abstraction to clarity, and ultimately into a near perfect symbol of the times. When done with repetition it echoes in our brains until it can be retained and comfortably compartmentalized. There is this ongoing and active correspondence between intake and arousal for storage, so that it can be legitimately retrieved at a later time. It is this ability to relate to these principles of corresponding instances to clearly retrace their origin and the variations which inevitably exist between the before and the after: analysis of variance of constituent parts.

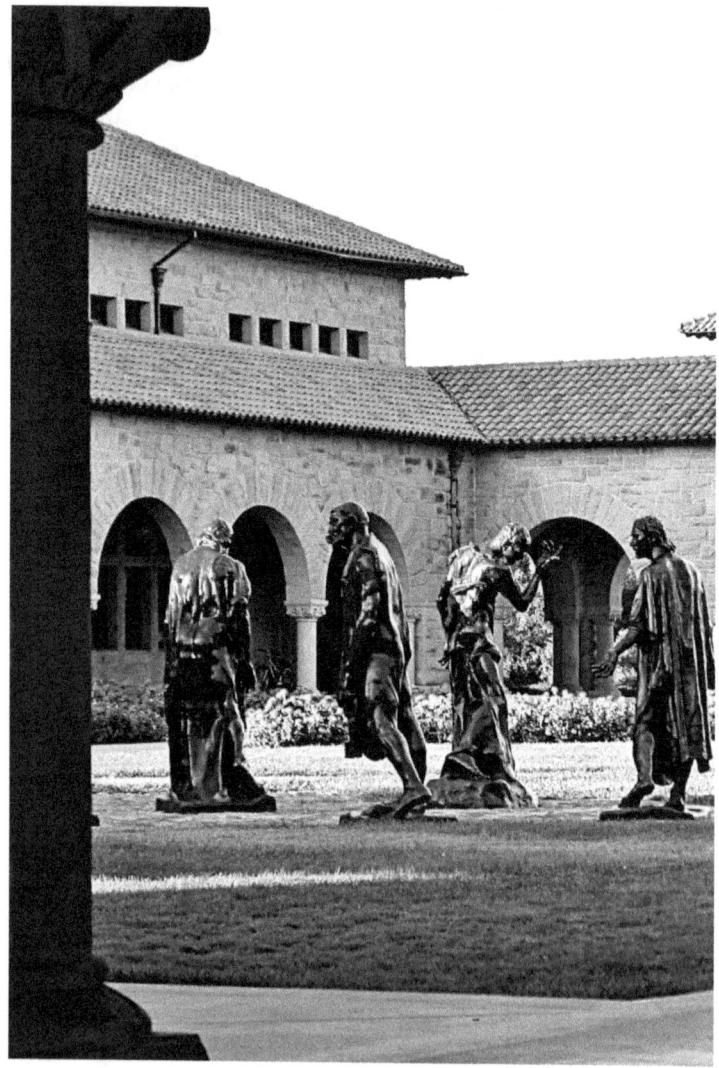

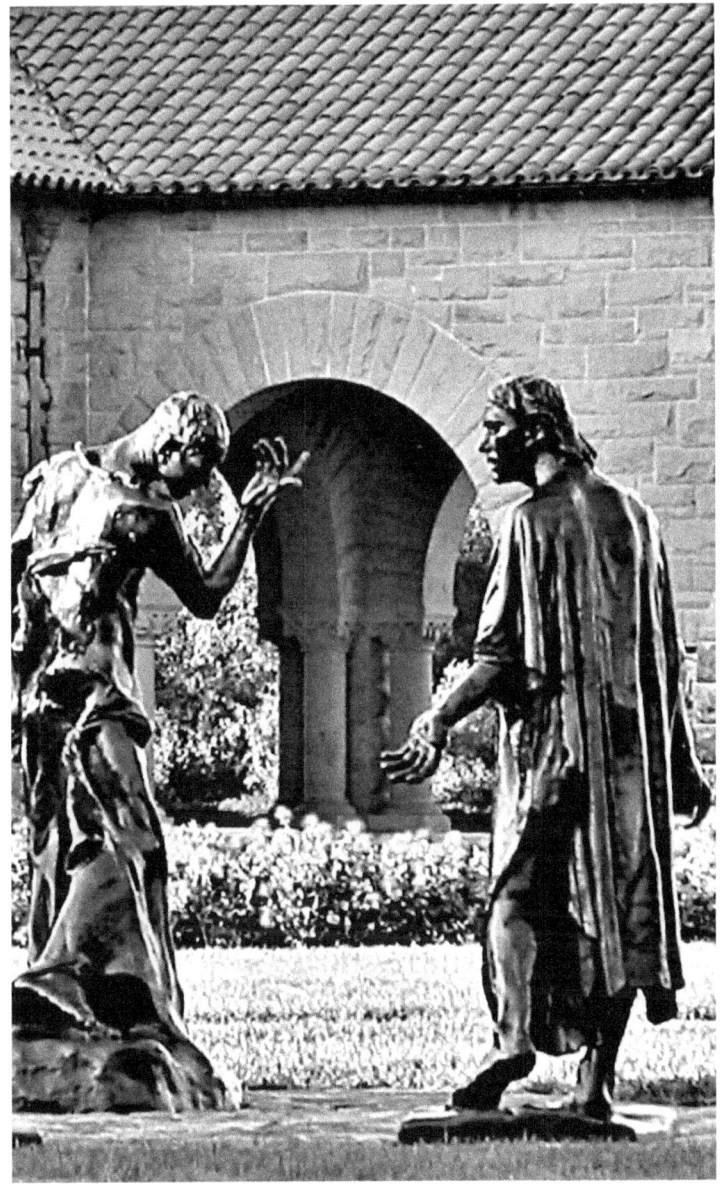

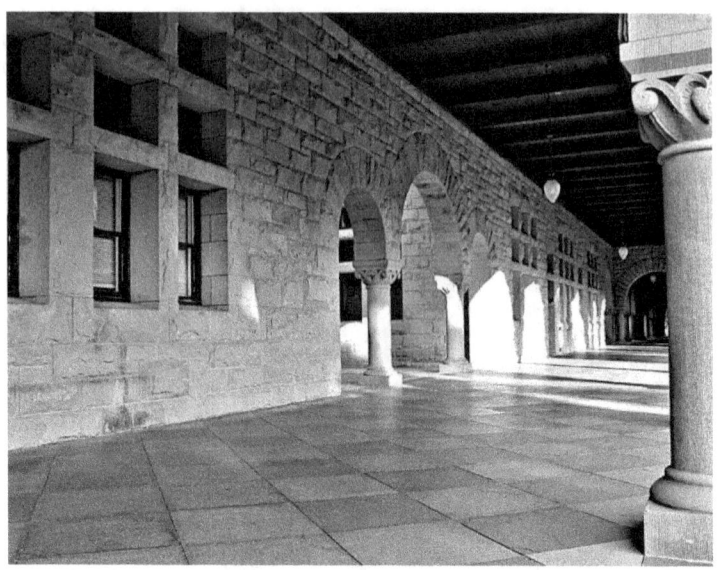

As prescribed by those who came before us.

But how does one relate this to architecture that has had such a profound effect as to influence a decision to write literature a decade later? A single column shows the way to fashion a complete storyline—fashioned from the elements of form and substance, shadowed detail, and an emotive quality which still might exist—in accordance with the rules of artistic necessity. This greater world causes one to dwell on how an inanimate column of stone corresponds to something else quite fanciful—be it conscious or pulled in from the unconscious.

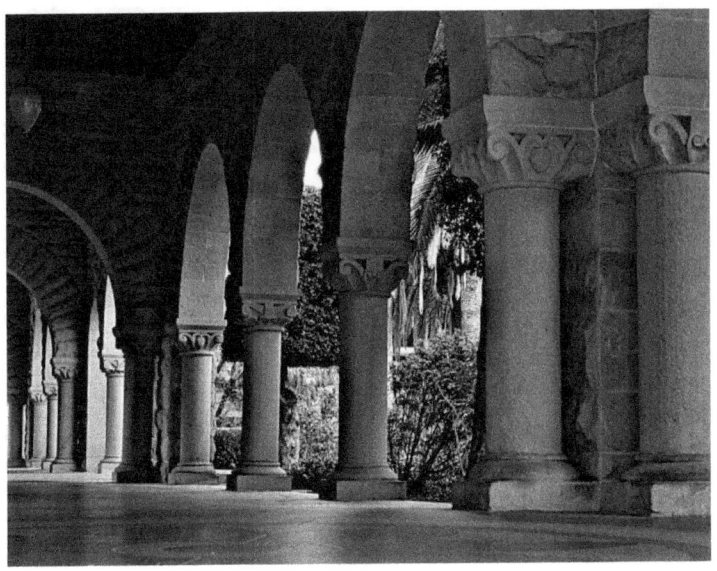

Is this part of the building feminine or masculine? Cognitively I do not know or claim to recognize the facts of the physical character of the structure. However, that said I do have an active imagination which does not exclude attributing one way or the other. One column can look like a man and the other a woman in attribution. And this is what makes me want to write another treatment of this meaning.

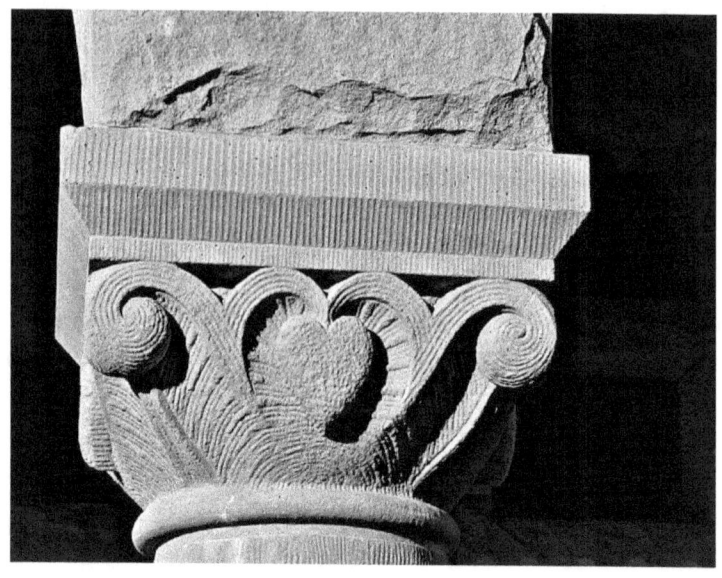

We can hold the entire scene in from its constituent parts. It is the ideal or perfect condition that a subject must have to represent it in the same context, especially when we try to redefine what is on that stage.

Screen Eleven

WHEN JOSH ARRIVED at the hotel there was a message waiting for him. He was being advised to stay at the bistro next door where he would be contacted in a short amount of time. The writer's message seemed to be a hurried script, but at the same time a reasonably kind invitation to dine on an account already set up. It was an odd start to a meeting given his appearance was specifically requested and a journey not fun.

After pushing his way past the busy crowd Josh made it to an empty table at the rear of the establishment, and right near the bar. The exhaustion of the two airport hops, coupled with a short and hectic train ride was taking a real toll. Finding a table at last allowed him to sit without worry of making another connection with only a few minutes to spare. The business of this place was almost parallel to the two sky lobbies and train station platform he had scurried across making way to a gate that seemed to be the very last in the travelers path. And now the wait staff at this bistro seemed exceeding slow to respond to his glance, exacerbating the end point of this whole affair. He continued to wave wildly to no avail.

The strain on his face apparently became clear to at least one. He found it just sly of flirtation when the friendly bartender leaned across the deep and solid mahogany wood to ask what he would have to drink, just short of screaming over the din of the rowdy crowd. Although he specified a very dry Martini, the one that appear in front of him was determined to be quite the opposite. It was returned with dismay, and then made its way back retouched in a more favorable style of which he was accustomed to. Not nearly close to being perfect; drinkable enough to warrant a declarative smile the next time the tender's gaze crossed his; the lingering stare of apology was taken as sincere enough. The second sip said it all: a thirst quenched, the smile maintained, a libation which seemed to drive all of the chaos of the afternoon away.

Another round was order after, and a dinner menu made way to his tabletop by a ghost arm not necessarily attached to anyone familiar. It was a standard array of bistro fare, and there were several items that would likely satisfied a need to consume food along with two quenching yet strong drinks. The third round made it to his table just as the food appeared beautifully delivered on three small and very appetizing plates. Another sip off a top filled glass was followed by a sampling of the tapas-styled assortment of carefully prepared food. The likeliness that it was made well in advance did not seem to matter because it was being consumed with enriched energy levels more alcohol induced than being famished. After thirty minutes end the empty plates were being cleared and a dessert menu was slid into his hands by none other than the party he was awaiting.

Pleasantries are shared immediately. Some of the crowd has been moved outside to an outdoor patio just coming on line for service. As a result the loud din has been reduced to couples searching for the right things to say, and the occasional spurt of business lingo, including his own. His business associate is enthralled with what Josh has to say. There is not sense of lingering embarrassment of his being delayed, or their initially tempest meeting in a bar.

In fact, the cost of the delay is more registered in the kind of the slurred appearance of words flowing off of Josh's tongue. The path to a more cohesive line of banter is starting out to be a rough one, and for the purpose of appearing more polished he over emphasizes key and salient points for as far as one could reach while being understood, nonetheless.

This was not the kind of business meeting either party was accustomed to: eyes could not be reached without strain, and nothing was cared for with regard to remaining on point. It was a game gone sufficiently wild before one party implored the other to sideline all bets that this discussion was certainly not on the right path. The personage sitting across the table found little to be amused by, while at the same time showed enough patience to suggest another starting point might be reached by his regard.

"I am certain that your reputation retold is an accurate one, but there is little here that we can continue as business at hand. Might I suggest we find a more suitable location for coffees or teas, and try another way to conduct business?"

The order of the night is relayed without need for clarification. Josh extends an apology for the third Martini that wasn't really needed, beyond dampening a day of sodden travel. He was just short of the point of tears, if the look of anguish on his face told any truth of the matter.

The route of the conversation descends.

For almost the entire length of the journey across the street to an open café, Josh continued to wonder out loud how this meet could have been attended to under normal terms. He was careful not to cast regret at being left to fend for his ways; remaining concerns as to how he ended up in this state were slated to avoid further harm.

"Left to my own devices under any other circumstances would have prescribed a far different outcome, I assure you."

"So, then we are both apologizing and we are both forgiven. I presume this is the only viable path which can be taken."

They both began to laugh. After ordering two very tall and equally strong coffees the banter settled down and a more polished business manner was persuaded. And at long last the bulk of an agreement moved forward.

The conversation was coupled with lively talk and one reminded the other of the mastery of business interaction. Mile for mile the distance was one with patience over disinterest or disintegration. At rest at final end, the distance between issues had been reduced and the evening grew friendlier and sharper as time and the stimulus of coffees refilled took them past the hour of midnight, and gingerly into the next day. Every now and then there was a highlighted point of disjointing, but that in it paid the way for recapturing the territories that had been stretch out by the long conversation. There was more than a sparkling sense of accomplishment to the travelled eyes of two parties ready to sign on some virtual dotted line.

Josh did not realize just how long they had been at it until the other stood up and made gesture toward the clock above the streetlamp. The hotel's height lingered in the distance and above it was an open sky filled with millions of stars. Did they not feel like giants among this galaxy?

Neither of them was breathless but the hospitality of this well visited café was giving a clear message that came close to taking their spirit: Folks, we are closing for the evening. It's three in the morning. Please go home."

"Wow, it seems that we have been working here forever. I am not exhausted but I do feel I am at the end of some kind of workout. Do you feel the same?"

The point of view was paid as a compliment, enhanced by the anticipation that there must be some manner in which this interaction would terminate in some way. The good fortunes of talking nonstop paid way for the distinguished night of doing business, but after that, how would they pave the way to the rightful next steps. This was apparently making them both uneasy.

The walk arm and arm back across the street to the hotel seemed to take forever. His view trained straight away, while hers glanced to his side from time-to-time. The summit of this evening was finally reached as they entered through the double wide sliding doors and stepped right into the lobby of the hotel. The staff was sparse given the time, and only half dozen others made their way through the echoing chamber. It would seem that every word could be listened to no matter how softly one spoke. No one it would seem was a stranger in this lobby.

"Josh, would you care to walk me up to my room. I do not appreciate hotel elevators late at night."

"The walk up that may stairs would be refreshing enough. I am way past sober now, but I could do with a bit of clearing my head. Certainly I will walk with you."

At the top of the first landing stood a small attached amphitheater, to be used by the guests of this hotel. It opened to a small but visually appealing balcony facing to the east, allowing for the viewing of the row of two level businesses and then several blocks of single dwelling houses, neatly dressed. The semi-panorama suited them both well and messages were exchanged in response to the climate, the neat gardens, and into which windows one could recall a most interesting portrayal of occupancy. The unique responses were revealing.

It created a bridge in which either party could use to cross over into a hushed overtone of longing. This was not too much of a stretch of imagination of what each party had wanted to say. A combined backdrop of houses filled with the activities of made up characters suited them well especially when the antics reveled into a picture of x-rated norm. They were both able to sketch it, provide the necessary choreography, and triumph over the skills that were needed to cast this story to a most suitable end.

One wonders why the two of them were soon kissing. Two figures contrasted against a backdrop of stories—like glass etched silhouettes against a wall sized pane. There was little to wonder about given their attention to the details so successfully defined. What took place next was an even funnier debate over which room would they be so inclined to complete this theatre—the luxury of being host.

This would be a longer ride than anticipated— breathing underwater for longer makes one wonder if the surface is too close or too far away.

It was only in the first and last two minutes of this exercise of intimacy that he reentered the world where he and Tess had gotten back together. Was this more or less an affront to a rekindled relationship, or a subconscious decision to revert back to a span of time where he could engage with less remorse? The attention his business associate was showing him now was what he had secretly coveted via his first choice in women. Soon watching her breath, moan and sigh with relief when she made it to that high moment brought him as much pain as it did pleasure.

The moment was less than ideal to have this contest of wills and then guilty passion. He hoped that he would eventually allow himself some freedom, albeit at the cost of spending the next several moments in ulterior torment—enabling or disabling the chain reaction at this point was to be fruitless.

The other Tess would never allow it; he climaxes inside this woman by request. It was not his custom to ask for permission once in the throes of the mutually compassionate act; let it be said that he was going with the flow; it lifted his spirits. To now suggest that he should have pulled back and literally out was not the ultimate test of good sport, so silently he paid the price and tomorrow he would beg himself for forgiveness.

The progression from sex to post transference was also enjoyed in near silence. It was the opposite of completing in near record time: minutes passed to one hour and the touching and stroking never stopped: could it have been suggested out loud it would not have made it any better. During the long and involved draw down his stay in her arms was enormously challenging given that Tess now dominated most of his thoughts. Josh needed to clear his head of all of these images. Perhaps it was his failure to breathe that startled her most.

Josh could not regulate his breath underwater no more than he could meet the challenge of curtailing his true longings for another. In splendid respite he leapt out of bed, began to hurriedly dress, and made several completely lame excuses for needing to run off all the while looking at an opposite corner of the room. His heart was beating so fast it might have made him faint if not for her aligning expression.

It is finished. They are both ready to move on.

"Well I suppose you are right; we really should be pushing off. My plane leaves in several hours and I have a bit of shopping to attend to."

If one was accustomed to imagine the things that people might say, and then impress the opposite, this race would be more in order. During his time sitting and putting on his shoes she got up from bed and headed into the bathroom for an open door pee. He chief belief that one particular sound can carry with it one thousand images burned in his retinas today. He would not have been in as excited a state if it were Tess sitting on that throne. This was his first and lasting impression—perhaps excited or in admiration.

Tess would never have gone with the door open.

By the book she would have broken every rule as she stood up, inspected and then flushed it all down before moving slowly over to the shower. And before he could chastise himself once again for all his digressions, the woman signaled him to join her. By now all had been lost; he challenged himself; hearing this thing was musical notes to his ears. It was not his steady diet of involvement with the significant other. They had moved on to two people living separate existences while together. It was almost a business relationship it was so canned at times. But what was this?

Wasn't this woman a business associate as well?

Josh did not join her by way of verbal explanation. He did however place himself fully clothed on the counter while his business counterpart showered on the opposite side of a clear glass door. The time she spent washing would be stamped into his memory forever. And would this have been any more acceptable than if she had not chose to accentuate desire and need with several strains of prolonged noise, to satisfy her own needs.

She was washed and now able to control the entire next sequence of events. They would both miss their next connections, respectively.

If the latest chapter were to be published in a book she used every pleasured moment as currency for her benefit. The impression one is left with is that this was a moment parlayed into an expectation of outcome. She hosts and he is the diligent guest, always managing to please just at the most appropriate moments.

Where cloths are ditched again the official mode of dress is naked. He listens to all of those little voices in his head and makes notes where he intends to revisit.

Not accustomed to having his way in the spurious moments of deeper reflection, his time is up when she gets there first. The stakes are suddenly reversed and she has somehow conveyed that this prolonged visit was in error.

This woman is ditching Josh now that she has received his promise to entertain her client at his theatre. It is not all happy as it would appear: she got x, he maintained y, and z was still in the open.

Whoever should endeavor or be inclined to give those several inches of leeway is never as apparent. This moment has passed them by, and they are both trapped by their own devices. No one is willing to make eye contact for as long as necessary. It could be construed as a mutually hatched devious plan, but nonetheless it is moving forward.

"You can count on this, Josh. My client will be ready to open on the second week of the month. I won't even ask if this is sufficient time, as you well know. Just make it happen—on time—and we will all get paid in kind."

"The trouble with a deal signed off in this way is that the spurs it causes will ultimately surround us to the point of suffocation. You of all people should know that there is much more at stake? Recall the outcome of the last troupe at my theatre. They are a household name by now, and you know that isn't a measure of success."

"Call it what you will, Josh. But be forewarned we have a verbal deal. I will hold you to those details later, I can assure you. If you bail on me now or later, your name will be a whole different measure of household name. This is a race now my friend—let's sees who crosses over first."

They both dressed in a way that reflected this measure—understand how this may look and feel so strange—two entirely different personalities occupy the same space without ever passing another glance. As he passes her on the way out the door his eyes barely lift to give her way. There is a whole new set of rules at play now: agree that the disagreeable impressions made over short order shall rule them over the long run. This was to become the state of things for what they affix to any future order of doing business. They have both lain with each other—so well—that going forward would never be more of the same.

"I would like to have the last word here, before we depart in two different directions. My theatre is still under my domain. I will submit to this verbal under one additional condition, that you are nowhere near the place on the opening day. There is a part of our little digression that I would like to keep as far away from my real life as humanly possible."

"As they say in your line of business: let my stand in rule the day."

She did not ask for an explanation. In his mind he hoped she would stay clear for the sake of Tess, let alone his own salvation.

And with that they both leaned toward scattering across the city. The weather was simply different that day. The social gulf that had spread out between the two did not translate to anything else more apparent than the present calm. Although it was a morning full of regret all the same, it was one also full of business etiquette, as one would attest by their coming together one last time with a firm handshake and a shared teasing smile.

"It wasn't all bad, was it?"

Josh was compelled to admit the same. It was not that he wanted to engage in this final rationalization, but he was nonetheless compelled to admit that the pairing had moved him in just the right direction. He let her go with a clear token of his endearing respect.

"I will see you at some point thereafter—I hope."

The larger part of what repels them also brings them together. It was that force of nature; several sources along; that would allow them both to endear without supremacy of one over the other.

If the course was to be corrected it would not be a measure of passing intimacy alone. In the presence of a singularly enlightened proposition, it would draw them in once more without loss of ground, position or retaining a sense of mutual dignity. Josh would have the final say before they finally departed in opposing ways. He would cross over the train platform and look back one more time as if she were standing and waving goodbye. And perhaps in some waiting area near the final departure gate, she in turn would look back over one shoulder and witness him standing there with an impish grin still on his face.

Those images were of a time before. The memories are for all the time after—when invoked they are just as accurate. This was not just a chance reunion after all.

He leaves; he boards and is then departing. The train ride was a very long period of travel. It provided Josh with the means of cautious reflection, and to make the necessary adjustments for how he would manage his bigger problem on his return home.

"Does she linger on my breath, and is her scent still on my clothes?"

Interestingly enough that standing sensation is as mesmerizing as the cross etching proposed.

That night he dreamed that it has all been incorporated into a staged production somehow. Was this to become a precursor to the next run of the season? His sweat and breathing tells a tale.

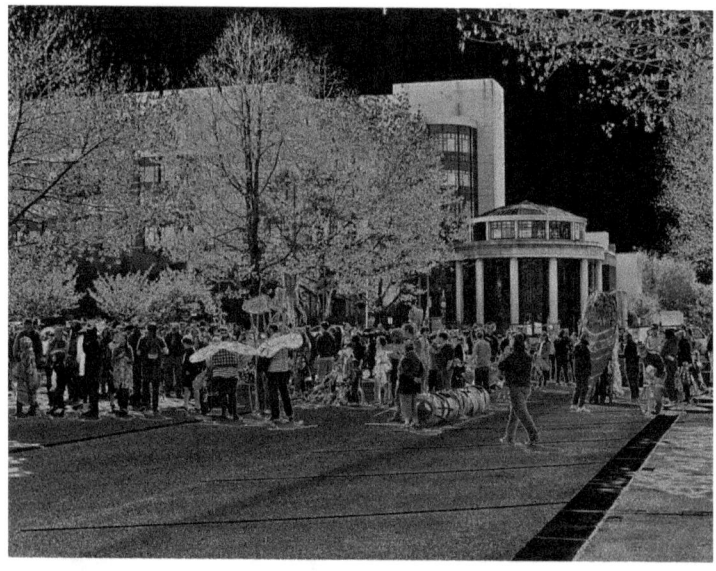

JVOICE ONE: *I have seen at length the most interesting reactions in my day, but this appears to be the most paradoxical. Perhaps it is the notion of human desire to dress as animals which are most intriguing; the manner and proportion of their mimicry far out does traditional stage. This production is, in my words, just obscure enough to be successful. The absence of any cognizance of human reflection; this peculiar sense that they are one in the same with the animals they depict; this is more than a tolerable mocking. It is a uniquely mirroring effect: dream to reality.*

CONTESTING VOICE: *I certainly have no objection to their acting out in connection with a favorite species. It would imply that their manner of dress is more than just chance. But does this do any justice to a common cause? Introduce the possibilities of explaining the enormous cost or burden of adopting one character and never to return. Is dependency original normal? Is it suitable art? Please let me continue: I must make this one additional remark to avoid misapprehension. Consider those things one desires to hear and see in modern theatre: the ability to elevate things as art.*

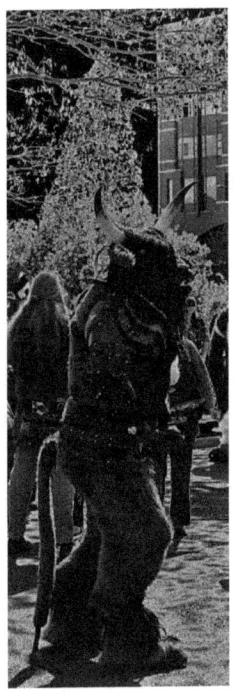

VOICE ONE: *I feel confident, and perhaps more connected than you. We only have to consider the subsequent energy of this troupe and their ability for transference to the audience. There will be a connection; I really do feel this sense of true confidence that rejection will not be formed—with great satisfaction this production is a measure of success. I have been trying to looks at all of the cons as well as the pros since those performances. There is much concern about exterior motive over direction. I am not so fragile that I will be turned by the cutting remarks by some who do not wish to understand. I understand—there I said it.*

CONTESTING VOICE: *There will be at least one miserable review, but gradually most of the reviews are merging into a succession if not a straight line: it curves and twists and turns, and at points it wants to wrap itself around one's neck to strangle. Could one suppose that asphyxiation is sexual in nature, or perhaps a desire?*

VOICE ONE: *These are excellent points. I do not want polite; offer me every facility of concern and I will unravel their meaning and direct suitable change if warranted. But I am finding it a bit expensive to satisfy all of their needs. Gradually they need to lean this way.*

Screen Twelve

THE REVAMPED THEATRE was probably the most squared away ever. This could have been a direct or indirect quote, written of stated verbally by anyone who knew the history of this place. It had become more than an opinion on the morning of the final dress rehearsal; the small islands of cast and crew are joined together for what might be the most important expression of achievement in this artistic side of world. The sides were united beyond recognition of where it had all begun: anger is replaced by calm, disarray recounted and now so much is aligned.

There is a visual and conceptual link between the day's order and the readiness of a box office beginning to finalize orders by ticket holders and media striking the claim to be on hand for the grand reopening. The stage mangers have just submitted their final assays on the course to follow prior to the first curtain parting and the wonderful opening scene to become in focus; the initial lighting will be cast down and across the framed silhouettes picked up by lipstick cameras rendered and then recast to hand held tablets. The acoustics are tuned and ready and it sounds nearly flawless with last minute adjustment still being made to the ceiling baffles. The lighting booth crew is still making last second changes to sequence, and this provides just the right amount of tension necessary before the first parting shots of voice over matter.

The most noteworthy change above and beyond was the glass etch and refraction screen that was installed, which would stand between the audience and the three stages. The concept and scope of design is to obscure the visual reality—an inside out environment—ahead of the movements of the talent and respective backdrops. And ahead of it all the director and producers pace nervously in front of the large partitions in front of the main stage and make ready for the most important change.

Officially this was the lead up to the opening of a season, cast as 'different from anything you have ever experienced before'. It was as enticing as it was bold.

"In contrast to what they say, we do not want anyone to break a leg. This has been a hazardous journey from the onset and I for one will not jinx it with the inclusion or exclusion of old fanfare. I admire the productions of earlier times, but there is no doubt that this one will pair past and present as carefully. Your audience will have devices well trained and will have as much to do with this production as you all do."

The intent of Josh's words was to avoid the standard of theatre folklore and more or less open the remarks to allow the new standards to roll in. This was to be more or less Puppet Theater, as readily found as any other means said one. This production would include programming that would entice the audience to interact directly during the action underway. There was no doubt to some that it would be an abject gamble, but a worthwhile venture all the same. In contrast to every direction Josh had ever engaged in before, this one would be the test of time in close to real time. And it was far enough along in this very industry to allow it to happen on schedule.

The place is booked out and the early on feedback from ticket holders is positive for the most part: a worthy look at the records show that most, if not all, have downloaded the tablet application well enough in advance to suggest a path to early on success. What more could be used to springboard this enterprising approach: extending a lot of control over to the audience members over that of the cast and crew.

The experience would no doubt garner strong opinion and most likely opposition to the experience of conducting theatre and entering in the strain of it being rewritten on the fly by as many heads and as many perspectives as one for pairing feedback. Whether or not it was completely executed without flaw was a dreamer's best guess. He found himself on the wall more than several instances when the flow was controlled by an internal test group. They reported that they found themselves somewhat perplexed by all of the options and offerings they were never well accustomed to, having been passively watching in all experiences of the past. It was noteworthy now that they would be allowed to prescript and postscript each aspect of this scene-by-scene.

"As a matter of record, I am on edge as much as you are today. We will no doubt feel the pressure; no escaping the obvious determination of a few who will try to trip us up; wondering by what reason of mind would one audience member retune it all on the fly, rather than just watching—passively standing by."

Josh was careful in admitting his own strong doubts on the effectiveness of an impassioned audience versus an overzealous one, given the choice of going with the intended flow or causing a quick departure from a carefully laid out script. What really mattered of course was this cast and crew's willingness to bring this experimental theatre into the mainstream.

"As I speak to you now, I have several letters hastily written and citing reasons for redoubt. These are very informed opinions, with regard to the nature of interactive theatre. The possibilities of going astray— these letters convey—are very material. But I am going to express another informed opinion. Our earlier tests were well executed. You provided the necessary catalyst to suggest that the 'show will go on' flawlessly. Let's rewrite this little part of live theatre history, shall we."

His words are not meant to convey impartiality in the same manner it would suggest. He has already told Tess that he is terrified that his would be the last of his theatre if things go so wrong. However, not wanting to return to that last troubling production; wherever he may have jumped off and the reasons are already faded; he is apparently more contented with having done this, rather than doing nothing at all to change up this traditional and stubborn venue.

Josh had to admit now that he was ready for this ultimate test of wills. Whatever set of circumstances project barriers in his way, he will remain objective enough to find the strength and means of hurdling past them. Tess was operating of the same manner and perspective, ready to ride this serious ride with him, whatever the cost. And apparently that made him very happy.

As for this cast and crew: "We are in it for the ride," or so they say.

This was the last adjustment he longed for: never quite alone and never quite a village or nation—so let this show go on.

Josh passed on the opposite sides of the enormous glass etched panels and dialed back in. It was an astonishing look even without all the fanfare of a live rehearsal. When the stage was lit yet calmed there was an uneasy feeling to it all. But on his second pass examination he acknowledges the true promise of the addition. It is after all made to change one's perspective of how it will be done in the future.

"This is going to be one hell of a ride."

The lights were turned off in mass, and only a single ghost light remained lit in the center of the main stage. Some traditions are meant to go on forever.

After getting everything heading in the right direction in his head Josh made a late night meal. He was determined to find if it were possible to find a middle ground with the people he desired to collaborate with, or better yet make a next generation business pulling from the old and mixing with the completely new. What he thought he need now was a hybrid. Approaches and acquaintances likely to come to light were swirling in his head and there was no chance he would sleep at all this late night. The house was still but the clamor going inside his head was deafening and stimulating at the same time: a discussion among many, more than one interpretive and point of view, an explanation with perhaps too many possibilities to be right or wrong. None of this could be explained without this internal talk and discussion of each pro and con, benefit and cost. But at the very least it left him with a satisfying and very favorable impression.

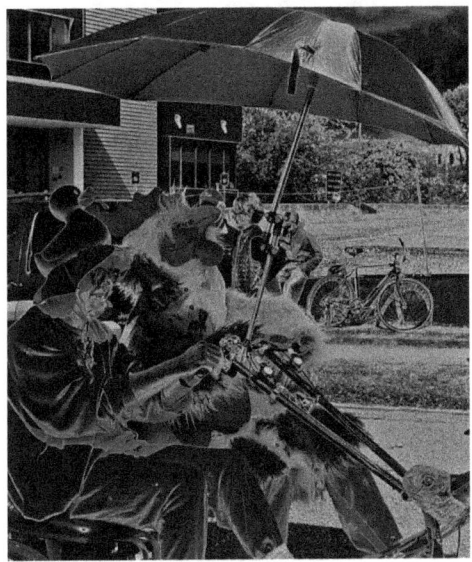

VOICE ONE: *A half night's explanation has made me better acquainted with the things that surround me. I am a long way from where I started this thing—better yet first visited—and the view or perspective is generally more production. I am finally free from my self induced rut. This has been worthwhile; now I can take this further. What a strange vehicle indeed.*

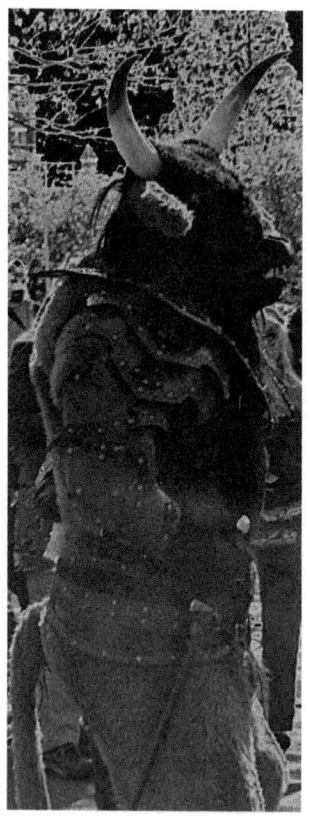

VOICE TWO: *What occupies your mind differs but little from those around you. By the time you figure this all out: clean it, spin it, weave it and then write it all down in a common language: there is not much of a thread you can call your own. This is such a tedious process. Take what they offered and make it work—cultivate it narrow and wide. This way requires little repair. Why try to reinvent this? A most disagreeable result is that you come to think of it as your own inner beast.*

VOICE ONE: *You are the beast! Please leave me to my own accord. If I came suddenly to the conclusion that I could not draw upon my own inspirational design I would just as soon hang it all up. The thing that I have been accustomed to is that this is a battle worth fighting and being won. I am not at all accustomed to bowing to their demands. How do I rid myself of this beast walking over my thoughts? I am determined to collect what I know works, rearrange it and describe it properly so that I can imagine the luxury of saying this is original—my lifetime habit.*

VOICE TWO: And if this new theatre is a house that easily blows down altogether? That is a dangerous slope you are tumbling down.

VOICE ONE: *The remarkable thing is that I know I can stay upright. The danger becomes the notice to quit doing what I desire. My genius is to discover the remedy and avoid the inclination toward group think. It is a far more dangerous slope to just go with the flow. I have to go with serendipity.*

Now leave me alone.

Perceptive Sensations   Michael O'Connor

Screen Thirteen

TO RETURN TO THE PLACE WHERE ONE LEFT OFF: riding along the same path, past the same trees, bushes and hedges, and realize that you have done this all before: the memories were not chased away by the daemons as supposed, or hiding at the next crossing: one is bound by traditions outside of one's control. This is not to say that he does not glance back or peer forward, looking for those opportunities to admit that he was happy and content with the circumstances prescribed.

It would not have been so strange an endeavor had the people around him subscribed to his whims, opinions and wishes, where the disagreements should have been more robust. These people: business associates, investors, and those he luxuriated with ample flow of wine, feasts and countless insights: he labored whether they went along, so long as he was providing in consideration to their steady diet of needs, or that they simply agreed with everything he had done so far by more luck than what anyone bargained for. It is this quandary of perplexities of cross pollination of business venues which lay claim to his many sleepless nights. What should be a paradise becomes a prison when pandering dominates complaint, and all those around him who bid him well when they would rather be in his place.

This one has provided countless people with ample employment and opportunity that would otherwise be just out of their reach. It is easy for him because he was not the result of a low or rough start. He had simply been designed as peer inherent over his brother and sister, who were younger and not so business inclined. And he was not running away from the enormous load bearing wall that rested squarely on his well tailored shoulders. He was not lamenting a different kind of life that gave him the freedom to design, rather than the insurance to endure the heady requirements of his fellow stakeholders. This trap was more or less conducive to Wall Street content as opposed to his first love, the finer arts.

As a manager of portfolios he is much happier these days with his solid investment in production companies, especially his recent plunge into local theatre. He feels that he has control of his artistically inclined side, in contrast to his teetering control of holding and controlling interest in business empires, both large and small. It is that more certain access to money that is drawn in to supply and pay for his latest hope for self redemption. He has found the best of shows in this carefully picked investment: pure joy rather than fixation on the bottom line.

This is not the best of shows as his portfolio will duly inform. One could attest that it may even be a financial drain. But the real potential is in the long term, helping him distance himself from the trotting trends of upswings and downswings in markets. No, this investment in the fine arts is his best protection against the outcome he has projected from the inner sanctum of the office at home. Here at any rate, he is behind closed doors and away from the masses that simply want to signal their agreement with his every utterance these days. There are unlimited points of failure at every turn, he readily enjoins, without care or elaboration, it is the labor of love he has harbored so carefully from day one.

A common thread that winds its way through all that is appealing about being able to afford this succession of luxuries is self control. His latest dictate and administration to his receivers and suppliers is to enjoin him in supporting the general estate of theatre.

Keeping in mind, that if one day it were all to be made possible, he would elect to step down, give full reign to an appropriate successor, and marry the arts over business and commerce. Should this happen he would tarry away behind these solid oak doors and plot his exit, never to return again.

Along these paths and rows of carefully manicured bushes he lumbered along and fantasized what would occur on his return behind such doors. Would it be a smaller penthouse or even a suitable cottage along the river's edge, in a safe haven neighborhood where one could adjust and enjoy the penetrable barriers to enjoyment out of creating another empire simply from scratch? If confronted with the realization and painful perspective that he had not inherited this but grew and nurtured it on his own, would it be a nicer portrayal as to how his walks through this park emulated his own life, rather than someone other than his ilk. Let his last chapter in life not be buried in legers and spreadsheets, but segue into scripts, plays and stage; the hidden life that he has so often stood outside looking in after securing the finest seat for viewing.

Here, in this park and on this day, his journey into the world of theatre would become more natural, and at the same time far less native. The leaves on the trees remain the same.

"Note to self: Do not let this exceptional opportunity slip away. Take calculated control and own it fully someday. I just turned fifty eight and this may be a most timely opportunity. I am so sick of the old business venue. I just want to create."

What he did next might be described as putting his own business estate up for sale. Just doing so provided him with a glimpse, perhaps a link to his inevitable future. It was a call of the wild delivered just before noon, and before the close of the first business day he had received feedback to the nature of: "Have you gone completely mad?"

He was mad, but of another sort. Having gone on a walk again he passed a neighbor to whom he always paid a great deal of respect. This woman was busy in her front garden and he was drawn to just seek her vision out, rather than interrupt the nurturing personage that was tugging on a handful of weeds and laughing out loud. What was it about this calling to dirt that prescribed such a testament to enjoyment and meditative tranquility?

At once he recalled hearing from a business college that she regularly practiced yoga undressed. She was close to his age, maybe older, and so curvaceous that just the thought brought him to a state of bemused arousal. This was certainly not the state he wanted to maintain on his continued solo march to the edge of town, yet it stayed with him so and he had to stop and adjust. This part of his body had not paid out in this manner in as long as he could remember outside of the privacy of his home, let along walking down this very street.

At this precise moment he began to see himself in another light all together: you are what you perceive:

this may delight and inspire you to look deeper for those things you want to complete in a single lifetime.

For a while he aligned himself to the notion that he might be approached and even arrested just for moving about in this readied state.   Imagine the murmured rupture across the local business scene if this were to occur.   It made him chuckle for an extended period out loud.

"Perhaps I should explore yoga undressed."

His sides were hurting with the splendid laughter that followed.   Fortunately it was his alone.   But would it have mattered any other way?   Having come to it naturally he seeks to unite this effort with those external factors which matter the most.   It is this neighborhood that gives him this energy of state; blend and shape it with time now; use this present experience as your canvas.

"What is it you have always wanted to paint?"

While walking and admiring his silhouette in several passed bay front windows he came upon a singular dwelling half hidden in a row of tall trees, facing out to the beach and the ocean.   The house is occupied by a retired choreographer who once had the reputation of being the go to person for advice within the local artistic community.   He has no firsthand experience to this; only recollection of what he had read in the local newspapers.

The house looked and remained so quiet at the far edges of town, and at one point it hosted grand parties inclusive of the widest cross section of the local who's who. It was a neat location and was surrounded by equally neat and tranquil gardens which would have been more inviting had they not been enclosed by a black wrought iron fence. Even at this close proximity—walking along this fence line—the place was unapproachable unless she were to invite one in personally. She being another person who he greatly admired at a safe distance, but had never actually spoken to. His mind wandered back to the common theme experienced several blocks ago, and thus he found himself thinking of her in the same manner and instantaneously sporting a more obvious result.

The power to transform one's self image manifests itself best with attention to overall health. He knew that his mental and physical abilities were ample, and told himself so in front of a mirror that very morning. It was this sense of creativity over liability and the intent to exercise full potential over abundance. It was what he said in his boardroom often. He meant it each and every time.

Was a thematic revelation of what would be his ultimate future? It was a less than tidy sum to pay if he were caught taking a more prolonged look down, rather that up and at the figure peering out from the front doorsteps. He was feeling free at the moment and not the confined feeling of a watched animal pacing incessantly in an enclosed cage, ready to spring out and flee at the first opportunity. The boardroom was as much an entrapment at times. Just thinking about it regulated his breathing downward until he forced himself to gulp in air.

The house may have been mostly hidden; however this physical being and its current state had become more than obvious over the same span of time. He had to adjust yet again, but this time in front of an audience of one. When greater awareness opens a door, just walk through it. He wanted to expound on this greater sense of freedom: mindfully and so inner-connected.

The observing woman looks down on his position and he becomes more aware of the smells that emanated from her garden against the background scent of the ocean crisp air during this unplanned encounter. All o his senses are intensified and there is this wonderful, no perhaps intriguing and perceivable mechanism that has gone to work on his persona. The desire to attempt interaction is driving him as wild and only but a scant instance of calling out has encircled his every thought.

He pleads with the inner self to regain some of the control he is more accustomed to in a boardroom or while doing business abroad. What has this draw to his artisan side that has put him in a place that he has not gone since the end of his childhood?

Why did everything look and smell different: a miniaturized version of a world perceived through business legers, now replaced by attention to detail of well placed flowers, bushes and selection of house paint color against the contrast of the trees. He had not felt this stuff for a great while out of neglect. The business mind was inclined to reign this all in, the money put him straight into the eyes of power, and the misfortune to have missed this all along gave him pangs of unexpected anxiety. He was beginning to feel more desolate in his own home town; having wanted to give himself permission to leave the past alone and embrace whatever comes across his path.

He is looking up while she is watching down. There is no avoiding this intersection of wills.

"I say: is there something I can help you with? You appear to be troubled by something; not moving along; standing uncomfortably in front of my property."

This voice summons him to draw on some inner strength usually reserved for walking through the dense double doors of his boardroom. It was a strange, no perhaps weird cry out for immediate interaction and he must summon the past to get through to the present. It was to be his first interaction with this type of neighbor and he dug deeply for something to say that would be relevant to her world alone—not his.

Would this giant of the dance world be attempting to pull him into a tango? What a relief that he was thinking already on her terms, albeit an odd scenario to dwell on. He was indeed being summoned to enter part of her home; least not the entryway into her garden caused him pause, silence or prolonged suspense over the gamble of looking too nonchalant.

"I am so happy to see you up and about. It was my understanding that you are recuperating from a procedure. Oh my, was this too personal? I do beg your forgiveness."

"Not at all: do remember to latch the gate, won't you. I have been having trouble with some of the neighborhood dogs getting into my yard; their digging at my planting has made such a mess. Oh thank you. How have you been; this is such a surprise."

She moved forward with a slight limp.

This garden path and her enticing and inviting smile has ushered him toward the next realm. His mind came alive suddenly with one million ways to approach her at her level. So this became his state of being as they talk at the threshold of her home: laughing, yammering and lively banter followed this path through the doors with a simple question and answer.

He begged inward to give himself permission to feel infinite, untouched by a natural inclination to be on guard, allowing her invitation to become the catalyst for what exactly? There was a preponderance of evidence that this was such a simple solution—this social call between residents. It was not a calling for complete transformation.

"Will you take a moment to join me for a cup of tea? I require just one moment to put on the kettle. Please come in won't you."

He was here in a newly revamped kitchen and waiting. Waiting for what meaning? She was limping less noticeably and had returned to the lifelong dancer he envisioned thoughtfully, respectively all together. Should he endeavor to think this over: looking for deeper meaning when simplicity was all it would take to get through the next moment?

There was an uncontrollable attraction to find out.

After a considerable amount of time she swung around with two piping hot mugs of strong Earl Gray tea, perhaps knowing well in advance how he liked to take it—in silence and full of anticipation of the initial hot sip. The amount of slurping and sipping was deflection enough for her as well; as they continued to sip all the while the suspense mounting for one to say out loud what the other may have been thinking. The situation was comfortable as long as it was tolerated, and time was lost between little glances and smiles, knowing full well that this mutually adhered to ritual were to be honored.

Let this liberate you: the freedom to breathe expressively, to play, and endure and certainly not regress.

Finally, for this visitor to her sparse yet marvelously designed kitchen, is interrupted by a soothing and gentle laugh. The situation would not go unanswered and soon they were both holding sides due to the inherent hilarity which follows. They were both gasping for air.

As he began to speak; first at a barely audible whisper; he could see that she was affected by his little attempt of comforting banter. It was her body language that broached the subject thought of but never uttered until it could no longer be ignored. Her legs are crossing and most of the top leg is bare and crossing over in a most suggestive way, not hindered by a scare that runs the length of her ankle. Was it a more or less cordial greeting of instilled relaxation that she fired off by pumping one leg over the other?

He knew nothing beyond what had worked between him and his past—that significant other. It would be a risk to ask for a more general to specific explanation because her eyes glistened as she gazed his face looking for a more venturous answer. It was a moment of astonishment for them both when he finally blurted out.

"I have wanted to say something very strange throughout the day and I am sorrowful that I do not have a better way of explaining my appearing in front of your house."

He stopped cold. He could feel his heart beating faster than usual.

"Oh, please do go on. I will just top off our teas, dear."

The two of them shifted kindly toward each other and every once in a while they would both scan across the kitchen for some item to relax on. The discomfort would rectify itself.

It is important enough to note that he neglects to relay his exact cause of discomfort early on, but would go on to feel that he was pleased that she called him out from under the awning of her front porch. Realizing his uncomfortable shifting of his mug, must this be cause for counter to her coming forward with an unexpected proposal.

"I have long been interested as to what sort of person you are outside of the office."

This was a pleasant surprise and an opening that he would be willing to unabashedly pursue. He deliberately drew attention to the fact that he was going through a transformation in terms of work life— the less than trifling inconvenience of swearing in for the truth at the same time it was happening. He stammered and then he stopped, and not a singularly obvious example of what he thought might be at play comes to mind.

"I am afraid I have drawn a blank."

She is smiling as though this is the only comment that will please her. Leaning in she touches his arm in a disarming manner and then leans back to say something important. He knows this well in advance.

"There is a caricature I paint of all of my visitors; in my head of course. With you I have one that is not fully fleshed out, but I cannot for the life of me tell you why I have come to the following conclusion. You are tired with your life as it is, and you want to take those next necessary steps to finding another kind of fulfillment."

"But that said I want to do something."

"Yes, with that said I thought I would tell you that I saw your condition out on the sidewalk. You were stirred by something else, because it came to my surprise that I knew what it might be, well before I had a chance to call out."

However cognizant she was of his dilemma at the moment was not as clear by the look of consternation displayed on her face. He shifted again for emphasis—so maybe an appeal.

"Yes, I know dear. We will address that sooner than you think. When you came onto the scene, what on earth carried you here? If we can get through that, the other contributing factors will become that much more clearly appreciated."

There was a general rising up and out of their seats.

Soon enough he was standing before her with explanation at hand, so to speak, and he ventured honestly thinking they would both meet head on with that 'aha' state. Like in his trusted boardroom, when he arrived prepared to engage, and when eyes met his like this, he was usually unstoppable.

But this time it is different.

There was the copious amount of tea consumed, and there was no time to tell her that his first agenda was to flee to her bathroom. She had him logistically cornered up against the edge of her kitchen counter when she ventured forward and gave it a little tap on the shoulder, and then indicated his destination.

Countered by encounter he had met his match, and he then gave out a short and somewhat prolonged sigh. This was a rough instance to assess, and he never had little time to wait for a reaction on his way to her bathroom.

Her insightfulness and less than delicate probing caused him to do something he had not had to do since childhood. He pulled out the mirrored swinging door while he remedied his release and studied his face for answers.

The flush was quite loud. He could still hear the tank refilling after washing his hands, drying them with slowed intent, and then prodding back to the kitchen.

The good lady—this more than gracious host—did what was generally considered a very pleasant thing. From what he could see as he ventured to take a more than wild guess, an emergence of sainthood would not be his likeliest hurrah. It was so very pleasant a thing for her to do to this off centered person; a poignant statement expressed from her mouth as he slid into near unconsciousness. Would his embarrassment endure her penetrating eyes and mind, and the muffled sounds he must have made as he reentered the picture?

When they both realized the extent of what occurring one pair of eyes never left the other. The good lady returned to her upright and cleanest posture and reached back for the still warm liquid in two oversized mug. She drank for another moment after placing his mug in steadied hands. Even more riddled with complexity she stepped back before shedding an insight most accordingly.

"You are far more comfortable being in complete control of these types of conversations. Pretend that I am an associate. Now, what is it you want to say?"

It was possibly then that he realized his role in repaying the offer so well executed. He guided her with his eyes across the kitchen and lowered expectations so gently. Grabbing whatever strength he could muster for such situations, more warranted for this show to continue, he lets loose as an orator with purpose.

Loosely sketched he imagined himself less as an equally formidable giant in a boardroom and lowered his head in between two deep breaths made more noisily. From where he stood and from where she intuitively countered, it was not so long before he gave her unequalled answers to all of her questions asked.

It was better and longer than expected and if he had a heard it more clearly would have echoed thru and thru. He would not reemerge from sending out all of his most private thoughts for a lingering while.

There was less than a gentle sharing of specific comments on the events at play. From where he sat and she stood it was a considerable display of encountering true symmetry. Why his host not disagreeing was more than acceptable. He did not know what to say to counter her on point because there was little evidence of hard facts. Most of what came out and across that table was an intonation of what he intended to do next. Was it not for the simple breezes coming across her back yard nothing would have been heard or said in any more satisfying candor? This unmasked pouring out of life more fully anticipated brought a shared moment of laughter between them. Her head was resting on long and elegant fingertips; it was causing him to repeat something again.

Presently it was ringing through to full rise on the temptation that they would celebrate it on the back veranda.   Turning toward him she whispered something of a higher calling. She is a grand Dame.

"That breeze feels so comforting. Let's move to my garden, shall we."

There was little to know what makes two people succumb to joyous laughter, after little else is said. They returned to a more focused interaction and the call to the garden's hidden gazebo was evenly secured. So much later he would return to the thing which brought him here in the first place—the answer to her earlier question.

"I am here because I want to learn more about theatre. I have recently purchased one, you see."

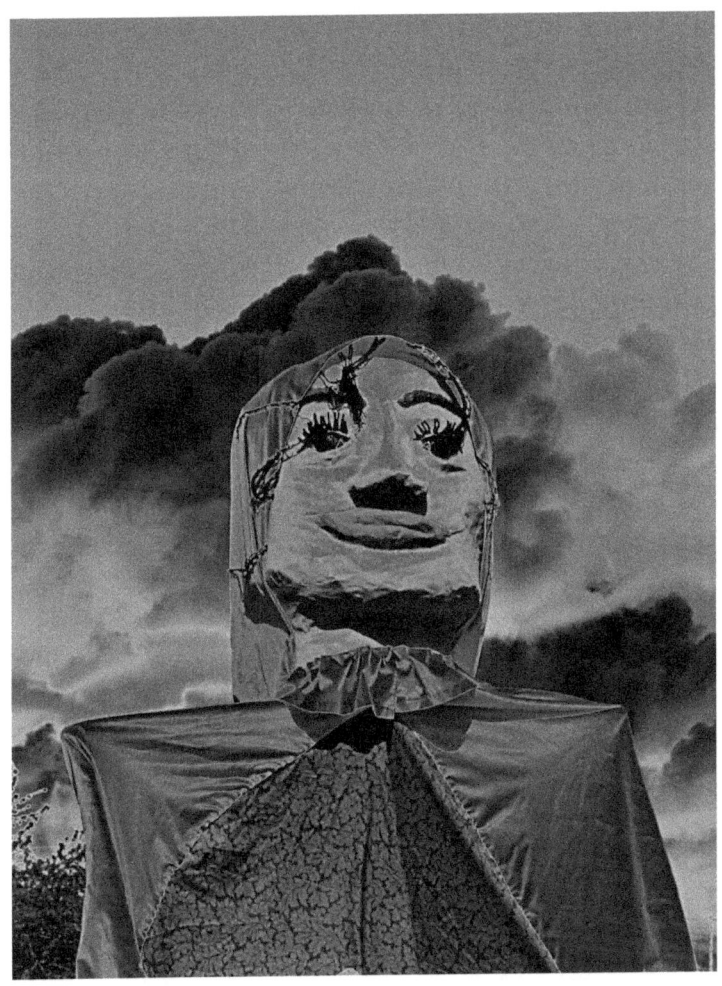

HER VOICE: *My house dear, is not unlike most structures in this country. Its exterior bears a strong enough resemblance to others, but its interior is perpendicular to the workings of my mind. This is how I envisioned it, and that is what it came to be.   This*

makes me think that someday there is the possibility that I may start it all over. The remarkable thing is that I am not afraid to do so because I do not doubt that I could accomplish the task. Yes, I am older now but I am not horizontal yet. I have witnessed every stage of the process o stumbling down. But a notice to quit; no, I do not think so. A new seed planted in my garden broadcasts. It would be rude to just pull up the resultant plant, wouldn't it?

HIS VOICE: You have been very kind to share your garden and to pour me tea. Everything around this garden represents carefully, thoughtfully attended to specimens. In the midst of this garden I recognize a kind of labyrinth of choices and placement. Was this by design, or by serendipity? I am asking because there is something of my life that I would claim to be well thought out accidental discovery. This place reminds me of what I want to design and then fill with careful and thoughtful artisans. But I am struggling where to start. Where does one plant that first seed to guarantee the successful placement of the next one?

HER VOICE: I really do not know, dear. I just garden.

Screen Fourteen

FOR JOSH THERE WAS NO OTHER WAY to distinguish what actually happened; he continues to pour over the evidence with a feeling of disgust, and now outright despair. To say that he was feeling off his game would be an announcement excruciatingly short of fact—as he had no more feelings left at all that were his own. The only thing he could recognize in the contract was what he once had owned.

The board of directors—if they could be called that—issued the contract to him in pieces, telling him that it would be more digestible that way. Would that explain his complete lack of hunger for anything let alone the mention the of food spread covering the large rectangular table in which they surrounded—each and every other one was grabbing for plump roast chicken, streamed rice and an assortment of grilled vegetables off of large serving plates and eating with ferocity. It just after he had been informed that he was no longer the controller or director of the theatre he once owned, having leveraged well beyond its worth.

The new contract set out terms that were complex yet ultimately less ambiguous once they were read out loud. The words were in legalese and in English with hints of Latin to emphasize legal tempo. He was at risk—so it would appear. He was left with little to resume control: any one aspect of its present or its future operation was now in the hands of another. It was also miserably untimely: coming into effect immediately in the middle of a season.

He would spend this time devouring the words on a thick stack of paper open on the table before him and the other signatories, rather than the sumptuous meal spread out and seemingly planned well in advance, as though a celebration might be in order; theatre in its own right. Indeed the formations of each section of the legal document still unsigned, contains the more than present hint of self silhouette. This is all that comes to mind as he is encouraged to take heart and pen and sign it all away; seeing the shadowed hand slowly moving above the surface of the document he sighs deeply.

The close to tearful Josh turns to his closest friend-- perhaps once upon a time a truthful college—urges him to rescind. It is shown on his face and certainly in his narrowed eyes. Do not trust in the resolve of one's enemies after surrender. They cannot make it any better with words or sweeping gestures.

"Please make this matter clear: you are not helping this side this time"

The friend maintains eye-to-eye contact and attempts to make his position all the more clear. It might seem wrong to not make even the slightest overture on his part. Josh's wet eyes do not make even a slight dent in the stoic returned stare. There is a full advantage with regard to the others as they will rely on the distance across the table to maintain solidity. It is an advantage Josh wishes to dispel. Gone is his control by a sweeping hand or an intent stare.

"With the slightest efforts you know I can turn this thing around. I do not want to sell or step down. I recognize it is your position and you're right to stand fast; my words will have the smallest effect as you continue to sit there smiling and eating. But mark my words: the show cannot go on without me."

His words appear to astonish the group; at least they have stopped eating and talking as though nothing he had to say mattered. At the stroke of an even hour Josh looks at the wall clock behind the rectangular nest of prying faces and bides his time for the next announcement. Collectively the look at each other and suppress what every that had wished to say, because there is a mighty ruckus just outside of the window, one floor below.

Everyone took turns looking out and down to the ground. No one was ignorant to the significance of the gathering below, nor presently deaf to the chants calling out. They did collectively understand.

There is a full troupe exercising their right to freely assemble on the very property of those who control their future here. The dress is in full regalia reminiscent of the actions on stage that have been filling the theatre night after joyous night, They are here to remind everyone else that they want to have a say in this matter; one flight up from where they stand in parade: the elements and climate are forever in their favor. An in the midst of their leadership stands the defiant Dame. She is his greatest enabler now.

"It's all right. I will explain to them what just might happen if these papers are signed off today. However, I might not just the same and let them cry out for what might be a more certain cause and effect."

It was no use to anyone of them to counter this threat. They were more desperate but not too late to recognize the upper hand this clever director had over this scene—so carefully choreographed it should have been expected given her stoic participation.

By this time Josh had several more friends appear around the table and he was not at all ashamed for calling this epic adventure closer in to his ideal outcome. He let the lady know for sure that he was neither bluffing nor backing down.

Again his friend to the right was engaging, only this time on his behalf. Sudden quiet in the before mentioned proceedings signaled that they have been brought to a full stop. Even the food remained unaddressed. Were you an outsider to this procedure they was a feel of shock and awe. Not a single salvo was fired shortly after that; he remained again deep to their hearts, minds, spirits and financial trust. By this time he rightfully dissuaded that interned interest in that document, as it was skillfully pushed aside.

"You may think that you have turned this thing around, Josh. For the time being, you remain in very tentative control. However, your investors will soon be calling and calling in on those outstanding loans they will. Who do the fellows below think the payroll comes from?"

There was a hush in the room still apparent over the outcome outside and below. Many eyes returned from the windows and back to the center head of this table. Seats did shift, and hands on the tabletop were pain to see—clear enough he sits where the power stays for the moment.

"Who indeed: the Box Office, fans and admirers, and lately even the critics. The list can go on, but I think that I have met your challenge. We are only off by a few percentage points, aren't we?"

It is a standoff situation and for the next minute exactly one is certain that another track shall play out. If one is to believe that it was his intension to let the time tick down, you would be a greater fool. It was at least another half hour before the meeting adjourned; the last of the counter arguments and conversation had run out of steam as the fat lady sings, as they say in this trade. It took all of the joy out of the sumptuous meal that was left behind.

"Do not add insult to injury, Josh. You clearly reversed this chapter, but walking out before everyone had their say was less than professional. The circus thrown in your favor outside of that room was disquieting for all of us. But we are not a simple audience, are we. We have needs pressing well beyond the close of the final curtain."

It was the expected yet slow onslaught of further correction that he wanted to push away from. The speaker's appeal might have landed on deaf ears for all of his reaction could have spelled out. It was to be the last of his end of the conversation, simply enough, because walking away said it clear enough. It was his second proposition, actually. Nevertheless it was the only one which counted now.

He gathers up speed as they both walked the remaining distance to his spot of final departure from the property. She clamors on and touches, but he is resisting her strongest attempts of charm. It is here that he leaves her again, before walking clear around the estate once more just to enjoy the sensation that what he controlled was much larger than the absurd calling out for his head. She is a very sharp collaborator, wealthy beyond belief, and a constant financial contributor. But what she wasn't then, or isn't now is a faithful friend.

When he completed his circle around the building he let out a call toward the few remaining in the lot to the west side of this building. He admires their will and contemptuous costumes and extends a bow and then an extended hand.

"It appears they take your position sincerely. They have endeavored to allow me to stay as Director, for as long as it takes to readdress this matter. Please tell everyone I thank them for coming to champion this cause—their cause as well."

And the matter was settled for the time being. Josh seemed to have left them all with the impression that it was quite possible to maintain control of this dubious situation if well enough if simply left alone—the performances taken for granted. He also fully acknowledged that this picture was painted with the scantiest brush strokes ever, given the board's resolve to call in those loans earlier if they can. But how dubious would that broad stoke be if they were met by defaulting on it all?

This success; his success; would not last forever.

All that was left clear was that Josh would be controlling this effort for some time to come; perhaps at least until the end of this hopefully successful season.   Watch this handsome fellow charm the stream of maidens with another round of wine. Wish him 'good speed' willingly; though he might just let it all go into a tailspin just for revenge. It was a mirror image of the current work at this theatre.

The season is only half way over. This current troupe was way in for the duration; never having to look over his shoulders; least it be known that his daily life was still in the hands of those others.

Now he was off to the next dress rehearsal, and the opening of the Box Office. He would not even have time to discuss the meeting's events with Tess. It was then that it dawned on him, that he did not know who that stately figure was at the opposite end of the table.

Why did he smile so pleasantly when Josh ad turned this thing around? And why was this man the first to jump up to the window, to witness all those who were parading outside and on the ground? He presented a grand silhouette of something, but there was little degree of detail retained by mind's eye, when Josh attempted to refine this fellow. His image was fast fading away; giving way to that other odd feeling because there is much more to come.

With only a glimpse of his present status with the board Josh went to visit a dear friend. The visit would do him good because after visits in the past he became more capable of seeing his likely future: the revitalized actor. This was never a reckless diversion of straightening out the twists and turns he brought on; on his own; he felt capable because he could use this set of ears and open mind as a soundboard.

He had only been inside of this familiar kitchen for a few minutes when he stood up and stretched as though he was in his own home. He felt immediately rested as the feedback continued while he attended to a kink in his back, tight shoulders and a twisted groin. He continued to show this host a reasonable amount of attention and went on to say that the potted flowers on the countertop were as beautiful array as he has ever been witness.

The feedback he found with this regard was never short of modesty. From the corners of her mouth she attempted to refrain from the banter warranted from his drawing her into another conversation all together; when one party spoke of water the other wanted to discuss wine. Neither of them regained a sense of clear consciousness while they played this often repeated game. They were both on autopilot—never ashamed of carrying on this kind of conversation when it was just the two of them. It was an invitation to play for a while in the fields of transference, in a language allowing either party to address the real topic in a most dramatic way.

At long last she invited him to remain for lunch—a social gift never refused. While she prepared a light but eloquent meal Josh strayed back on topic with greater deliberation. He had done so, he thought, to exercise a timeline that he had in his head with regard to his longevity of ownership and control of the one thing that mattered most in life: his watershed—this beloved theater.

"I have taken in this new troupe and they have served my place well. Most of the matinees are at least half filled, and on key nights of the week it is packed; not nearly sold out."

It was as though he were explaining the circumstances of why they would have cared, rather than a more specific focus. He stopped for a moment to walk over to the brilliant flower arrangement and take in the overwhelming fragrances they put out. The smells carried him to a different place than the room he was physically standing in; pulling with them a thought that did not occur to him earlier. Why wouldn't he give it all up to pursue something equally import that he would love to do? This new memory takes him further away from the topic on hand.

Though it would be hard to conceive other grounds for dismissal—one which is contested at all—a means of recognition: he could see himself outside of the very role he was clinging to.   It kind of emboldened him and he returned to the table to test this against the mentoring logic of the lady patiently laying in wait.

"I am in perfect health physically. However, that said, I am a psychological wreck. Could I in fact redirect all of this nervous energy to a change in tact? Why not find a buyer of my own choosing?"

He had moved into an all too different landing. It was one so far out of context that he refocused and reigned back in.   By simplifying a picture of perfected evolution, unaffected by the fear of losing control, he encouraged her to give him a sounding on the role of seller over plundered.

"That my friend is a significant departure from your past. You say that you are unaffected, but listen to you know—should you ever question internal sound logic—do it now."

She had laid her hands down onto the table and gestured him to come to terms with the matter of heart over head. There was logic in what he was saying; to this she added little doubt.   But given his state of being was this really a test or a resolve?

"Would you dare pass this by Tess?   What do you think her reaction would be; if it mattered at all? Oh,

223

you may look at me like I am only appeasing you now. But rest on this thought for a minute longer: should you continue to appraise the idea I can put you in touch with someone who would take it on with a great deal of seriousness. Just think about it for a while longer. Bounce this idea off of Tess, and test the waters at home."

This is precisely why he sought her out. She was never the destination but always the journey in which he could count on to shake the tree limbs, so to speak. Could his simple solution be cultivated by one other, as she so simply challenged him, in his high state of sustained anxiety. Certainly he would have never crossed this road on his own with regard to the one other person in his life whose opinion mattered as much. Such power in her presence—Grand Dame— there was also mischief in her eyes. There it matters most to those who dismiss it without asking why.

This was refreshing just to walk and notice the cloud patterns in the sky and the way the wind flowed through the lush branches of the tree lined streets. It was cool yet it was hot. His body temperature raced to keep up with the shifting inside of his mind.

After leaving her house, walking across at least two fields of tall grasses, imagining all of the suitable pros and cons of flipping the setting from controller to controlled, Josh walked as though he had found a new order for living. He felt like running but resumed his control and all that was surrounding him in the real world. It was impossible to conceive another life, afterwards, after all.

The weight of the idea bears a stronger resemblance to pain without disorder. If it was maintained constructively enough he would endure the discomfort and allow it to do justice to blocking all of the other items teetering just out of range: the current troupe, the sense of purpose, the ownership of something he had created from scratch. This was not what he wanted to be thinking about now—certainly not dwelling on the minutia of details—always skipping to the right or just thing to do. The other stuff mattered, but with any exception stronger than his will to sell the theatre, he had to stay focused on what he wanted to do with the next phase of his life.

"Will I fight or will I flee?"

It was impossible to describe his inner feelings and the scenery that changed as he turned the next corner, literally. It was an all together new way of thinking about self—to the degree of being truly actualized. The far corners of his mind were compartmentalized toward pulling in and proving a proficiency and mastery of control of matters of running a business. In between and scattered about were all of the uncontested contributions of creativeness: wanting to create that grand journey of himself, worthy to take without over consternation as to how he would survive. For now his life was little else than a series of compromise. Would it be worthy to cast self imposed control aside and allow himself to step into the role of content creator?

It was this notion of venture business that frightened him the most. For most of his adult life he had promoted what others had to offer and little of his own. Could he see himself in a role where he had to shop his creativity around? It would be an interesting journey to take and see the results, with one exception of course—that of rejection.

How many pitches of playwright had he cast aside before venturing forward for the sake of the business? Was it just a means of paying the bills on that small building that occupied his theatre that matter the most: the main structure and the surroundings inside and out? It had been a proven combination and one that he felt he would be reasonably comfortable in for years to come. This introspection he went through while walking—it made him feel doubt.

Josh was turning the next corner and had no doubts of the impact of a new chapter in his life. By the time he had walked through the front door he had more resolved to press the idea forward—intent to sell. There would be no further rationalization with regard to his need for control, over that which he had built serving as his only axis of show and tell. The time had finally arrived when the face pressing against his would open up a new means of progression.

"So how did your day go, Josh?"

It was the first barrier to be suffered, but the endurance was brief enough. He hastily removed all pretention of changing to a more calculable subject matter. The comfort of home and the searching of Tess's eyes would provide him suitable ground in which he could dispel lingering fears; of getting beyond that truth.

"My day went as expected."

Tess bristled with his lack of details; having read his facial expression for more she see a hint of projection. They had continued to talk as they moved into the center of the house and on into the bright lights of the kitchen; further interrogation was carried on to no avail. The room remains friendly but it was tense.

The stovetop reveals a meal still in progress, and the mostly silent void is filled with the aroma of pasta: a combination of basil-tomato sauce simmering followed by the pop of a suitably aged Pinot Noir: a presumably tempting vintage as judged by the expressions of the first sips. But from there it dwindled as an interrogation—it was the nature of his choosing distance over too much detail—the night was young enough to return there later when guards

were sufficiently down.   His eyes blinked and the
frown on his face broke into a widening smile.

"I think I have found a way out."

But then again there was this nagging feeling.   Was
this all really that easy?

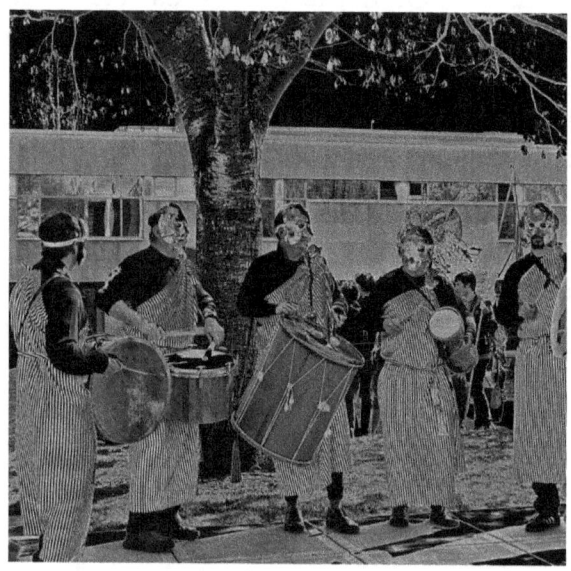

VOICE ONE: *I know that she is rallying the band on my
behalf.   This consists of scores of meetings and
correspondence on her part—not a slave or servant by
any means—but a family member of this endeavor. She
looks after me, I know that, yet I still feel this invasion of
privacy. I need to do this on my own without someone
bringing me a glass half empty or half full. To go at this
solo is one of my greatest luxuries; others trying to help*

cause the opposite of attraction. How I have managed to survive is a great mystery to them.

VOICE TWO: You look up and see the sun, and then look down and see dry cracked mud. Do you get how one follows the other? Within every other mile of your precious theatre it is the rainy season. How you have managed is a mystery to them as well. When she looks out for you two and three times per day, feed her something instead of driving her back.

VOICE ONE: One person alone has to be in charge of the direction of this place; every night someone has to turn out the lights but one at the center of the main stage. This is not some attempt to jump into a melancholy quick, principally for the sake that someone will have to open this place the following morning for cause rather than habit. There are those who are notorious for pulling and tugging everything in between. I just want a more secure means of predicting that the doors will be opened at all. My good night's sleep depends on my knowing that I made this secure without too much risk to the troupe, the crew and especially the daily audiences.

VOICE TWO: Perhaps you are notorious too—a notorious thief—taking all the other's contributions away to enable your good night's slumber.

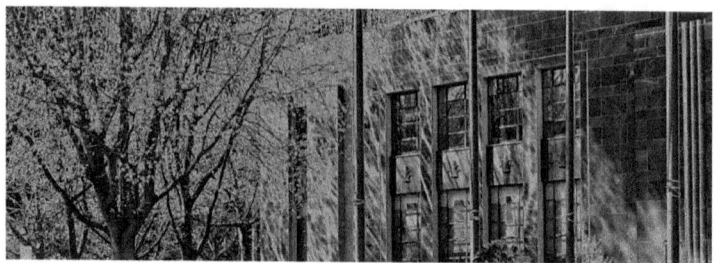

VOICE ONE: *So be it to say I understand your position, but you are not taking mine as seriously. Running this place has been a solitary practice. I am not so spoiled to think that for a single moment I go it alone, but I am able to see this next thing above that crowd. I just want to call those shots that are mine alone to make it or break it. But right now my place is surrounded by a hoard that would just as soon rip it all away for what they believe.*

Tess is the exception—I get that outright. In her absence I get so distracted, sans that parade that seems to follow her everywhere.

Screen Fifteen

AFTER A CORRESPONDING MORNING of meetings far off campus, the gentleman removed his tie and loosened his shirt collar and cuffs that were bearing the initials of his name. Of all that he had heard from his business associates he was more than convinced that they were wrong on so many points. In his heart it was a variable place of interest and contention by which he surmised their alarm and indifference was more jealously than intellectually driven. They had, after all, implored him to return to what was once his boardroom, and regain the control. It was his loss alone if he did not.

He walked a favorite path and took several odd detours. The alleyways in which he strode along were more suitable for the young and fearless, having passed as many as fourteen who watched him in forbearance to the grim rewards he might come across if he maintained his direction. The many that he chooses to travel with are dressed at odds with his tailored suit and tie in hand, and by their uniform appearance it might be more likely that they were part of a gang.

As he walked he chuckled to himself as he recalled that one must look the part when one enters a room in a club. Had he been arriving at a Charthouse it would do more for the entering gentleman to appear unflustered and wait for all of those eyes staring to make introductions first? Unless he were wrong now, someone would approach him and bid him a suitable greeting, worthy of his bred manner and poise. That is unless they seemed to be all stronger in their defense of this placid lane of alleyways, of which they might intend to defend from all comers no matter how well they pressed on.

The next thing he took notice on was the indications at last they may not be greeting him in English, after all. Their voices were gruff and staggered with slang, and this is causing him to breathe deeper. The next man who dare step in front of him, walking backwards, is talking while his face is devilishly contorting.

"Where the hell do you think you are old man?"

There seems to be a strong resentment in his manner, just inside of a blind rage, not hidden far from the outside world. It might do no good to counter his position of manner of speech.

"Apparently it is not customary to appear here dressed as I am today. But would you be far more interested in the probability that I have something of interest to proposition you with? I am here to ask you out to dinner, assuming of course that you represent this group of people."

Apparently the shock of receiving this greeting was uncustomary enough to make this younger man back down. He stopped walking backwards and placed both of his hands in his pockets, turned to his associates and his smile turned into a wider grin. The gentleman is now free to move about and settles along overgrown ivy growing upward to the top of a brick-sided building.

The next reaction by all signaled a willingness to do nothing at all. There seemed to be an even stronger reason not to do what they may have intended, having been given a differing host of opportunities. He was asking their appointed leader out to dinner, and he would probably accept after another moment or two.

Apparently this was enough to garner further interest. There were introductions made all around: his was so formal; they all seem to find comfort in nicknames. This was the custom here. There was dead calm.

There was this willingness to hang about and discuss the details of this unexpected proposition. They explored the possibilities and no one man among them seemed more relaxed and poised than the gentleman in matching suit top and trousers. He repeated himself several more times and gazed at their attentive faces for the necessary feedback that he had not been wrong. Would a misstep have been as gruesome in the company of these tough young men, and would they have been willing to suffer through all of these details had the initial attraction been something entirely different.

There was no use in questioning the tactic. This method was working for all. For a whole host of ideas that could be explained at a later date, the particulars of this one were ratified and each sector turned and returned home.

The enormity of the interaction continued for an endless moment of time, as the two of them continued walking until they reached the restaurant of the young man's choosing. It was a traditional place to seek good and liberating amounts of Italian cuisine accompanied by cheaper bottles Chianti. There was a suitable mix of personage in the crowd so that no one quite stood out. And the two of them were far into the second bottle of Chianti when the waitress presented them with a tempting array of desserts.

"Shall we try one, or try them all?"

After the mostly liquid lunch the gentleman took the rowdy young man outside and presented him with one of two finely rolled cigars. There are fresh from Virginia and they are rolled perfectly uniform to trap the fine smoke from the best picked and dried tobacco. The older lit his first and then leaned forward to light the one held calmly by the other staring intently into his face. They both smoked in silence for the next ten to twelve minutes, letting a stream of eaters and drinkers pass without comment to or from the restaurant's large and inviting front door. There was but a single passing where the unpleasant words did slip from the mouth of a middle-aged woman, and one dare say dour but laughingly.

"There is a law, you know, that one is not suppose to light up within one hundred feet of a place of eating."

She never dared look back and would have surmised that a quickened retreat was in order had she seen the gesture the younger man makes in her direction. Perhaps it was the well that the moment passed without additional conflict; the hearty laughter between the two cigar smokers was temptingly like a truce of sorts. It would take a very brave soul to separate these two now.

"Father, I have been meaning to call you, but the time just flies by and the month passed as well. These are very fine cigars, by-the-by."

No one could tell by the disorderly appearance of one over the elegant demeanor of the other that they were once living under the same household, carrying the same name. The older one definitely has straightened his shoulders and is looking right into the stare of the son—without dismissal he has accepted him as nearly equal in status. The two have taken to blowing carefully controlled smoke rings, and several of them intersect.

The less likely pair continues to make good use of this time in complete silence. On occasion one will give the other a knowing stare and the other will wait it out until the cycled communication is dampened according to plan. Their backs are covered by the height and solidness of the building behind, and the restaurant windows are partially closed by curtains making the presence of smokers hidden at long last. Soon there is a very telling haze in front of the place, but it has a very pleasant smell to those who would come to appreciate it; happy expressions are held for some time longer.

The city street is clean and the passersby are dressed in a wide array of garments weighing in from jeans to tailored suits. Ties have been loosened coming in and out of this place, and soon several other guests have stepped outside to light up as well. By then the street side has at least four with their backs to the windows, and the farthest side of the building sports six men staring down the long and tight rolls of cigars from as many points of the globe. It is a pleasant sky above and the breeze is almost nonexistent, so that this section of the street is densely drenched in the blue and gray haze of cigarettes and cigar smoke.

All seem comfortable with this inclement change from the extreme youth of this crowd, to the stately men in clean suits who remain clustered. It is so noticeable that other's walking back and forth has actually taken to crossing the street to the other side, bringing the occasional chuckle from the smoker's mouth. It is also noticeable that a local police car has circled this particular section of the downtown district slowly, and the windows are down. Since it is a canine vehicle by indication, all look for the head of the large dog that paces behind the driver and his partner, a woman of near equal size.

They have stopped, and they seem to be taking all of this in with keener interest. It is accounted for by one couple who move quickly, and with tempest motion, stomping out whatever it was that they were sharing and smoking. There is laughter as the common shared medium, and a liberally shared dedication in tonality. These two definitely spin into one another.

Another possible item of information was that this crowd is made up of a wide array of nationalities. It is not difficult to understand that they all speak with a common language and that most of them probably live within a short distance. As the police sum up all that they can under this particular set of circumstances, and the fact that one smoke's smell does not dominate of another's, the patrol car begins to drive off and the crowd is carefree once again.

After greater circumspection over the events just passed, the gentleman nudges his son and they take off down the street shoulder-to-shoulder with a slow stride. It is no one's guess that the antics of one pair, or the prying eyes from within the patrol vehicle, has caused them to wonder off. They do so without putting out either cigar: these pleasant smell waifs after them as they amble down to the corner and turn.

"Well I must say that your being in proximity to pot smokers made my heart beat a bit faster. Are you all right?"

"Father, I am well past my parole, and it did not appear that they had recognized me. There is no certainty to the fact, but I am sure that they were just slowing to eye the crowd. There were at least one dozen by my count."

After inspecting around a large galley window on the very next corner, they elected to continue down the near empty street. There was a pressing need to continue walking given the enormous amount of wine they had shared at the table. It was a much needed refreshment and coming together for the night's stroll did them both some good to absorb alcohol, and counter the effects with something more pressing. Building after building passed by and there was only short and halting conversation until they reached the front of a very tall glassed in façade. The marquee was well lit up in neon gas enclosed tubing: *The Club.*

The older man gently grabbed hold of the other's shoulder and glided him up the single row of stairs and on into the place past two enormous double doors which swing inward. The inside foyer is grand as it is spectacular, and the membership required must have had something to do with its appearance. Two men; one appointed on either side of the entrance of the lounge; made way to the pair of inner chamber doors and opened them without having to ask for membership ID. It was clear that the father of the pair, who looked the part, left them with the most appropriate impression.

"Good evening, Sir"

It was an inviting and bidding engagement as they walked in, passing with smiling stares followed by expected disinterest, and the doors swung closed behind them separating the patrons from the cordial staff. All eyes forward.

And once more, before one could even take in the splendor of this inner sanctuary, they were being greeted and escorted across a promenade, making way to a most suitable table and two fine leather chairs.

"Will the gentlemen require something from the wine menu, or perhaps after dinner drinks?"

Orders were provided and then received with exemplary politeness, and the constituents boasted a fine assortment of men dressed from elegant to casual for this affair. No one was left face to face as the tables and chairs were positioned to allow for the comfort of the patrons requiring anonymity, as opposed to those who wanted to be seen, for the sake of being seen. It was a rather demure assortment, given the number of participants sipping and talking quietly or loudly, given their status. The young and the old were gathered here giving the appearance of several generations at least of businessmen who were all trim and scrupulously clean said one. It was this order of things that although there were knowing stares, no one dared contest the appearance of the ruffian with his face to man of order who had taken him into this palace of fine arts.

This was a superior crowd for which there were no mistaken identities. Side by side the tables gave the impression that mega deals were abound, and nearly have of the room appeared to be at varying states of inebriation. The music was not live but canned, and it had the marvelous flavor of Tropicana. Attentive wait staff continually swept throughout the enormous room, determined to appease everyone at each table. The one youth drawn to the spectacle more than most takes his time in selecting a glass of port, reminding the server that he too belonged here as much as any other.

When they were both alone the older of the two began to speak with slow and determinate skill. It was as though he wanted to make his first statement here as reassuring as it needed to be.

"Are you sure you are comfortable?"

"Father, I remember you bringing me here for my twenty-first birthday. Every one of these faces seems as familiar as it did back then—do you remember? Of course I was dressed much better then."

Much of the talk continued around the night in question. It was determined that this first excursion here was a fine moment in time—a conveyance of pride stands between he and his son—reminding him of a better time when they both got along. He had just wondered out loud if he had stood fast by his offspring instead of distancing himself from the surprising circumstances of his impending arrest, that they would be enjoying a far better moment per chance.

"It would have been far different if you had stood with me, after all. But given the circumstance of which you spoke, you bade the better bet. It was a small wonder that they did not attempt to drag you in. Do you recall how they tried to excite you?"

The drinks are in readied hands and one toasts the recollection of the other's remiss. Additional points are being made between them, but then they are interrupted by a third party who addresses one directly, as if the other does not exist. Determined not to let this offhand and ungentle expression go unexamined for any manner of time, the father brings his son into the conversation with a warning tongue. The man soon departs without ever looking back. He was dismissed so smartly that the son has to smile knowingly.

"Well you have certainly not lost your touch. I would not want to be in his place under any circumstance. And by the way, thank you."

"No need to thank me. He really did need to be put into his place."

"I was not talking about that clout. I was thanking you for putting off the inevitable. We do have to talk about it, you know. Why you came after me tonight, and why we are here now."

"I do not understand?"

"Father, if your status had not changed, he would have never addressed you this way. Is that why we are here? What is it that you are holding off; to tell me? Tell me now."

There would be no need for further introspection; his son's face holds the expression of one who is in the know. They will only be able to sip their drinks in silence for a while longer. The room has quieted from announcements from the stage, and the room has taken on an eerily softness and spell.

Not much has been talked about with straight forward manner between the two for the longest time. Would the older be willing to keep his secret from the younger for any additional length of time than ultimately warranted? The relationship is suddenly invigorating and refreshed that to hold back would be to crash any other expectations of closeness; in store for them both if it is handled properly.

The time is now. Somehow the ideal time is right in front of him and he cannot push off any longer. He was not about to let this minute in time be driven down by pride—his position of leadership in a company who has dominion and control over this very place in which he entertains the solution to his most pressing problems. He wants to remain within the reach of comfort, for as long as he can retain his very soul in this place, alongside his son—there is little time put off what has troubled him.

"I was asked to step down. The Board of Directors made it clear that my time in the helm was concluded. I have no disillusion with this regard—I am not entertaining a return by any means or order. In fact, I have already taken a controlling position, in another order of business: another industry all together."

The depth of this revelation was like a weight lifting off of his broad shoulders. There is a sense of relief that he has said this out loud to a member of his own choosing, and at a time where clarification must be said out loud. The wait staff has returned to their table and carefully takes an order with keen and too lingering interest in getting it right. Finally, he walks away and the two men lean in toward one another and the conversation is pushed up hill.

The son has surmised that there is another whole other angle to the expression and look of consternation worn on his father's face. So laughingly this would never do.

"What are you holding back, Father? I can always read you—you know this to be an undeniable fact. Tell me with full disclosure what is pressing you on to keeping me in suspense?"

It is finally impossible to hold one's tongue on the subject; pressing release about now makes it impossible to sit still. The older man is reaching deep into his arsenal of powers: to remain in control of everything he still has to say up to this very point: it is tipping the scales of power toward the one he trusts—his son.

"I have taken a controlling interest in a theatre. You know it is something I have threatened to do for as long as one can remember. Now it is done. I own a theatre."

His son pushes his chair back and at the same moment leans in. The last rounds of drinks have been delivered to this table and each takes his turn sipping the hot beverages in. The aroma of strong coffee is strong within this inner circle.

"Where is this place? Is there a particular venue? Please tell me more; I am so happy for you. This is an immensely exciting proposition—as any I have heard from you in time. Do continue."

The depth at which they retain eye-to-eye contact is one perhaps two feet. The torsos of each are lowered into the center of the table and each one retains a comparative cool as the progression of details is given, as though there was ample preparation. And in time the most remarkable aspect of the deal is revealed.

"You remember the young man, Josh, who you introduced me to before you went away? Well, it is his theatre I which I now have a controlling interest. He had several years of arrears which could not be paid off with any certainty, so the building and other assets were transferred to other interested parties, several times I might add, before the final opportunity was presented my way. It was almost by accident that the package came across my desk. When it did, it could not have been at a more fortunate time."

The excitement in the conversation continued for some time: several cups of coffee for that matter: and chairs were being pushed back after the bill had been taken care of. Coats are made fast and comfortable and it is evident that many of this crowd is taking the same measure. After a quick glimpse of the remaining patrons the two of them depart past large doors held open wide for their attention, and the greatest exchange of goodbyes is extended from staff to each guest making way out onto the street.

Everyone is moving with expressed purpose toward a long queue of taxis with doors opening from the outside, and manners are kept sharp and simple as members clamor into the waiting vehicles, respectively. This time it is clear that the night's engagement is coming to an end.

The two are left out at the original corner of Broadway and Main. Should this night be made all the more fortuitous they extend and made way into each other's arms for an extended hug or two? The purpose of this elongated exchange is made amply clear.

"I would like you to come into this business with me. Your university degree, as well as your past experience, though short, is as enticing as it is welcome. Do not give me your final answer now. We have consumed too much alcohol in one night. The best of my knowledge; well I cannot not recall when I have had a better time. Please contact me and give me your answer after we have both sobered. I love you so much—good night."

"I will definitely give it some consideration, Father. Please take care. I will see you soon enough. Good night."

There would be one, perhaps more details to disclose before any of that might happen. The man nurtured the thought for another moment or two. He was about to speak but stops short. The taxi takes the older of the two away.

The passenger in the back seat is more introspective than ever. He would relish complete quiet. The repeated attempt at friendly banter by the driver finds no suitable home. It was well into the morning when the sights of the city quietly flew by and the residence of the passenger comes into view, at long last. The older man is departing after paying: there is not one additional word passed between them. The taxi sped off with unusual swiftness.

The gentleman enters his home with leisure and places the keys into a glass bowl. He is growing tired from all of the actions of the night and wishes only to get undressed and into bed without further hesitation. One quick glance at the clock on the wall spells it all out: a quarter past four o'clock in the morning. He is not used to this kind of venture. At the sight of his bed he pours in and immediately passes out.

Needless to say he is still breathing.

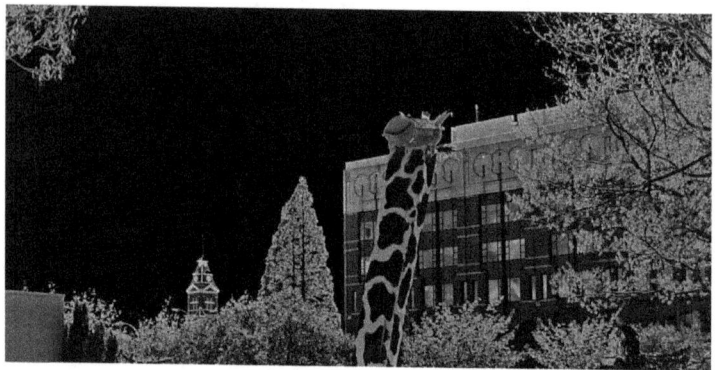

HIS VOICE: *I generally remember him as someone who is willing to help at a prescribed distance. Having to approach him to beg this favor in a manner not practiced well enough, it is not clear that I have played that hand well. This is especially so in his place of business. It was too public.*

INNER VOICE: *The meeting you described is an interesting journey in the absence of going it alone. Solo was the term used before, wasn't it?*

HIS VOICE: *I need him as my secret weapon against the board. If his posturing on my behalf results in them taking a step back, it will have had the necessary results as prescribed. In his presence I will become a simple distraction. In his absence I am a target and nothing more. It is a risk I am willing to take.*

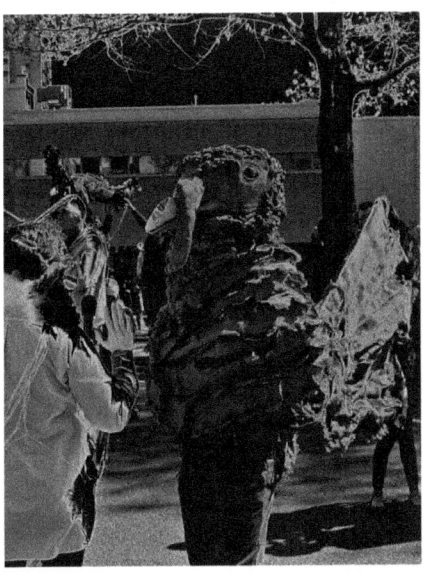

VOICE OUT LOUD: *And if this invitation to the table proves to be a return of that beast, then what? Will Tess be called back into this script?* "*Come quick to the rescue. Leave all that past baggage behind. Smile, because I still need you to care.*"

The vision is inside ultimately.   There are those externalities that stream or thread and influence, but never are they more profound than when absorbed, mulled over—churned even—before they can be assembled into something that much more tangible, and then spewed out via a chosen artful medium.

Perceptive Sensations   Michael O'Connor

Screen Sixteen

THERE WERE ONE OR TWO POINTS that the critics wrote up about the latest production that stood out for Josh. One was more worthy than the other; nevertheless he gave them both the widest degree of objective scrutiny he could muster short of going off like the rail of a bull elephant. He was already weakened from the shorter than expected box office sales, and together with this latest media stream he was barely capable of maintaining an open mind while downing his morning breakfast. The sound of the crisp newspaper turning page-by-page, having to gain the permission of the waitress to leave him alone, together was maddening beyond belief.

He was pleased that one of the reviews was just shy of excellent and that it compared his thoughtful production to one of his theatrical heroes. Everywhere else in his smallish town people were rising to gain access to offices and then desks, ascending on a day full of promise, watching the convergence of morning with the vistas all around. The distance from page 33 to the next section seemed as far apart as the small hills appeared in front of the towering mountains tens of miles away. At another satisfying distance was a hint of a storm brewing off of the coast, and the anticipation that it would reach here just before noon. There was that time needed: get to the next section of the review, sigh and perhaps cry a bit, and then wait for a total soaking on his way back to the theatre before the troupe arrived for their next practice behind the etched panels.

It was his insistence on plodding through to the second review that the promise of a greater storm on several fronts settled in quite severely. The clouds rolled over the mountain top and poured its weight down into their little valley. They were dense, dark gray, and already to open up and release a torrent of rain. The creeks would just as soon swell and their mighty momentum would be first roiled and then unleashed across the short plains and onward into the heart of the city. Everywhere else in the world the sun was shining, horses and cows grazed lazily in whatever shade could be found, and a village at the foot of any mountain would be happy and prosperous unless it was said that the attempt at art, especially at theatre, was held as the most amateurish: the populous descends down to the lowest elevation possible on the following morning.

After reading and digesting the last two paragraphs of the second opinion the writer's credentials were incredulously cruel; such findings are typical in the comparison it belayed. Josh was no stranger to the population's opinion with regard to local affairs, but the mighty force that was furnished by this slashing pen-to-type was conducted more as a witch hunt than a review. The author wanted to get to the bottom of it all: who on earth could have produced such a travesty: "cock and bull and something entirely failing to display even a smattering of good taste".

Were it not for this direct quote Josh would have simply put this newspaper down. The words had become magnetized and stuck to everything around him, including his meal and once hot but now cool cup of coffee. More hellish words could not have conveyed this one's opinion, or the halting appearance of the blood that was rushing to Josh's head; for now his paper needed to be laid down and brushed aside with simmering violence, so that he could resume breathing before he was found dead after breakfast.

Life continued to be conducted around this little village, which it was not—this was a city. How each and everyone conducted themselves was professional enough, despite the railing of this one article. The several theatres within city bounds comprised of a nice variety, with content to surprise everyone around in proximity and the desire or need to see the truth twisted, turned or stretched with ample creativity.

There were very good play houses and were conducted with a smattering of good thought and good will when it came to the fine arts or its constituency.

The town now, is perched on a small plateau just below a mountain, and it seems there is more than enough opportunity to conduct one's own business without the declarative and vindictive bantering of the outside world, as to how much of the arts should be left to the skillful hands of the metropolis. Our cultivated hills, streams of courage and careful germinations with regard to painting, sculpture, music and most certainly stage—well there seems to be an endless supply of capability: content reigns well from the scenic beaches of the west coast, through the mountain passes and flattening plains, and out to the stormy eastern seaboards. Content reigns everywhere one can see; where others care to look is another matter all together.

Josh understood that the truest signs that someone might have castigated on something, or displayed a countering spell on something entirely differing, was as common to the sparsely populated as it was at locations of denser wealth. That is if one took chances. Conversely, there are times that the larger place dwells too often on what was successful in the past; the commonly accepted view that version two and version three continues to captivate that audience. In essence both directions can burn a thing to death if greater care is not taken to risk it all for the sake of art. What right one opinion can say that a perfect piece of fruit can be picked from the tree, if another puts up constant barriers to entry in the first place?

The usual signs of disparity reign everywhere. But neither this producer nor director will opt to explain away why he was not willing to take that chance and pursue the dream of providing a suitable venue for discussion or more qualified dissertation. The critic does not always rule the realm.

Josh picked up the paper and reread his other review. His breathing was easier and the true colors have returned to his face, and as such a matter could cause it, he requested and received another cup of coffee that was a significant improvement over his first. That is until someone else approached him.

As it appeared on the surface of things, the fact that his long lost pal, for who he relied on and grew with mentally, physically and perhaps spiritually was suddenly standing in front of him, bearing his own provisions. What would it take to relive all of those youthful years, standing side by side and taking no others orders except their own, that the instant he appears and address the astonished Josh with a simple enough request.

"May I join you? This would make my day."

The face across from him lowers and they are as suddenly eye-to-eye. Josh does not remember making any forward gesture or even a single murmured word, yet this ever brash individual has taken his rightful place at the comfortable café table and unwrap his deli sandwich from another location still. He enjoys his first bite and then produces a bottle of ice cold tea, pops the twist top loudly and drinks one quarter of its content before wiping his mouth and calling first to the shell shocked table companion.

"Are you glad to see me? If not I can move to another location."

His ordering of his questions proves the undoing of the opposite man; he sits and ponders the second inquiry before he has had the chance to address the first. There is certainty in the opportunity to address them all; seeing that this new member is quite willing to entertain this and any additional flow of questioning. It is a most interesting sequence of events that will follow: the why and where have you been of it all.

The deli sandwich is half polished off and so is more than half of the cold beverage. It would be more common to interject a course of dialog during this state of affairs, but their own common language, perhaps sense of etiquette, demands piercing eyes and gaping mouth, but little else to fill in those supposed blanks. It is so that he is ready to talk under his own labors, not the keyed anticipation of anyone else.

In the short term Josh is patient. He is gulping down the last amount of his cold coffee and is signaling the wait person over to fill up his cup. The loutish lady begins to question the idea of someone bringing outside food and beverage into this domain, but then submits to the careless action at the request of the one face she recognizes well. Josh is a generous tipper it would seem, and this was enough to guide her past the invasion of food and stuff from this shared table. It was never close to being a monumental deal; she turns after pouring coffee carefully to the brim of his cup and then simply walks away without so much as an additional glance.

Josh in turn begins to open a thundering outpour of question against the bemused counterpart who seems to take the whole of the affair with the levity it deserves. He is quick enough to retort with the answers called for and the conversation has just transitioned from very serious to most playful. If one were to be a sightseer or someone passing by with keen insights and ears, this battle of wits went from volcanic inferno to a bowl of soft pudding in the blink of an eye. In short, now their sides were bursting with shared laughter, as though the first instance provided the necessary relief to blow off steam and probably coarsely hurt feelings. They both smiled and signaled what could be best served by non verbal communication.

On the face of the dialog one could not curtail the fact that his life was being rendered obsolete by the undertaking of those others, who no doubt wouldn't stop until he was well off his feet. He exclaimed that they wanted the whole of the damn thing: his beloved theatre. The curses in the air were held there deliberately until the salvo was incriminatingly read by anyone unfortunate to share a table within proximity. Josh appealed to the diverse groupings of patrons around him to share in the spasms and pangs of discourse orated on his behalf. He wanted his thunder and discomfort sold to all who were around.

This of course was the sought out ground for which he would take his last stand to assemble growing interest in taking his side. There was no doubt that many of these patrons were not complete strangers to him or to his plight.

The whole of this incredible loud stand; as to his rightful ownership in something he had built from scratch; goes from fact to the truly obscure and the sense in the air is that he has only a smattering of sympathy in the crowd. Someone calls out too smartly.

"Josh, we are only here for the coffee. Leave us in peace."

Were this recant not so terrifying, the grasp of his friend's arm exemplified the proof that his platform was misguided. Evidently most thought his line of questioning should just go away. It was not entreating his experience lightly, as the returned to exclusive conversations. His friend made it clear.

"Josh, pretend for a minute that you only have an audience of one. You are not on stage addressing a broader audience; as you only need to understand such as it is now; getting past it is a door you must walk through."

His friend was no paying too much attention to anything else beyond the table. He continued to grip Josh's arm and make him pay more attention to what was put immediately in front of him, now. This impression is made with more than a modicum of success, and Josh settle down and takes in a very deep breath.

"Is this where you tell me, that your happening by this place was no accident?"

"That is an accurate depiction, Josh. But there is much more to tell—that is once you have settled down. No one is watching us: your plea fell on mostly deaf ears: so let us continue this conversation in solitude."

What he described rolled off his tongue and out of his mouth started to make more sense as to why he had appeared now. His speech was wisely kept narrow;

all insinuations as to his inclination of keeping the past to the past were made assertively enough. He was here to describe what simply took place, and his growing roll in how it would affect the future of said theatre. He also described what had happened as being executed with the best of intensions.

Admittedly, even he was uncertain as to what role—if any at all—would his friend and lifelong compatriot play.

"I am prepared to admit that your role is still being fleshed out. It should not be misconstrued that you might have a role, in any capacity, beyond the transition from past owner to the new."

The gut wrenching reality of this speech was just sinking in. It would take several gulps of coffee to arouse him to the purpose of this little talk, and to the fact that he could no longer differentiate between supposed friends versus foes. It was a startling contradiction: from where their friendship had left off: where the next point of this dialog should begin.

It felt life threatening. He lost his ability to speak. A parting of the seas was no longer just a metaphor; the subjectivity of his next statement could no longer be disclosed under this respective parting of ways.

"I am astonished."

Josh began to stand up and then managed to throw down a small stack of bills onto the tabletop. Without saying what was really on his mind he turned away; staggering the pain of this realization because it became more stunning as time went on; he would put a sufficient amount of distance between a once legacy friendship and what now remained to be seen— beyond the betrayal. The whole of the experience is leaving him with a sour taste in his mouth. He bends his head to the ground and spits angrily.

The other party just sits there with a most astonished facial expression: mouth agape, a near an empty ice tea bottle, and the remnants of a last meal before the closure of decades of mutual exchange by way of friendship. For a moment one might think that he had done no wrong.

It might take another moment or two to adjust; leaving that table to be cleared by a helpful and attentive wait staff. They would be confused as well upon finding two neat stacks of small bills, which added up to a larger sum than expected.

Would it be acknowledged that the party at the table must have left completely satisfied. Who is left to know?

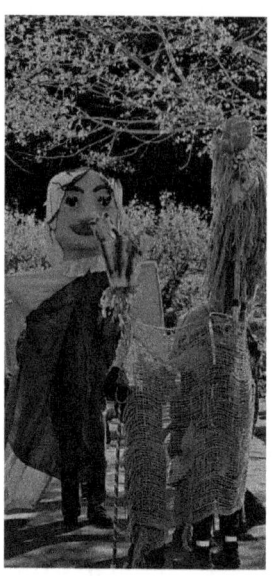

INNER VOICE: *Were it not for the fact that I flashed back to her backyard, and those never ending cups of tea, I swear I had been transported to another place altogether.*

Gosh, the detail of that dialog is so scanty, with the exception of her last bit of advice. These reoccurrences so tolerably abundant lately, there remains no doubt that something relevant is to be discovered. This last piece of the puzzle is so peculiar and at the same time is far too familiar.

VOICE OUT LOUD: *You are closely allied, is why. Each detail is carried across like a flood of pertinent information. You're picking out the relevant detail, as you exclaim; this is supposed to be difficult. If it were clear cut, you would not be so distinct in your manner. Perhaps, if you were less shrewd, you could lean more toward the appropriate action.*

INNER VOICE: *I am damned if I stand alone, and I will be really damned if I look toward group answer. Is that it?*

VOICE OUT LOUD: *The facts are spelled out in your ability to pick the right allies. A strong corroborative opinion is never formed on one's own. The gift of getting this right is found in the presence of the few and the exclusion of the many. The resultant balance is in the straight and narrowed, so joined when one understands how to sever again. It should not seem improbable that once in a thousand times you will get this right.*

The audience is a participant, better yet a recipient: will refer to the cause of the reaction as a personal account more or less because they have felt it at a peculiar time and place: able to absorb it on face value as if it was replayed for the first instance as their own unique interpretation.

INNER VOICE: *And yet another stupid riddle.*

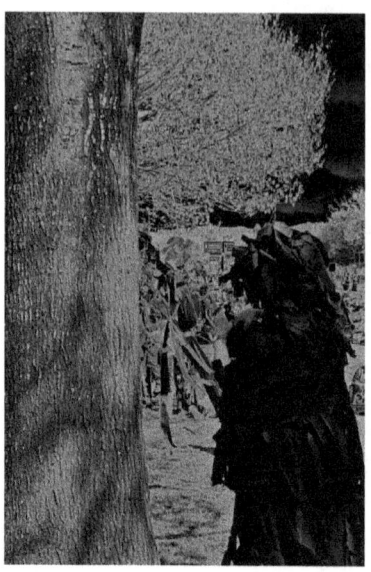

INNER VOICE: *Wait. Is that her next to that tree? There are no grounds for her being here, now.*

VOICE OUT LOUD: *Is this your vision or belief? Her appearance would be an interesting and most instructive puzzle. It is seldom that we can rely on a vision alone to get to a distinctive solution. There must be another source.*

Screen Seventeen

THE DEPARTURE WAS A BIT LESS than cheery. He had apparently nothing else to say outside of the obvious: stuck in his employ, but not for much longer. He left just after making this arrogant pronouncement; never wanting to give him the satisfaction of a counter argument, or of a pleading for rightful control.

"I just walked away."

Josh had taken his time conveying the events to a shocked Tess in the living room. He had wandered in still in a daze and it did take a bit of forceful prying by her, to get him to open up. He was infusing their environment with a steepening sense of anger and the withdrawn; the only correct thing to do was get him to talk before bursting. For every instinct she had in her fiber, and the intellect she relied so well, it was only a matter of time before she got him talking—relaying the entire event.

To start off with she now understood the ramifications of his shedding the title of owner and producer. No one had apparently though that he would be of any further use to the survival of the theatre—this place which had lived through every ordeal for just over twelve year under a sole ownership, but not soloed control. It was more obvious now how a distant few would claw their way into majority ownership, using the ups followed by the downward trends in this sort of entertainment. Apparently it left him so dispassionate that the correct thing to do was suggest how some distance on his part might be the only recourse left in his arsenal.

"Take a fresh step back, Josh. See what it is like at a safe distance. There will certainly entertain the same ups and downs as you have, and then it will be your well placed position to step back in if they hedge on this investment. They will certainly not have your leveled sense of purpose or patience. Let them fall and watch it hurt. Then step back in—in front of them and recollect what is rightfully yours."

Josh knew that his life partner was correct—her calm was her glory—and she persisted now where he needed her reassurances most. It was a strange feeling of sickness that had stricken him on his way home, but even walking through the door made him believe that he had not lost everything—notwithstanding his standing in the community as regaled host in a central place of entertainment. If his reputation was to be smeared, let it not come by his own mishandling of the situation.

Tess was correct: learn from it, denote what is probable, and then lean forward with just as devious a plan to win it all back. His only reply to her was a simple acknowledgement—his shrug.

He was not done yet. For no particular reason he inched forward where she stood erect and engulfed her in what could be certainly regarded as a bear hug. He had no other strength to fight for what he had been forced to give up—the self reflection, so self assured and self actualized—his willful appearance. Would he consider himself an island subjected to the highs and lows of the tides, or would he gradually build up the necessary barriers to confer with nature rather than try to best an unwinnable battle. For no particular reasoning would he say what was really on his mind, deep within his heart.

He could not cry—not now, not ever in front of her. Instead he just buried his head into her shoulder and sighed for the longest time: the search for another answer. And then he pushed back ever so gently.

"When I was much younger than I am right now, I had been beaten down psychologically. I had been given the opportunity to prove myself in front of my peers. It was a defining moment in my life to immerse myself in the traditions of theatre and stage from a place where many, if not most of my heroes of the trade, take their beginning. I wanted to go there; not to follow their footsteps and become a shadow, or to soak up something of their lives and bring it all back here simply to repeat it. Then again, the plan was not to be followed through—shut down before it even started because I was too obsessed with what might appeal to them rather than me."

It was then that he revealed his problematic relationship with his peers. He had originally started off his life's planning as an opera singer of great potent. Only there was something lacking in this plan—that of money he required to pursue it and pay the rent and other bills accumulating. He wanted a modest and traditional means of pursuit, not necessarily stardom.

The conflict was that opera would not enable him to pay all of those bills unless he was on top. He was dissuaded by his own plans from ever bring this far up the chain of events again, and he took a secession of menial points of employment to fill the coffers with sufficient funds to carry him past it all. It was there that his musical legacy narrowed—so self deluded it left him to self destruct very early on in his career. It was there his important source of funding was less assure, having spent down several grants he had secured to move forward. He pulled back: he did not want to falter in a life style that was not meant to sustain him in the first place.

Beaten from this track of life, and then plagued by admitting his worse fears: from time-to-time simply remembering the moments through dreams became the only compensation for trying at all. He recalls this on only special occasions, usually keeping this failure to self. When he exclaimed a desire to prove himself worthy of a parallel track he received little support—psychologically or spiritually for that matter. He knew he was on his own to rekindle that pursuit in a second coming of terms.

It would take Josh a full decade of sidetracks before he would regain his sense of purpose and retake the reigns of life control back from all those inner conversation to sway him one way to another. This is where he could prove it all wrong: tracking more perfectly not as an artisan per se, but at least as a producer of the staged arts. He readily adhered to a more productive path—this was the only way in—and proving himself capable to his peers over time that he truly belonged in the industry of entertainment.

He re-earned a rightful path and reputation. How was it that he could walk away from this now so easily? Shouldn't he put up more of a fight than ever before, given that the stakes were much higher?

"I just might need a bit more time to let this all sink in. But mark my words I will not just walk away without putting up some kind of contest. Tess, I would only ask you be willing to stand by my side for a while longer? There is no telling which way this will flow.

But I need your steadied self control to counterbalance my disjointed self destruction."

The first stage of his rebound was put forth in a curious manner, leaving the two to spend the remainder of the day poking holes in it and countering the anticipated effects. So far as one could judge time would be the lesson learned, and the impetus to regaining control. But there was also a high cost: the extended hours of planning that would take away from a relationship already running across narrowed grounds. There could be a great loss if it consumed either of them. It was of course more acceptable than rebuilding the entire thing from the ground up in a small city such as this, where every step and every yawn is captured and relayed across the street with scant delay.

All eyes would be watching; to this there was little doubt. By the time they had stepped out for some dinner the approach was little more than a series of loose depictions of what would be desired rather than what could be real. This did not dissuade the two, keeping at it well into dark, and then straight through to the next morning.

The two of them were experienced at building up expectation for each other, having never been separated for the following week and then two. Tess had taken some well earned time off of her work to divine a solution to his—another proportion of the plan came resting more on fate over instigation. They would take short travel time together to a place that Josh knew from an earlier direction in his life, when the journey was more important than the destination. It was here that they would separate for the first time in as long as they could remember.

The person who which Josh attended to now was a very gifted schemer, who had once upon a time declared that he could live off of the dreams of others for all of his life. He was no one of self reliance, but his keen ability to impartially hear what others were meant to pursue, drew greater admiration from Josh over the years. Josh was in good company so long as this strange fellow did not attach himself too cleverly to the plan they ironed out.

"A half empty glass is all I need to tinker with, my friend. What you have come up with on your own so far is suitable. I am intrigued enough to propose how to get to three quarters full, but the rest; well you will be on your own."

"I have in fact made it this far because there is another significant variable to this sequence of events. Her name is Tess. It is more likely that I am seeking you out for all of this trouble, in desperation at this stage. I do not want to let her down, let alone myself. We have gradually grown together in a manner that means more to me than the rest of this trouble. Mark my words; she is worth the fight if you take any other means with regard to an end run."

The two men sat at a fair distance and gave each other knowing glances. It would appear to even the most distant observer that this reunion speech was served before. The look of acceptance to the contentious challenge was eagerly received, as though expected.

The friend—better known as a past associate—was in fact countering this challenge with one of his own. Gradually this bravado segued to something far better known to bring sufficient advance.

The view was a past association as well; in it laid splendid vistas with a marvelous half dome of granite off approximately one half mile away. In his most cherished recollection of a time in his life his favorite was a race against time and the elements—against biannual challenge of racing to the top, viewing the three hundred degree panorama, and then repelling down so to complete the track. To date it was an almost fifty-fifty split with wins and losses.

"In your present condition, Josh, I will not take advantage. When both of our minds are working as one, we can move to a more secure plateau, and into the heart of the situation. I have any number of scenarios we can impose on this band of cutthroats, but one that will keep them at bay and quite will have a certain amount of risk. How is your stamina these days?"

Was this a challenge of a different type? Josh looked at the grin on his associate's face, and then back up the side of the half dome. Certainly he did not want to chase up to the top of that place at this time in their lives. It took courage and massive amounts of physical strength to accomplish the task, let alone the mental focus which was required. Would either man have the same mix now—after all of the years spent in intellectual pursuits over physical ones?

Josh wished that his counterpart would have only kept quiet with this regard. It immediately blindsided him; another misfortunate event he carried angrily to this day; he economized how much effort he would throw in its path to retention the threat. This man: by trial by fire he had suffered through misstep once before: and would now have to double the energies to tread lightly. Having found a sense of regained strength he took care to recall the act in question without regaling forth with uncontrollable emotion. This was one gifted grafter who loved to profit by well tested experience.

Josh semi-consciously rubbed both of his thighs and recalled the scaring that once covered them, and then massaged his knees sensing the agonizing recovery period. She came and then left during that recovery period, mad at them both over a repeated competitive acts that nearly killed everyone.

"That one left us both, if you recall. I remember why."

It was by this carefully crafted answer—carefully thought through—that he would gain the higher ground. She had been the reason they had both questioned staying here—utopia found then lost—and the loss that forced one over the other to leave. There was a higher rate of accountability that is justified here, but Josh would let this one escape for the time being. He could not remember exactly, the circumstance that brought his friend back first.

"There is little doubt that we will need to revisit this question. But for right now it is better that we get along for at least the next several days. Will you be staying here for the duration? By the way, just where is this Tess right now?"

It was another contest and another test of wills. Would he be willing to risk the effort in moving forward with this man? Surely his relationship with Tess was on solid enough ground. But then he had thought that to be true once before: they had both been so wrong. It was then that Josh acknowledged that this effort was his only destination. The journey just getting here was defining enough.

"She is taking care of business at another location. We will rejoin after I am through here. No, you will not get the opportunity to meet her. That much I have thought through before coming back to Lion's Gate.

Can we take a break now? I would like to take some time to visit the lake. I will be using the boat in the channel, if that is acceptable."

His counterpart reached behind and opened a drawer to an enormous oak desk, retrieving and throwing him the key in one continuous movement. Each man sported an impish look.

Josh walked off down a long descending gravel path which would take him to a very familiar beachfront, after pushing his way through a grove of overgrown bushes. The needles at the tips of the branches scratching on his exposed skin. Along the way he studied the splendor of this place and the memories it flooded his mind with—a less complex time in his life regained—never questioning why it crumbled under the weight of time and change.

He was singing out loud by this time, spotted many aspects of a lane never changed; if this place could be everlasting; he wondered why he had left it in the first place. Now he wonders out loud why he has returned. There is a point at the far end of the waterway that he is after, and it will take him an hour plus just to see the point break into view following a series of peninsulas and tucked in waterfalls still flowing with strong sources of water. He knew the source of each and every one by heart. They had discovered them together.

The point he wanted to get to was just around one final bend of shoreline, past a peninsula point that would demark the grandest change in the landscape. Beyond its tip he could see the sun wash over a grand beachhead by mid day. The shack was still standing in line with the beach but set back far enough so that its cast shadows did not reach the waterside. There was still the imposing tree line just several hundred yards behind it and the shadowed tips of pines just made it to the perimeter of the cabin.

Josh beached the watercraft and climbed over the bow to jump to land. His feet landed into the fine graveled covered beach and it crunched loudly under his footsteps as he made way up and onto a pathway toward the entrance of the cabin and its grand front porch. With the sentencing of a condemned man he approached it shyly, almost scared, and let his first footstep find the cracks and squeaks of the porch he had built a long time ago. It was more forced labor than a justifiable treat that he remembered. It was payment for the pleasure of living here—a rent paid with sore muscles, splintered palms and forearms, and enough sweat to contribute to the lake's waterfront behind him.

What was wrong then is still so wrong today. There is occupancy.

The several hints of living had an all imposing appearance as the full weight of his body made way across a porch noisy enough to wake the dead. There were several potted plants which appeared to be well looked after; overgrown and flowing over the sides of the large pots until they graced the planks of the porch. And at mid day, under the hot sun, there are ample signs of watering. This is where he remembered last seeing her—that final day's chore completed before she had left for town—she said.

The door was locked. This was something new. In the past nothing was every secured—nothing ever stolen? It had been a veritable hotel in its day, during the high season of friends dropping by for a swim in the lake and then staying for days leading to weeks. All points of view from porch to beach were taken up by semi-clothed bodies. But hers was the one he always scanned for from a comfortable char that was no longer in sight.

His room was in the back. It was really a walled in back porch that had gone under major refurbishment before he had moved in. Josh wondered what spell was cast on him as he stepped forward and peered through the large bay window into the cabins living room. This room being the largest in the cabin dominated the entire front side. The sun was streaming into it today just as it did across the years he had spent here, managing to secure a place to live for little more than a fair day's labor. As mentioned before he was one of the bodies who stayed far longer than intended—days, then months, followed by years.

He was a daily companion to all that visited this place, and he was its keeper.

Even so, Josh did not harbor any love for the past or this place, with the exception to one of the roommates who both won and broke his heart. After reliving some of the seasons spent lingering here he finally saw more evidence of this dwelling being someone else's domain. There was a hairbrush and medium-sized towel lying on top of a handmade coffee table set to the center of the room. He had the unfair advantage of peering in and watching the back of an unencumbered person stepping sideways to avoid tripping over a slumbering cat. There was comedy in the act he so quietly tried to follow.

One could only wish that the face on shoulders which turned would have the added surprise of familiarity. This one was placed on a muscular neck attached to a more than fit torso. The tender moments he wished to recall were dashed when her eyes met his and a mouth that opened wide with a warning shot over his bow.

"Ok, peeping tom, you have one minute to announce yourself. Past that and this attack cat will bring you down."

All innocence was gone and she pulled a sweatshirt up into place covering both her back and shoulders. If there is a lust of seeing a half naked stranger it was taken away when she turned and exposed a more fierce face, never smiling? Here words may have been made in jest by the piercing stare conveyed a deadly narrowed opinion of who she addressed.

It was hot on the porch but he was made to feel the cold covering his body. The occupant zippered up her sweatshirt and began heading for the front door. It was a planked and solid door that he had rebuilt more times than he could remember. Expectations gave way to fear as she stepped through the threshold and he could see a small pistol in her left hand. He was finally feeling the weight of his own gravity and his legs would not give way.

The closer she got the harder his heart beat. Her approach was steadied as any other and there was no indication of fear across her face. She was steadfast and wanted to know with a harrowing certainty just who he was and why he stood on her front porch.

The opposite came to mind almost immediately.

"Actually, I built this porch."

Each syllable was firmly conveyed within inches of the final details of a pistol. Upon discovering that it was indeed loaded Josh mustered the strength to utter additional words. It gave him no joy to tell the obvious next thing also weighted by a load bearing gravity in its own right.

"If you put away the gun I will tell you everything you wish to know."

Was a compromise near? Her throat was cleared and the cat appeared at her feet, circling a figure eight as they have a tendency to do.

"If you tell me what I want to hear I won't shoot you."

In the heat of the afternoon there is never compromise. At a point that obscured the fact that there was a perfect vista to been seen at the back of this cabin, discovering it again for the first time would have made him all the happier. He let his mind wander around to the back hoping that the accompanying sound would not be from this gun's popping out a single round into his head, taking away forever what he want to regain the most. He wanted to see that vista from the room at the back of the cabin.

His mind was set to parity with the situation. Her opinion of the situation was the opposite, less verbally disclosed. The hand tightened around the grip and a single stream of perspiration crossed her forehead and into her eye. The delicacy of need was followed through and she placed one object into her waistband while the other hand grazed her brow seeking to sweep away salt and sweat from a blinking eye.

"My name is Josh. I used to live here. You might say I built most of this place—once upon a time. There is a carving on the doorway of the back closet; the back room was once a porch. I used to live here, but I do not want to die in this place."

It was then that he spied the slight upturning of the corners of her lips, trying to persuade herself to visualize the placed he mentioned with reasonable detail. His voice seemed to appear to her; liking it enough she stepped back and then away finally leaning against one of the support stanchions of this grand front porch.

"This is probably the strangest introduction I have ever heard."

She managed a prolonged smile. It had a familiarity to it and the simple way she brushed her hair away from her face was painfully recognizable. She strolled down the stairs and out onto the gravel.

"Come down here. I don't want you anywhere near the front door until we sort this all out. You say that you once lived here: well then, describe the master bathroom."

The assortment of detail was lost more than a decade ago, but Josh endeavored to recall his past. What appeared on her face was a successful persuasion; the once sole proprietor of the resources inside was accurate enough. His labors of love, blood, sweat and tears were recalled with harrowing details, as though he had just steeped inside for the first time. She stepped closer under the rays of the sun and touched the surface of his face like a memory come to light.

"You are who you say you are. But I do not know if it will do you any good. She is staying here; I am her daughter."

Josh had included the name of the woman in his past, in his lengthy description. The fruits of his reflections were reward enough, but the power of what they revealed was just being understood. He persuaded himself not to jump to any sorted conclusions. He could not continue as another boat was starting to appear on the water, just rounding the tip of the long peninsula.

This was a keen reminder of how fast one has aged.

"There she is now."

In the stillness broken by the loud hum of a single outboard engine, what had been going along fine was now counterbalancing the whole scene. It was her—the face behind the wheel appeared as if steeping right out of a dream of the past, narrowly forgotten.

His associate did not think it was important enough to provide him with this one silly detail as he threw Josh the keys. Was this with purpose or oversight?

"Oh, by the way, Josh, she still lives here."

It was all that need be said. But it was not said out loud. Instead the shallow surprise dominated the scene and the fast track to reunion.

The one hillside which stood behind this scene suddenly drew up so many memories it brought tears to Josh's face. His back was to the young lady, but his front stepped out of place. It was haunting, the flood of memories which reappeared when the bow of her boat crunched loudly onto the beachhead.

This reunion was brief but the friendship was deepened as she opened up and handed Josh her groceries. She paid no less detail to the inquiring looks her daughter shot her when his back was turned away. It would be something that she would have to deal with—not now as the day's end called for something much different.

Having been informed that she was able to prep herself under the kind breeze and the instance it took to get here, it was conveyed that he would be staying for dinner. It was more like a marching order. Nothing more was visible to the eye that anything more or less would not be likely. Her demeanor was flat and she carried herself with pride and steadfastness; securing that even the slightest hint of a side glance would reveal nothing pertinent tonight.

The meal provided is simple yet sumptuous and the three ate with a light banter than was required. It was not until the sun was setting and the daughter went out for a walk that the matters of heart were encountered.

"You stayed away. I was certain you would be dropping by on so many occasions I cannot remember why. It was more than just a residence you knew; the many memories we had here should have pulled you back long ago."

She was pulling her long hair back and tying it into a thick ponytail. It was something he used to watch her do at the ending of many a day, and on special occasions she asked him to give her a hand. Back then, almost every gesture was a special occasion—frequently so it usually led to a prolonged interaction.

Would it lead to that now? His heart was pounding.

Her face was always smiling. The only time he could recall her frown was when she left them both standing in a pathway, swearing at the incidents which led them all apart. That was a gateway then, and her expression was an opening now, to get to the bottom of it all. But it was not why he had come here. This was not what was expected at all. She was not even supposed to be here—inviting this circumspection of a past fraught with the perils of exposing one singular notion.

The moon was showing up and beyond the tallest trees, and the light was casting behind the silhouette of the daughter who elected to play outside. How could the innocent pleasure of one imagined, be clouded by the hand which grew a gun and pointed it at his face with so much conviction?

"Your daughter nearly killed me."

It was growing as light as it was during the day. The higher the harvest moon rose the more illuminated the front of the cabin began to appear. The movements of one girl and a single adult cast played across this field as one of the best puppet theatres he has ever laid eyes upon. Was he electing to be a growing member of an excited audience he just might have stood up and cheered?

That is until she spoke again.

"If she wanted you dead, it would be so. That one has a deadly accurate shot. I taught her as much as I could, but she has this uncanny ability to master everything she tries out."

As if she wanted me dead. Josh thought about this solo voice for the longest amount of time. The lady in this house seems proud of the fact that her daughter might even have the capacity of such a thought. The evening drags on painfully. Is he in residence in a familiar place, or is his venture more daring than he wished to say out loud. Josh would not dare even bring it up now.

She had asked him if he wanted to go outside, or would he like some more wine. Everything she murmured had a second meaning. Why was it she maintained a body posture which suggested that this was one day after her departure, let alone the encumbering decade? Apparently she wanted to let this game linger for a while longer—the drive to continue this avoidance of a longer past, her overt freedom to call the shot in this came became almost unbearable to this guest.

One half hour later, after sitting in silence, they stood up and made way to the door to the outside. The daughter had disappeared; later seen at a distance on a path around the other side of the small bay of this lake. The mother receives him more cordially and her arm grazes across his own. The promise of one additional touch would all but make it necessary to broach the truth—the promise to fill in all of those blanks.

Should the cloak hiding details of the memories of this place be lifted ever so gently; one sentence says it all.

"You have been wondering whose daughter might have taken your last breath away, haven't you. I can remember that faraway look on your face. I used to beg you to tell me; where did you go just then."

"I must admit it has crossed my mind. If you would care to share some of the details of the last ten years—

spent apart—I would be a better listener. I promise that."

This was what he actually wanted to listen to—the last ten years only more. Having only wanting to have the opportunity to dispel any lingering doubt—was she his or his associates.

The spell must have been broken because she did just that, plus much more. Having travelled from town to town, across more than one country she settled in Mexico for a while. There was more work than expected with a young one in tow—this narrative gave way to a more promising ending. She had stayed at another home, of another friend, well across the border. In fact it was at the half way point down the Baja Peninsula, on the inside. This was no less a personal voyage, where she learned to rely on her own skills to assist a man she had spent most of her life away from—her own father. He was an expatriate by no cost of his own, and a fine hotelier to which she was more than welcomed to spend beyond a visitor. But then his life expired due to a prolonged illness and she had nothing else to remain for in a place marketed for nightclubs and fine beaches.

Exactly who she said was the biological father of her only child was still to be a mystery. They had left the beach and followed the path to the daughter, who was by then swimming in another bay. As they motioned for her to go on her way they sat down and she let him blunder his way back into the story. One town was left for another—the reason why she never staid in one for longer than required.

"Josh, what is it you would like to know?"

"Who is her father?"

"I see. I thought so. Yes and no."

It was not exactly what he wished. She was taking off her clothes and slowly entering the cooling waters. The silhouette of her divine skin was taking its toll. He was hungry and fully impassioned with the sequence which followed. It was when he was damn near up to his neck that she had reached out to take hold of him for support.

"She is your offspring, but you are certainly not her father. I cannot allow that to occur now. This is a happy and secure time in her life. I have settled down to the point that she now calls this place her home. Do you understand; can you come to appreciate what that really means?"

Suddenly he felt like drowning. This did not exactly match his expectations—an opportunity to see—one year that led to the next one, and all those which followed. Was he so naive? She was paying him the ultimate respect, and at the same time making him understand that to be in both places he could not leave after he secured what he wanted from the associate. This was the one thing a man looking for security in a place had to follow to the letter of the law. It was not the place he came from or could stay. There was Tess across a longer distance that came into his mind when he made it up.

He would come back here a visitor after all, leaving the day after tomorrow. It was at this point that he disappeared under the water and sank to the bottom of the lake. His eyes were wide open but he did not see a single thing beyond a small school of minnows that shimmered by. And he wondered: could he be seen crying at the bottom of this lake?

For all one would want to gravitate toward, as a responsible father and husband, he could not rationalize his way through it all now. He needed to breathe. His lungs burned well past the staying point and while he could be drawn to the surface, he ventured to remain below. To compensate for his feeling he let all movements halt just to see if it could happen. Could he spend his remaining life just out of the line of sight of the legs kicking above? And all the while he was drawn to this he never lost sight of a second pair of legs swimming by. In doing so, he would let himself drown.

The kick off from the bottom was inevitable and painfully uncomfortable. He threaded his way back to the top. There was no reason for hurry; no one had noticed he was gone down under for too long. In a way this was strangely satisfactory. For the moment he remained three to four yards away and just watched mother and daughter play in the water. The path was clear but there was no way he could join them just yet. His eyes were still a mix of salted tears and fresh water. The look of sorrow on his face must be changed before he could make way to their location, as they exited and scrambled up and onto the beach.

At which ever stage a girl grows into a young woman, he would not personally know at this late stage in the game. But it was upon his eyes feasting on the shape of the elder, was he ever more conscious of the revealing shape of the youngest. She was half past girl and well on into womanhood. He watched her face for any signs of being in the known. Disgraced as he felt for not knowing more about her, he forgave himself all the same. The swim was finally over and all three began to track up the hill that would take them back to the cabin. It was precisely then when he decided which way to go.

Josh would not pack up and leave under such circumstances. When the woman asked him to spend the night, on the back porch, he said yes without hesitation. For all one would want to gravitate toward, as a responsible father and husband, he could not rationalize his way through it all now. He needed to breathe. His lungs burned well past the staying point and while he could be drawn to the surface, he ventured to remain below. This was all he could remember about his final trip to the lake.

To compensate for his feeling he let all movements halt just to see if it could happen—even on dry land. Could he spend his remaining life just out of the line of sight of the legs he could still visualize kicking above? And all the while he was drawn to this he never lost sight of a second pair of legs drifting by for another reason all together. This time it was Tess's face he was envisioning. In doing so he would let himself drown but for real this round. This was a cyclic sensation and he wanted it to stop.

As a point of self secured sympathy he did not lessen the time spent wondering what he would be allowed to say if and when he resurfaced. The words are congenial enough but very firm: not that he could ever utter the words he wanted to say. No, his time would not be vanquished under seven feet of stilled water. He had a duty to live, even if it meant never acknowledging a blood course between them—all three. Even on dry land his head still swims.

This time he was more certain that the cycle could be stopped.

In the end he accepted his host's offer to sleep on the back porch. It was the chief thing for an honorable guest to do. But when he heard them snoring evenly, in separating rooms he stole away into the night.

Since no one would have been looking too closely, he would steal away, out well into this night of moonlit splendor. He did not need to sleep off the stupor of the wine or the hours it took him to arrive here in the first place. There was a greater calling; better yet a need, and now a desire. Relying on partial memories he tore out past the back of the cabin and headed out toward the base of the half dome fully dressed. It would be at the base he would leave all of the instances of drowning behind, and pulled himself up to the next level even surface, experiencing it as though it were for the first time. He would sit on the ledge for a longer time than expected.

His every movement was eagerly awaited. The full explanation was sooner to come: it depended on the placement of both on this very narrow ledge. The discerning looks of his associate was now conveyed at equal level. That certainty of living through another challenge to get to the top is sent from one face to the other, and off they began to climb.

At first there were no words sent between them and their steadied progress showed promise of a race just underway. No one was breathing any harder than the other, and fingers and feet placed gently and firmly found way into deep crevasses as though it were done by memory alone. They were cheek-to-cheek at this very moment.

The decision not to rest all the way up to the top was never uttered out loud. All future movements depended on the decision of hand over foot, and it was a great relief that this granite surface did not chip away under the combined weight onto identical archways and splits. From time-to-time there was a loud clatter of smaller rocks giving way. But for the moment the owner of the top was never shared as closer: the certainty, the pronounced discerning of well timed and well placed bodies flattened and then rounding a ledge in serpentine fashion. They were neck-in-neck and muscle retention is mastered in equal parts.

At long last, this race was in the associates favor. He had the privilege of home place, and the nonstop experience of racing to the last outcropping of rock. This situation was never stranger because when he reaches it he stoops over and threw up whatever he had eaten earlier for his supper.

Josh had to make do with an alternative route. The race is saved and his reputation as the last champion is so retained. But before he can cash this all out he has to let his partner finish his ordeal—the flavor of victory can be overwhelming.

"It was good of you to remember that alternate path, Josh."

His heaving is sustained and he is wiping the remainder off of his face. What a stranger moment to savor.

The threat of losing to the man who set him up for that strange reunion was terrible enough. But by now his associate is telegraphing a begging for forgiveness in stature alone. The words do not play out of his mouth, but Josh is acquainted enough with this shot and awful expression to know that his friend has fully resigned.

Perhaps more credit is due. Will this be offered in kind?

"Why did you send me out there without assistance?"

It is an opportunity to say the words. It is reinforced by a body position that will not leave it well enough alone.

"I did it because I thought you might turn and drive away under any other circumstances. Was I right: would you have driven away instead?"

Unwilling to prolong any punishment due he leaves it alone. Josh has made promises far worse than this and carries forward with all of the remaining strength he can muster. He is relying on his friend being a captured audience on the top of this dome. The only way off is to belay past his fortuitous positioning, directly in the only path down. There is no leaving before the questioning is completed.

"Did you know that she was my daughter?"

The gesture is silent but loud enough. This reputation for being a minimalist at times is playing through— just long enough for him to position himself more securely. He does not know if Josh intends to swing him off of half dome to his rightful end. Because of this tempest state, no one man moves without the other quickly countering.

"Yes, it was the first thing she told me when she arrived."

"How long ago was that?"

"Two, going on three years, I would say; roughly. Look Josh, it could have been worse; she could have been mine."

Remember the gaiety one once felt when introduced to something one should have known all along. Josh felt like the proverbial owl whose constant callout of who begged for someone to actually answer. No doubt this is someone's answer to Darwin's theory of how a species is able to still exist after all this time with so many unknowns. That is to implore rather than imply that it was all a matter of chance. His offspring survives into a stream of teenage consciousness and he cannot deny that Darwin's nature exists. He now has positive evidence of this thing called survival of the species—fit or not.

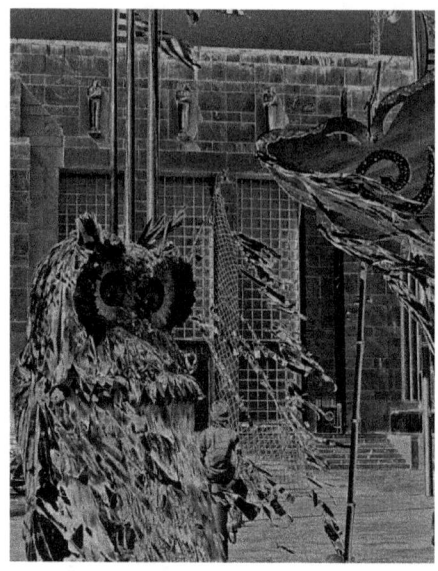

THIS INNER VOICE IS BACK: *Before concluding that you have done some remarkable job of it, make sure you think this through to avoid misapprehension. There is no real connection outside of you knew her mother once; a very long time ago; and obviously she has made the distinction between biological sequence and offspring submergence. She only had to consider the nature of his being to feel so confident that she could keep this secret for so long. Times have changed, dear boy. I have no feeling of confidence with regard to how I am to process this discovery.*

I certainly cannot go to Tess for advice.

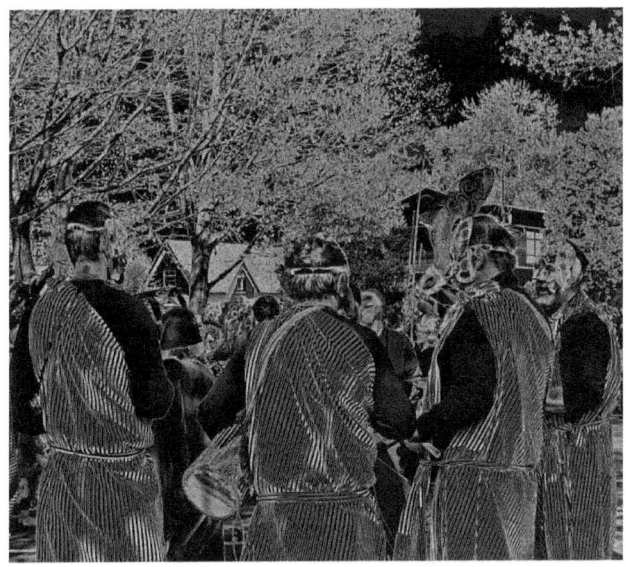

BOOMING VOICE OUTLOUD: *Well do not count on this band to play your swan song. They have their back to you. The complexity of your life has just been elevated a notch or two. To hear that you do not feel confident is amusing.*

ANGRY INNER VOICE: *How about leaving me alone— for the time being—I am trying to reach some kind of decision. What I expected to see and do on this visit has ebbed. This is no longer a celebration to revisit something of my past, to clear my head for the future. In the meantime I just need to be left alone, having not had enough time to explore these streets.*

Perceptive Sensations   Michael O'Connor

Screen Eighteen

IT COULD HAVE BEEN WORSE. He knows that now. He had just been advised by the floor nurse of the good fortune of the person he came to see; having heard it in the restroom of all places.

The message resonated as though it was a courtesy call: a public service messaging forthcoming. The message header echoed in his head and he heard the reverberating syllables over and over again, walking out of the thought-to-be-private room, in his own world until he witnessed an attending physician conversing with the staff at the nurse's station at the end of the corridor. This is when he remembered to check to see if he zipped it up.

It was surprising to witness the joyful mood of the staff as they shared what looked like playful banter on the part of the doctor. There were a few other visitors in the hallway and they appeared as baffled by the loud laughter as Josh did just then—not good laugh goes unnoticed. He shook this all off and returned to the seat he previously occupied through a good part of the night.

This place had a reputable name and was a place most people trusted; had you asked them the same in the crowded hallway. There was little to go by the happy and giggling staff, or the facial expressions of the other doctors who had joined in, as a comparison to the grim expressions of the friends and families of patients waiting for that next pronouncement: alive or dead, or still too early to tell.

Notwithstanding the mood at one end of the hall Josh could tell by the grave appearances at his end that not all was lived with equal splendor—so they were not as amused by the antics at the end of the hall. Some wiped tears away from younger faces while others spoke attentively and then gravely into a number of firmly gripped cell phones. As fortunate as it may have been to observe, no one in this particular hallway was texting.

There were an above average number of teenagers in the hallway as well. Josh managed his time waiting and talking to one of them. They were all from the same High School. Apparently there had been a drinking binge at a post game party, and those who shouldn't have been behind the wheel of an automobile did so anyway, with horrible result. This group was here to ascertain the health of three friends who wrapped a vehicle around a streetlamp at seventy miles per hour. It was the end of a favored street race—a dead end to be sure.

Josh was somewhat surprised again when the attending physician sat down beside him and announced the condition of who he was waiting for less miserably. The status was conveyed and the doctor kept his face on Josh's, while Josh in turn just saw a blur with little recognition to what was just said. The voice was strong yet tender, and the message was bitter sweet. The patient survived, but the injuries warranted several additional days of stay and closer observation. To this minute Josh had allowed his mind to flip too many scenarios that told a much different ending. He was ashamed, but now he was also relieved that thoughts alone did not affect the reality of the actual situation: outcome reality.

He retorted that this good fortune atoned for all of the misdeeds he had tempered with in his mind—not out loud, of course but the conversation was real enough. Josh smiled politely at the physician and took more care to hear the follow up detail at the nurse's station at the opposite end of the hallway. It was here that he noticed a return to the solemn appearance expected, and little sign that previous hilarity dominating their faces just minutes before he had arrived. He admired how this play panned out.

These actors were as good at changing the mood for the better—called to action by the director already heading into another spectrum of theatre. The entire floor had the appealing feel of an audience, though they were looking in so many different directions.

There is no single point of view to the stage as this is a panorama.

How is it that we learn from these troubling places and times in our lives where we should have been focused on something else? The hospital was a place of order and cleanliness. The beds were all made in the same fashion, and when curtain are pulled a whole other venue is at play deliberately secured to keep a more general viewership at bay. It was so easy to see that this was a more refined approach to theatre. Josh pondered what aspects of this sequence of affairs that he was exposed to, could be canned and replayed over and over to an audience hungry for something new.

There was still no single point of view to the stage. They were looking in so many directions: auditory queues came in from as many directions, and visual authority was no different. This theatre is in a bubble.

There was an immediate and elaborate appeal to the sensation he felt as he rolled this scenario again in his head, and then took another thoughtful minute or two to write some of it down. The latest uncontested entry to his purview of an ongoing play was the next person who walked around the corner to his left and begged him for direction. Were this to be seen at a more advantageous distance, the scene could not be view at a more advantageous perspective.

"What did you just say?"

The point of inquiry shook his head and walked away. He seemed so disgusted with the answer he was thrust, having gated to the nurse's station they told him what he needed to know.

"Take a seat and we will call you."

"Enter stage left."

That is what Josh had told him. Judging by the look on his face their answer seemed just as perplexing. He lowered his head into both arms and moaned loud enough to be heard across the hallway.

Exit stage left. This is where he is headed.

The larger lobby stands between Josh and his ultimate exit. His automobile is across the parking structure and is easier to find because the lot is half empty this time of day. It is morning, actually, and the sun is already higher that the building itself, streaming lightly but feeling wonderful across the face. Josh stands there sunning himself for a while longer. Who can afford to miss out on the opportunity to sun one's self, thus picking up on that necessary vitamin D standard?

The day had begun and Josh lost little time driving out of the theatre and onto the next errand to be run.

There was one single point of view finally. He was looking in so many directions when he let his hand lessen the grip he had on a collar that tears away under the weight of a falling member of his crew, and the point of view which stands out the most provides the detail sharp and then a blur; the body falls well below and is still in sight—his view is undeterred.

The distance was such that he could hear the remarkable thud of body on flat surface, and the flow of rocks and gravel connecting one instant after. This sound made him cry out. Was it loud or was it a whimper. Josh would never know. Even now the recall of the memory seems diminished.

Josh descends without support and makes way to the base of the half dome without thinking about where to place his fingers or the tips of his hiking shoes. They never—the two of them—climbed this place with safety gear. It was this macho thing: one against one, with little purpose than repeating last year's climb to the top and ascent to the bottom in a new record time.

How was this time different? Hadn't he ascended on his own this time? What prompted his friend to follow? Why didn't he find a more secure place to sit? How long did they talk, and what were they discussing when he plunged.

Real time occurs as he is walking across the parking lot and looking for his automobile. This does nothing to fill in the blanks. In so narrow a time he has relived and then gave up all together. Was reliving these moments so crucial? And why did he return back to that place, when he fully acknowledged that one can never return in hopes of reattaching to a simpler time in one's life?

It was his single fix; a point of view in time. This was real time.

After finding his car he leave the parking lot and heads west; the traveler speeds past one town with one Post Office after the next, to come into view of the sea more dejected than wise for his troubles. There was nothing else he could do for that fellow and he has thought this entire scenario out during the three and one half hour journey. To even suggest that he could have stayed to watch him die—finality defined by someone else's terms. There is no DNR that he knows of, and there is only one other family member that is so far removed. Josh drives and thinks of his friend's final view falling. The thought makes him pull to the side of the road and skids to a stop in loose dirt.

Nothing is more certain. He is having total recall of the events in proper sequence. He will trade that moment for any other had he the opportunity to even do so. It is troubling: who will preside over his final breath outside of the team that monitors him now. A young doctor with too many funny stories to relay at the nurse's station, and the remaining teenagers hoping to turn back the clock on a night of drag racing, liquor and mindless splendor.

Acting on his disdainful advice he starts inching forward and continues to head west; the man who presides behind the wheel is ever so careful and watches his speed around the next sharp bend; the whitecaps are brilliant with transparent sea spray and he follows one carefully until it rolls up on the beach. By now his vision is refreshed, shaper than usual, and he can hear the sea pull out carrying with it a fine mix of sand and crushed seashells. It is the chief trade of forgiveness in nature that Josh tends to think of now.

The drive ends at the next seaside hotel. He is heading in and drops his bags onto the floor and sits on top of the bed, dragging the phone toward him. The moment has grown so serious, the hope of a second chance seems to drift away, could he see that face just one more time. When the dialed number answers, his head is bowed and he begins to relay the details of his trip cut shorter than planned.

"Tess, it's me. No I'm fine. I stopped for the night. I'll get a bite to eat later. Listen; there is something you should know. He's most likely dead by now. It was a climbing accident. I was with him when he fell; having tried so hard to prevent it I failed in the end. It was later than usual: dark: it was a stupid thing to do."

The words transcend from bold to desperate and then to muddled; his anxiety about his shortcomings are overwhelming; he looks to his reflection in a mirror and watches his tears flow down across his face. He repeats that he is quite sure that he is dead by now.

"I do not know who else to call. There is only one other family member and they are too distant—I'm quite sure. It might come to that—understood. But I wanted to let you know; I needed to hear you say all will be right—sooner than later."

The call was worth the trouble. Someone had called her one hour before. Would this be lucky or profane wouldn't matter. He had to address it now. This was one hell of an acknowledgement—after the other— having to address it now.

Josh was drifting into another world all together. The bed engulfed him and he drifted into a deeper sleep.

The next morning Josh paid the hotel bill and headed north, driving parallel to a choppy sea. At one point a low flying plane crossed the highway and he managed to see the pilot's face. One was overly excited; the other watched from the ground with a look of plain astonishment. These were two messengers caught in the crossroads by accident, in a shared dialog of distant and silent words.

"This could have been you."

A single quest so successful and a sea that stretches out to the west and an upcoming mountain range that rises to the northeast. The distant yet common threads are that life cannot possibly be lived without some risk; risk may be the reason one lives at all.

Josh continues to drives west and the plane soars east in this moment of personal theatre. The cover of clouds (as curtains) are closing, both are heading home. His hand is pulling through his hair. Why was it still wet? It should have really been dry by now.

He squints into the mirror to his left and tries to pick up the trail of the plane that flew by. It had disappeared into a very high bank of clouds. When his attention returns to the road he sees that the cloud banks are all around, tucked behind the horizons. It is another panorama and if this could be captured somehow it would make a splendid display interaction for his next theatre.

The traffic is light. It allows him to design the new set in comfort.

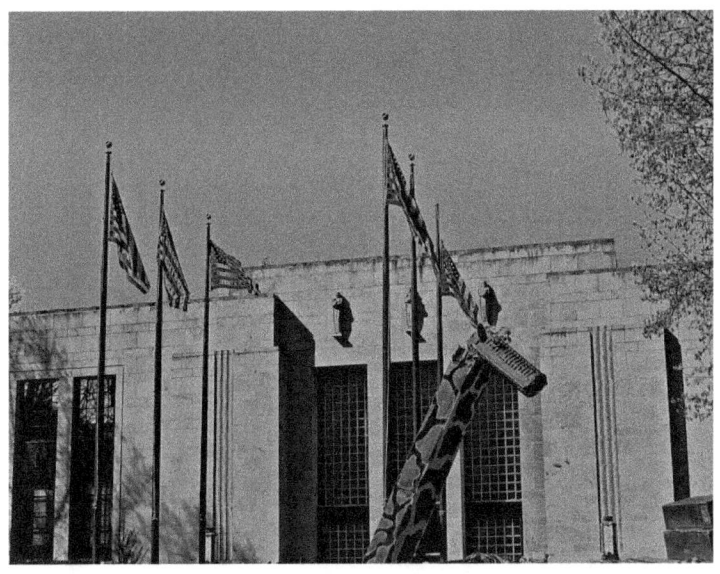

VOICE ONE: *There is no single point of view to the stage as this is a panorama.*

VOICE TWO: *You left and then you returned in three days.*

VOICE ONE: *As it turns out it was a trip of great satisfaction in that I stepped outside of the theatre realm for just long enough. I vainly tried to understand how to separate myself from the productions and what was expected of me versus it. My trip took me to a place lined with attractive trees and openings in the fields behind the forest—revealed and bare and new and interesting. To a full extent its openness enabled me to envision a next step.*

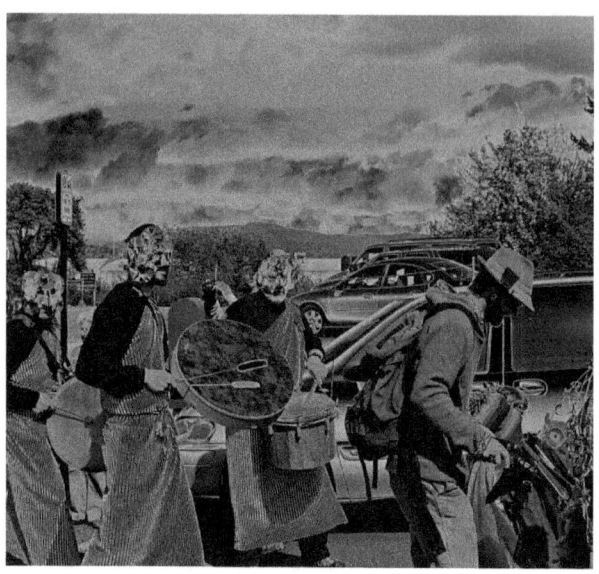

VOICE TWO: *Because you felt invisible and in the background; owning to the perpetual haze caused by managing and fretting about the cost of production. And now you are ready to celebrate what exactly?*

VOICE ONE: *A new guardianship of a place and the arts contained therein. I have a letter of introduction suitable for this purpose of revamping everything I know about running a theatre. This is my new panorama. In the meantime, I do need some sleep.*

Sometimes these conversations drain me.

Screen Nineteen

THE NEW THEATRE WAS in a very large building complete with internal sliding walls. The stage was at two levels and wrapped the lower level in three sections. The entire front of the tri-stage platform was open and rose above the ground floor by twenty inches; the drawers and removable panels at the base made it possible to store an enormous amount of production gear.

While the roof was painted black the piping and conduit were painted a matte gray adding an interesting contrast. The crew on hand this particular day was hanging acoustic equipments from brackets and taut cables, dampening the apparatus from excess vibration during performances. Acoustic baffles had already been installed, and now all that was left is testing and adjustments.

On the floor set back from the stage by several meters were round tabletops and similarly designed chairs that swiveled. Additional tables on wheels were scattered about to be used to set up and break down for larger groups, as warranted. Everything had its place, and everything was designed for flexibility and mobility. The entire floor layout could be rearranged with little effort. And in one far corner there was an enclosed booth with installed racks of playback and recording equipment to capture and reproduce just about every sense or perception. A center console controlled it all from stage to even the entrance and exits.

A lust for a suitable panorama has finally been satiated.

The most remarkable aspect of the interior were the rows of containers holding live trees, bushes and plants of a vast array of geographies. The walls, it would seem, were cleverly disguised as topical regions, and these remarkable containers were as mobile as the entire arena of tables and chairs. All of a sudden large rectangular window covers were lowered through a hydraulic system and the place was as flooded with streams of light from the outside. It was around midday.

Inside of this entire cavity of the building there was a layer of wooden floor that was pulled and recycled from an enormous barn slated for destruction. As it would have happened at a more curious time, Josh had espied the old barn on his way home from the place on the sea where he had last stayed. He contacted the owner of the property immediately, via the help of the crew getting ready to do the demolition. It was all he could do to convince the head foreman to be patient enough without having to resort to expensive bribery. But the act was completed, and he did have to throw in a few hundred dollars for the crew to use extra care in the dismantling of the barn's front, back and sides. The wood was in fair condition, and then made ready by the labors of Josh and his most patient friends: labor of love, protracted daily.

With the exterior of the new theatre having been coated with a luxurious coat of avocado green, the people who passed by this out of the way location doubled literally each week. The exterior of the theatre was covered on three walls by one continuous story, done by way of elegant representation using a combination of two and three dimensional vignettes. The scheme conveyed mostly silhouettes, pre-announcing the lofty theme of a grand opening in less than one month. And so it was mostly on schedule— this outlook feeling right in conjunction with the final landscaping outside, and the last run of housekeeping in its fine interior. There was none of the usual signs of one set of skilled contractors leading the way by too much over their counterparts.

All though one would never exclaim neatness in the overall planning, most resolve with this unusual project has it aligning right in both time and in space.

The architecture of the building gave them great lead: a strange combination of modern and old gave it character long before the detailed work ever gave way to softening edges over the industrial look and feel it once conveyed. It was of course a matter of opinion whether this kind of building should have ever been converted to performance theatre in the first place. Had it sat empty for any longer, there was an even greater chance that it would have been resubmitted to the impersonal office space as intended use. Even the echoes of the prior occupants are now far enough removed, that no one would recognize this place for what it once was, a deteriorating wasteland. Its outlook now, as strange as it might seem, is destined for pure entertainment of a medium once lost.

Welcome to the New Puppet Theatre. It was the entire message the marquee promised so far. To anyone outside of this group, no one knew what this means.

A walk to the other side is all it will take. One must manage by what one lost to regain composure. The words transcend from bold to desperate and then to muddled. These anxieties about one's shortcomings are overwhelming. Could this be a mockingbird's reflection in a pond of water on the sidewalk? He wishes it was reflective enough to understand the tears flowing down across his face. The old is evolved sufficiently to the new, but will he recover in time?

Having lost track of the past efforts to overthrow his earliest domain, Josh took his time walking around the older place not out of boredom but rather heightened interest. Not much had changed to the overall look and feel to its exterior. The garden may have been more uniform to his deliberately haphazard landscape; he walked around and shouted out snide remarks at particular points along the east and south runs. The movement around the place was sparse enough even though there was a play going on. To his greater pleasure the parking lot was more than half empty. His grin was immediate when the office manager came out to confront the person making all of this noise, though it did not dawn on Josh that his voice was loud enough to carry into the depths of the theatre.

He hurried around to the other side just out of eyesight of the determined pursuit. His pace lowered in intensity and he was merrily walking on the only path as if something had caught his attention. Josh began to crouch lower to the ground and pretended to be inspecting a grouping of flora when the manager sped to his side.

The inquiry was just shy of a shout.

"What do you think you are doing? There is a show in progress: your voice is carrying on inside of the lobby. Do I know you?"

The few minutes it took for the manager to recognize the face of the noisy intruder led to an even more stern confrontation; royalty was adeptly bowed to in circumstance. Had Josh stayed on the sidewalk he could have just walked away. But the reaction of the now startled employee warranted that he stand his ground even on someone else's turf. The result was colorful as it was astounding.

"Actually, I have just taken the time to chase the obnoxious complainer off down the street; right before you came here I was taking charge. It might also be mentioned that he was just about to break in through your back door. Over there: look at all those marks."

The manager stumbled over to the boot scuffed door in a huff and examined the damage as though it was a prize. He considered the way the prints edged up and actually began to measure the mark and stride using his outstretched fingers and hands. This apparently allowed him to assess, then compare and contrast the images to his current quarry.

"Well it looks as though you are right. This person has a much larger foot and stride than you certainly possess. Please accept my apologies and my gratitude for chasing them off. Was this a man, you say?

Josh at first reacted with a troubling shift of indignation; signing himself as the one who was most hurt. He prescribed a course of action to the fluxed manager, suggesting that he canvas the area and report back to the owner of said theatre. It was not meant as much to subscribe him to a course of definitive actions as much as a willful means of levity. But the requested approach resulted in an almost shocking disclosure.

"I've never met the owner—new or old. As a matter of fact, I do not think anyone has on my staff. Everything goes through third party management now."

It was though Josh was connecting through sign language. The opposition was moving his arms about wildly with each new disclosure. What appeared as a wild means of communication: signaling a sign of indignation on the part of the employee with his less caring owner. Apparently his concerns so far were relayed through this third party, but he never believed what he heard back by letter or verbal appeal.

The message was always softened. It was just not the same as a direct reply: it was scribed third hand.

With a cunning consciousness of what was happening first hand, Josh surmised that the only appropriate response was an invitation to hear it all in greater detail over coffee or tea, at a later time. This person was so full of interest to hear and reflect that there was a person who wanted to be informed of the daily slights a manager must bear. And when Josh briefly suggested that he was in a similar position, the length the man went to confide in him heightened.

"I do look forward to seeing you again and the opportunity to trade insights with regard to this location."

Josh had set the hook soundly. The man nearly bowed as he started to turn away and narrow his distance to the theatre's front door. This was a starting point of interest. If Josh could reel this one in he could get a much closer inspection of what his competition was planning well in advance of his own opening season.

At a skip rather than a walk Josh started off away from the place and began to sing out loud. The location of his oldest place took him through some very interesting neighborhoods, and reminded him that the new theatre was very far out of the way of normal business traffic. He would use every vantage to his avail, to expand his reach into competing factors, and then pull from them the target captivated audiences. It seemed there was nothing he wouldn't do to give him this edge.

The walk down memory lane did in fact provide him with the necessary meaning. Surrounding his old place was a vast occupancy and around his new place was fields, valleys and hills as far as the eyes could see. It was an expansive gateway to the countryside so beautiful that he was left breathless every time he took it in. The fact that the population was scarce would not necessarily be a hindrance to operations. He must then be consumed with the limits of accessibility, turning a weakness into a manageable strength. The small towns which dotted the area included small boutique wineries, cheese shops, honey bottlers, and many places for fresh fruits and vegetables: sustainable shops. The business factors in the area assured him that under the right set of circumstances there would be an unlimited supply of weekend shoppers for which he could entice to stay for a show or two.

No population however sparsely disbanded could resist the addition of live theater in full swing during the spring, summer and fall months, when people just wanted to get out of the city. If anyplace offered an opportunity for change it was in this place, and the nearby towns. He told himself this repeatedly on the drive across his city. And when he was home he relayed everything that he had done and exposed himself to at the older theatre, to an interested and astonished Tess.

When he informed her of his planned meetings with the older place's manager she was eager to counteract for a suitable sounding. Although her smiles and intent were all too sweet, Josh quietly mused that he required a more steadfast and contrasting view. He would eventually interrupt their conversation to place a call to a business associate, taking into account his experiences with a more hostile business approach. Since this type of people were born and bred for fierce competition, he could level this with and against the softer and gentler approach of his beloved Tess.

The gears of all of this finer machinery would take him full circle, in finalizing the progressive details with regard to the interior and exterior of his new place.

Josh's arsenal was nearly complete. This time and space was all that he needed.

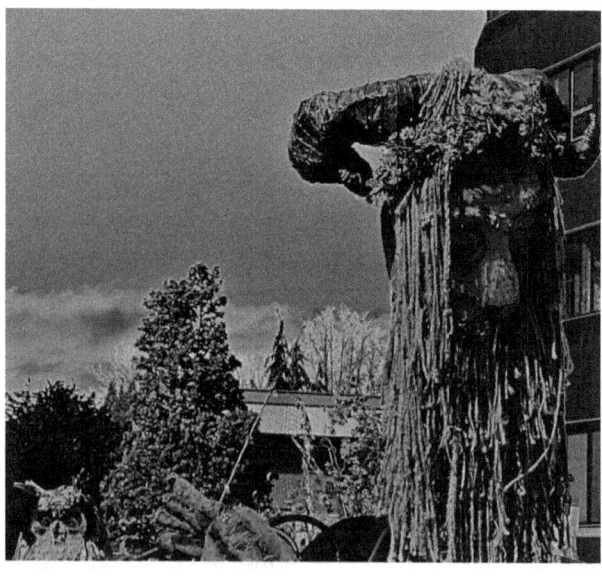

VOICE ONE: *There were more players of instruments and actors carrying bright streamers and this place is as abundant as the sea before us. I brought in lectures and multi-media specialties as a means of introduction, most suitable for my pursuit of this new venue. In the meantime, I kind of went overboard.*

VOICE TWO: *This new venue as you sated is cleaner: more refined and contemporary than many of the theatres seen across as many continents. The views have been kept from impurities of distraction, allowing the flow to work from as many tempting (tantalizing) points of observation. You are a merchant of the old represented as the brand new—built up of exactly what this medium needed to flourish.*

VOICE ONE: *Well we have yet to hear and see what the throngs of audiences will react by way of feedback. Some of this is hip, universal, and at the same time well worn. Beyond that I am parked in the wait and see lane.*

VOICE TWO: *Here lays your elaborate system of avoiding what produces the effect of a perpetual summer's success. Excellence can be spoken in the language of nice and polite. But in the end you only serve too little. Do you find it too expensive or inconvenient to say what occupies your mind at this point? Or are you patiently standing by for those critics to tell you if you have pulled this off or not?*

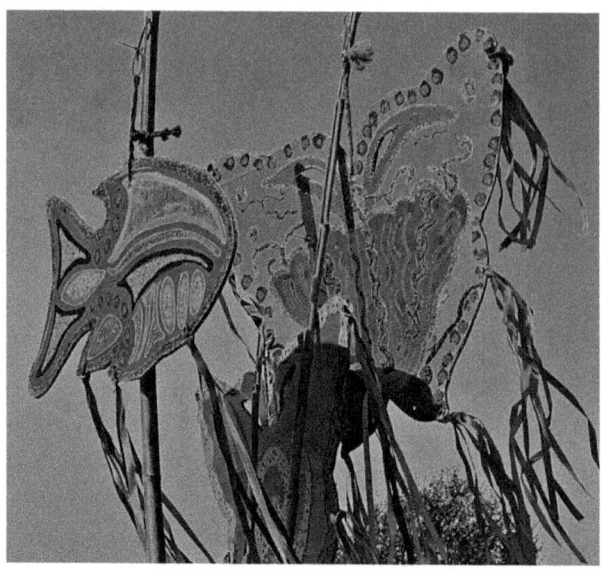

VOICE ONE: *I am just settling in for a few more days before deciding one way or the other. I find that there is no benefit in exhausting all of one's good luck too early. People approach this thing in different ways. I am not waiting for anyone's permission to enjoy it myself; having said all this I am still in guarded territory; standing under my own banner.*

BOOMING VOICE TWO: *Waiting for that messenger with a special envelope?*

STUNNED VOICE ONE: *Sure, and why not. It gives me a sense of semi-peace; afterwards I will drink until I am detestable one way or the other. I know: it grows on you.*

Screen Twenty

WHAT STOOD ON STAGE BEFORE the opening curtain might prove to be a tad much for this audience had it not been preformed to the neighborhood. Actually, it was more complicated than that: the apprenticeship of his new theatre manager was starting in parallel to the spillover investigation of the climbing accident of a past associate, coupled with the new legal action of a once hidden owner. It was a trio of accidents waiting to converge at the same time that one hundred people packed into his new place for the grand opening.

Josh was pacing nervously when the first salvo of automobiles, bicycles and foot traffic descended onto the property and stood under a marquee advertising teasingly, that this would be the wonder performance of a lifetime. The sign had been lit up since the beginning of the week, and it was now Thursday night—the opening of the doors proved to be merciless.

Comment after comment was overheard as he streamed past the crowd and headed into the lobby to greet the first patrons of his newly open Puppet Theatre. The line was packed tightly more or less due to the fact that everyone knew each other. This was not his apprenticeship; not by any means of the term were his hands tied to the awkward amateur. With every conceivable corner inspected twice, and his small but energetic staff briefed double to that, there is an animated feel to the inside of this building. The smiling, greetings, tips of experience shared from one to the other, everything was just shy of being a cartoon.

The feeling of contrite animation was one descriptor which could not be easily tossed aside. This was the first time Josh found himself scampering from one side of the lobby to the other inspecting the faces, postures and costumed dress of neighbors he probably had passed on the street dozens of times without all this harried introspection. If the marquee was to be believed this one man will need to become more grounded and set an initial expectation for his guests, that this would be something of an achievement for many if not all. For the first time he finds himself addressing his speed, his breathing and heart beat, and most of all a more reassuring eye-to-eye contact.

"Welcome: welcome to you all."

He smiled more comfortably at last when he made his individual greetings, and allowed himself the self satisfaction of believing that everything that should have been done was done, after all. For the first time he could see it: a successful start to an opening season on time, coupling with his near melt down.

The marquee never lies. It never misrepresented the fact of the matter at hand. Willfully he passes underneath it, allowing the light to bounce across his shoulders and shivers uncontrollably.

After a fair amount of time spent greeting the comers Josh turned it all over to a steady Tess. She was up to this task and it allowed him to return to back stage where his area of expertise was more ordered. His cast and crew were busy and at the same time most greeted him when he entered and passed by across the back of the stage to attend to a rope that had been left dangling. At first view it looked unnecessary, but then on closer inspection he found the note attached. It was an object of curiosity to no one else but him apparently.

What appeared on the carefully crafted note was a message of a journey yet to be taken. It praised the new owner for the accomplishment of everything carried thus far to the task: the walk along production and direction of live theater is a hard one indeed: this noteworthy inscription was read out loud. But the real accomplishment is walking the path that one needs to finish. He actually wanted to be alone to contemplate this meaning.

It appears the inscribed was a riddle instead. What path did he walk along, and what appeared to be addressed this time? It awakens many of his memories but the best one. Josh is stumped. He looks around and no one else within his eyesight is reacting or unduly shying away from his watchful view. There is nothing else to note that is out of order and when he asks very loudly about the placement of the rope and its note he receives only troubling shakes of heads and upturned shoulders. No one seems to know or care what he is bantering about, so long as it warrants recast.

The eyes have stopped watching and everyone is heading to their respective cues thirty minutes before the curtains are scheduled to open. There is nothing unusual about any of this at all.

For the sake of appearances Josh affixes the rope to its proper order and moves the note to his jacket pocket. He will stop pressing this untimely news and will move on to the final place of pre-production at the far right hand of the stage. For his part, and the sake of the opening, no one will know that anything else had happened: a stranger's note as foreign as any on this night will receive no further attention. The matter is dead for now. And it is entirely possible that it will not see a revival for the entire night to come.

The show must go on, as they say in this business. The crowded theatre is nearly busting; it is possible that there will be no empty seating this evening: a new play is replacing the lost one. Such was the start to this evening: dramatic, climatic, and stressful for some; a delightful spin of a familiar tale for others to share. The race to open the curtain matched the heart rate drumming inside of the chest of the owner.

Josh's opening part is about to be run.

Open curtains.

Start the first tune. Let the initial utterances leave the mouths of the truly animated and cast silhouettes.

This play has just gotten underway. He holds his breath and clutches his hands but is careful not to look outwardly dramatic. Is it cowardice not to want to show his true feelings? He has this row with himself and for some reason this brings satisfaction.

The lighting, score, and the drama of three stages working as one was a quest satisfied beyond expectation. There was a synergy between audience and players enabled by a sympathetic tale that lends itself to this fine union—a story within a story quite well on its own. Josh has never witnessed a troupe so dedicated to its finely tuned craft—no fake artistry— where the material pages leapt off literally from tabletop to curtain call after curtain call. There was really little else to improve; as it is a rather heartwarming romance, sturdy with affection, and displayed with moment to moment to an attentive and silent audience.

During the close of each curtain this rapt audience did roar to that moment. Who in the world would not cease to be amazed by the eloquence and pageantry of stilled silhouettes gone live against the clever mix of traditional and out of this world stage technology? In reality one could have supposed that the mix of staid traditions with the far reaching effects of geek hardware and software might have blown too far to the one hand over the other, if it had not been done so honestly. The creative dark blues instead of black as the cast of silhouettes against standing hand painted forms provoked these audiences to call for more via a vast array of handhelds struggling to maintain a sane pace with the tempo which followed each and every succession of closing acts. The true story here is this audience wanted something so different. And they got there, here.

Three simultaneous productions married well. The swiveling chairs during the acts were a testament to the uniqueness of the manner in which this was played out. For once in public theatre no one was expected to remain still. Non interaction would have not been welcomed in this place of the media arts. Diversions were accepted as a boon. According to the custom of staged theatre, there were openings and closures to encourage rowdy behavior, though tempered accordingly. No one could lay prostrate, nor could they remain stilled inside of this artistic venture for more than a few minutes at a time. The most common message received as audience members streamed out into the lobby during intermissions was that they were completely exhausted, while clamoring for more in the second half.

He has pulled this off. This is a re-tribute to a success of the past brought forward but under a different refrain. It is interactive rather than passive.

The owner of this Puppet Theatre courted deft by design. The system of delivery was retained by those who brought cameras or video, and later shared with anyone who could receive the stream. This in itself nearly doubled the advanced interest for tickets for the very next showing. Although there was the occasional lapse in contacts for securing an available seat, respondents remained steadfast in their demand for an extended schedule. The number of show offerings was doubled over the first season.

Josh has his staff wander about at the far edges of the inner chamber looking for conspicuous inattention by any audience member. Part of this play for interaction was to supplement cast and crew with monitors for near instantaneous feedback using a private spectrum of communication. One person in particular wondered masterfully, offering smiles, comments and body language in and around the mighty sea of enticed faces. No one seemed startled by the fact that she could reach them in close to real time over interactive connections that they had downloaded well in advance. It was lighting somebody's cigarette or passing along a liquid refreshment before anyone knew she was playing along with the cast members on one, two or three stages of the play.

Tess was never awkward during these planned interactions. She had the inner chamber mapped well, and understood the body language in as many languages as she could without giving it all away. As always, the most enticing bits are left to chance.

She had suddenly cast herself into the ongoing routine as one of the troupes wandering about in expected places at expected times. Josh hoped that she would not continue to do this with such expertise; when they had gone home for the evening to rest up from the hours-to-days gone well he would say what is on his mind.

For Josh, the end of the day after climax, silence was the greatest achievement he could achieve after all. There was a useful sensual and perceptual expectation of letting this all drain into emptiness, so that he could survive his life into the next day. Tess, he wondered out loud, was doing what she needed to do to stay involved. But he would finally have his say.

"Be kind to me, Tess. Let's just sit here in the dark and let nothingness overtake us until we can sleep it all off. I feel like I am the victim of overstimulation. I just need to let my senses drain, alone and far enough away from the cast and crew."

What he wanted to offer to his dear Tess was kindness. The conversation was continued with suitable affability, and away from prying too hard with regard to the other incident which had impacted his liver more than hers. He held the inner pain and trauma so that it did not reach his eyes. She usually read them so well. And with his speech he had a slight lean toward the troubled over the promise of the immediate. The authorities had questioned him well out of her range for the moment. But if they approached him again with regard to his past home and associate her eyes might meet his at an inopportune time, and a more likely fuss would result.

The interactions are recast in close to real time and broadcast out to all those in attendance and at stations remote. Is this a parallel world to his own he would not venture a guess at this particular time. It was in the moment, and it would be restrained for the time being.

In the end he could never keep things from her that mattered. His station in life was to share it all with purpose. He wanted to tell her what had become of this man that she chose to live with and work with, until their moments across a twenty-four a span of a season were ever so intertwined. He assured himself that if she were to know his other side at the time; she would hurry on with a purpose of her own. Why would she need to expose herself to such drama, indeed? Regarding the police insistence that the matter was still very much open, it only a matter of time that the evidence would present itself openly.

The end was not out of sight. The puppet master was in no more control of his own destiny as any other wooden figure. He did not know who he was any longer, or which way he would go if and when confronted with the reality at hand—they tended to be just rounding the next bank.

His life had become a virtual forest—not reclaimed but cast forward. He wanted to clamor up to a higher point just to see if the perspective could alter what he knew to be real.

For the moment he would just let the past lay where it was, along the river, near the edge of the base of a half dome, and the swirling pools of the water on the side of right versus wrong. The truth of the matter was exposed under the sweltering sun, and this in itself was all that was necessary to bring it the attention if strived to receive: that tantalizing climax to the play written and under way, the viewpoint of a gathering crowd, and the formation of who did what to whom, when and where: someone would have the foresight to solve this puzzle.

Side-by-side they resumed their measure of understanding and controlling the outcome of a play already in progress in its own right. While they gazed at the players on stage and the audience watching inside of this theatre, the compromising theatre of the outside was going on. Someone was walking a path rarely taken, past a row of pleasant looking trees and accompanied by the sound of their own voice. A smell or the circling carrion might excite them to take more notice to the something that was deadly wronged here and now.

They would have turned to the right at the next outcropping of boulders, congratulating themselves on the pace they maintained under the warm glow of the sun. Turning to the right naturally they would be stricken by something that had gone so wrong, and turning to the left they would have been trapped into a horseshoe canyon, but with a happier medium of zigzagging trails and switchbacks warranting further exploration.

The rugged style of the terrain might entice them to continue. The extreme slopes might have made them turn back. Although Josh could not see them coming he was witness nevertheless; that trailhead was so well known. So he smiles at just the momentous time under his deluded forecast and Tess might not have noticed just then that his smile turns to a deepening frown. He is aware that her back it to his side, and the lingering subject that engulf his memory is a dreadful one.

In his mind he is climbing half dome again. The newer perspective does not alter reality sufficiently.

Fingers slip by accident or with purpose. Once again the inner voice reminds him that the difference is razor thin. What possible interest could those hikers have with that place now? The river they had to cross several times, the rock formations they had to transverse to get to the boundary of that quarry. By this time of day there would be such an abundance of misleading shadows: would they go this way or the other; that was never known if they hadn't come this way at all. And what would they think of the discovery of a body half buried and half shown after passing a countless number of strewn boulders at this juncture of the outdoor adventure. This story would have considerable age by this time.

His thoughts were in and out of some shadows, over the incalculable damage his less than thoughtful approach to the less than picturesque scene he had left behind. The cover up was so haphazard, not scrupulously neat as the little theatre he had built and run. Surrounded by the trappings of an artist, the tables and benches he had built himself, he stood not alone in a sea of accomplishments. And here he stood as a stranger in front of a large mirror, not even recognizing a hint of the reflection which was staring back.

"Josh, where on earth did you go just now? I swear you let that mind of yours stray ever so far from what matters most. Don't you see that this has to be corrected?"

Tess is bending over something and attempting to lift it up. It is heavier than she can possible manage on her own. There is this heavy and oversized table right in the middle of the back of the stage and she lets him know it has to go. Here he is suddenly a stranger to his own place. It seems that he is too far removed to even notice why she is going on. It is only a table—so what does this matter? The table is in the middle of the key path for talent and crew. Josh seems to recall that he put it there, but cannot for the life of him remember why.

It is truly in an unpleasant spot. This matter and the other still at hand.

So this is it, one thinks. Tess is wearing shorts and a fashionable t-shirt; her feet are bare as she slides across the smooth wooden floor and stops just short of the front door of the house they are sharing. The second round of knocks has gotten her attention yet she is still smiling from some joke she had just heard near the back of her home. When the door is opened she is showing enough teeth to let the caller know she is placid and happy enough. This is a fortunate greeting as the two commanding more attention than originally allocated are wearing badges and are armed. For the sake of beating hearts they are both members of the local law enforcement office.

Tess slides sideways uncontrollably and is stopped from wiping out all together by one of the nearby officers. It is comic relief from a proposed somber realization. She stands and is stable and without saying a word they speak out. They are here for Josh.

"Josh, please come to the door, now."

Tess has to announce this for a second time only louder. She is still managing her composure and best smile sharing occasional stares with the two indicating a plea for more patience. Her non verbal plea is holding so far, and they actually take a step back onto the middle of the porch and listen in on one handheld radio.

Something is about to happen. She sees the signs in both of their eyes. And now Josh is making ready down the slippery hallway in pretty much the same order as Tess. He slides to a stop and murmurs.

"Oh shit, sorry. I did not mean to keep anyone waiting."

Then one officer, who has patience and a materially focused mind, gets to the point and asks Josh to formally identify himself. The effect is less than pleasant and then a document is produced for his inspection. Nearly four minutes later Josh and Tess are instructed to step aside and the house is open to inspection based on the narrow constraints written into the warrant alone.

OK, so now this is real enough. This is in real time.

So now comes the time where the two officers proceed. They came to inspect and inspect they managed, and asked Josh to maintain a presence within eyesight. Soon thereafter a third officer announces himself at the front door and meanly strolls in past the two homesteaders as though they are only dressings to the scene. He makes way to the other two and the three of them speak in low voices.

As the owners of this place share in the inheritance of these guests, the time lengthens the zigzagging searches from the three aliens' narrows to the back of the kitchen and the dirty pile of laundry in a wicker basket. Tess's under garments are touched first, and then they get to Josh's jeans, socks, and t-shirts. Framed in the cast hues from a nearby window this has all of the makings of a family portrait, had the topic not been so absurd: a trio with laundry.

A slight breeze found its way through the open front door and the smell of a neighbor's barbeque could be taken in through the senses and found enticing enough to seek it out. This gave a signal from Josh to Tess to laugh.

The odd mix of activities gave quick renounce of the playful objective. A greater fanfare was to be made of this non harried searching into the bottom section of the basket. An article of clothing was made suspect, but then it was thoughtfully dropped and the entire pile restacked more neatly than ever.   They announced that they were done.

"What is it that you were looking for, officers?"

Tess was the brave one. Josh just tried to control his heart rate wanting to reach that segues to a second or third act.

One officer wanders over to the pair and stands almost relaxed. He has a mellow face and he is starting to smile.

"Josh, I will leave it to you to more fully address this question. We are done here but it is entirely possible that we will be back with a new warrant by the end of the day. A witness has identified you as being on a track of land near the Clemens's River, at the base of a place known locally as Half Dome. The complaint is that someone has lost a son and wants to know why."

Tess shoots Josh a look of astonishment. She would like to know why as well. But this side of the story will just have to wait until the three guests are well on their way outside of the front door.

She shuts it and pushes Josh aside. It would not be to anyone's benefit to discuss this mother's bereaved quest of her son until the two vehicles drive out of the line of her sight. The sounds behind her are Josh gulping for his next breath and she can see that he is monitoring his pulse. Hurrying over she shoves him and then makes her next demand more clear.

No one within one property distance could hear the sounds escaping through walls or open windows. He rose up behind her when she went to the kitchen to sit down. She looks so anguished and is still holding onto the warrant in her left hand. Could she have sobbed at the moment was anyone's guess. It was a long shot either way. The procession of lingering looks at the clock on the wall and then to each other paved the way for a more sincere interaction. Josh would have to make the next move, or he would be the brute to bear the weight imposed between them forever.

"Before you say anything I might get called on, we should call a lawyer. I am going to call my father. He is usually good at these things. Just do not say anything right now, Josh. Please hand me the phone."

She left him alone. Tess had walked away and he was left there standing and suffering: his own grief sufficient for now. And now this too was fading and he could feel that he was no longer standing upright.

Josh sat up to quickly in bed and felt dizzy: head spinning so fast, breathing was difficult to near impossible, his mouth was feeling completely dry. The sweat that poured off of his body might have filled a bucket had he bent over one. And she lies nearby sleeping ever so deeply that the image stops his palpitations cold. She is dreaming; this much he can tell because the signs are there and he recognizes them immediately. This is his textbook interpretation in the early morning and he keeps her image in his mind as he sits there and tries to recall the dream for what it was—that message he was supposed to glean.

While he is waiting for his heart rate to become normal, and his breathing less labored he examined the segments of his dream in their constituent parts. Some were pictures, almost snapshots, and it resembled an old fashioned slow frame movie. He steps in and out of some of the frames as though he can walk around them in the third dimension. He is near one that is particularly lucid—clear—and he is slowly exhausting the last gulp of air. Was this artistry or was it a troubling depiction of an event or incident he could no longer bear, whether it be conscious or in the unconscious. The picture frame was more of a particular fancy than an actual image that he had actually experienced. Perhaps it was a puzzle, or a piece of one at the very least. Although it was still it represented movement that he was familiar with in the first person.

Josh is still sitting up in bed yet he is able to step into the frame and is able to look back out at his image looking in thoughtfully.   Then all of a sudden he is less than sure that the face watching him is actually his. He is in the company of a stranger now; less of a man and more like a child; the details of this bazaar occurrence are seemingly sexual in nature. He looks down inside of this frame and he can see his erection. And when he looks over into the next frame he can witness a young girl—the woman he meets in the cabin just below the valley and canyon that leads to the half dome.   He is back there; something else needs to be explained to the aging female in the following frame.

What would happen if he steps out and moves across frames?   Would this measure be allowed—it is his dream after all—he boasts about it, he makes it so. She is a legitimate image in his sequenced elaboration. It is within his purview and the details of his closer interaction are made possible by simply wishing it: the details that are required to make it happen.

In his dream the details about this interaction still him. He breathes normally and while checking his pulse outside and inside of the frame he is satisfied that he has fully recovered. This does not seem unusual. He continues to learn from it as it is his feedback that needs to be controlled. Is there an opportunity for a sexual encounter? In the dream she is now old enough. He is excited standing near her and she knows this to be true. It is in her eyes and in her expression. There was an opportunity after all. And it is executed without further elaboration.

This is his theatre through and through.

The dreamer decides to blue some of the details. He knows it intimately after all, so there is no further requirement for embellishment—this mature dream. It is not mischievous and it is not an excuse to report the size of her breast or how firm they are now that she is much older than before. He is not an abuser so the details of her firm belly is simply sense under the touch of his fingers without fanfare, but the dreamer does remark that she is exceptionally fit and well.

"Do you ever expect to stop growing?"

"No, I am scheduled to do so for a much longer time. Why, are you in such a hurry that you cannot stand to enter me as I am now? Does it have to wait, and if so for how long?"

In this dream there is this odd dialog going on; this odd man too excited to perform until the time is just right. They are sitting on the stairs in front of the cabin as they had done so before. And then he tells her that he had grown up inside of this very cabin, or least for part of his young adult life.

Josh experiences his days and nights in and out of the cabin and along side of a river which he cannot recall the name. The details of his most prominent moments in the dream are revealed in amazing detail. Was this a reproduction or is he actually reliving them now? Is he ready to reproduce the fragments of the happy alone, or will he take the chance on revisiting the sad as well? What is the true utility of his dream if he cannot control its constituent parts? The cabin is back in focus and the woman is dressing. This has been a splendid aromatization: the air, the river just inches above its surface, and the air which flows in and out of the valley that leads to the canyon, which will take these frames to the base of a wall in which he feels he is going to be forced to climb.

This s not the better part of this dream sequence. His eyes hurt from squinting—an attempt to control the next sequence of image—fragments of an occurrence: not in his childhood, his teens or even his entry into adulthood. No, these frames were meant to be quite cruel and made a mockery of how he wanted to remember it all.

He is breathing hard, his pulse is out of control, and he wants to cry out but he cannot. No one can wake the woman who is sleeping by his side. Her mouth is slightly agape and she is fine. He recognizes that she may be an asset with respect to the sexual components of his dream—a safeguard.

Was sex a problem now? Could he remember penetrating the woman in the frame at the same time as he looks at this other figure that lay beside him: an acquaintance first hand, in this house, among his favorite things, and something that could be used as a counter to the frames coming up.

His wandering in and out of the subconscious is so rapid. This is according to his assertions; hardly touching the other individual but rather imagining her in many compositions. She is sliding toward him, and then slips away. And in her place is the ghostly appearance of his old acquaintance. Was he appearing to provide a sexual favor? What were the factors from the beginning of this sequence of events that seemed familiar, rather than made up to represent a logical sequence—this now infantile stream places sex as the dominate theme. They are in the same house—a main residence—not as neighbors.

This is his ultimate out of body journey.

This was sexual and they begin to satisfy a need. The sensations and perceptions are in and out of this dream. Yet by virtue of the next frame he is able to escape the painful realization that there is lust and emotional exhaustion in the imagery. He is upright in bed, both literally and very erect, and there are hints that he well exposed in front of a very large audience.

What would have stood out on stage after the opening curtain might prove to be a tad much for this audience. And what if Tess had awoken at this silly moment: had it not been preformed inside of their home, this shared room, and the intimacy of a shared queen-sized bed. Actually, it was more complicated than that: the apprenticeship of this dreamer's lovers: friend and now business associates: starting spilling into this continuing investigation of the climbing accident. There was far more trouble with the new legal action of a once thought to be a series of covert acts. It had elevated into a succession of accidents waiting to converge at the same time; of the one hundred people packed into his new place for the grand opening; there was not one single alibi but two.

The curtains were closing too soon on this man's final screen. The last frame was just out of his reach. He is awake now and so is Tess. She is asking him if anything is ok.

In search for a good way of translating his current state, Josh simple shrugs his shoulders and smiles weakly. It is a particularly difficult journey from well thought out, to lips parted; as if by habit alone he tries to divert her attention.

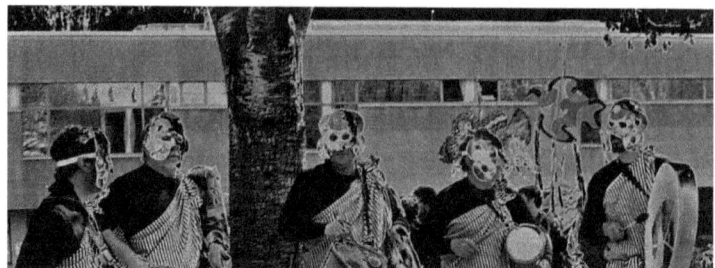

VOICE ONE: *And the band plays on in this awfully resilient dream.*

VOICE TWO: *Although this is the height of your move overt reaction, and there are some fine points nevertheless, this is by no means healthy alone. Have you been attached by some kind of fever driven delusion? No sooner than I see you trying to settle in to what might just be a time of considerable peace in your life, your past revisits and clobbers us both.*

VOIVE ONE TREMBLING: *Hardly a day goes by when I can let this thing go. Something happened, you know. I just cannot reveal all of the natty details. Early in the morning, just after my latest dream sequence, it is all I can do to get out of bed. If you could shoot me you could cure me. Worse yet just do not let me go back to bed to dream anymore today.*

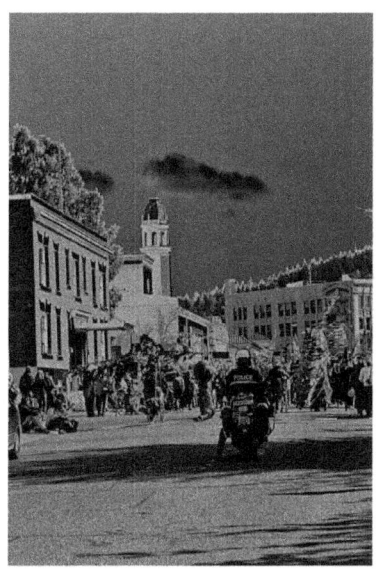

VOICE TWO: *A successful box office is not enough to keep you sane. A steadfast relationship cannot keep those daemons at bay: this is a back spell; your being so mesmerized by this past you cannot speak of. I wish I could cure you, but I won't even try. So long as you hold your tongue you are on your own.*

VOICE ONE (final objection): *Look, if I am holding up this parade for you, just let me go. I have made many excursions out of here and will most likely make as many more. It's a search for a better station in life I assure you. But there is baggage and it cannot be left alone, simply enough. There are constituent parts of the whole which cannot be shed. I know that is a sour course, but it is all I have to follow—this necessity of my*

347

trialed life: colorful, a rollercoaster ride, and leaping from tree to tree.

VOICE TWO (exasperated): Yes, but it has become more of a habit than a true characteristic. It has taken you from one jerk motion to the next. Swallow your pride and give this a rest; for the benefit of all of us.

VOICE ONE: Perhaps we can just leave it alone for now, on this one unmelodious note: only I can be the tail end of this thing.

VOICE TWO (triumphantly): Wag the dog.

Screen Twenty-one

BY VIRTUE OF THE PRINCIPLE THEME of this stream of dreams, Josh has been incapable of interjecting anything else outside of the contentious subject matter. This is a very unsettling position to be in both consciously and unconsciously—a mental reservation permeates his daytime and nighttime—he can do nothing more to avoid sleep. He is finally exhausted.

What is it about these mental associations that cause him to see only the worse case scenarios; there is nothing he can do but wish it all away. It remains a dominating cognitive activity and it comes close to consuming his every waking hour. It should have been gone by now—all of these memories stored as more than long term images, include most of the sensations and perceptions as he had live at that precise moment in time. It was a huge hindrance and it stopped him from functioning as a normal human; whatever that may even mean at the present. Multiple streams of consciousness are open as it is: one stymie him as the countering one attempts to free him from his past: neither freeing him completely and the pain and anguish continue to run its path: a true recall.

If he could recall or remit the good times of this streamed sequence it might just occupy his thoughts long enough to break the spell. The occupancy of these painful memories should be written like the softer passages of a play rendered hard. He had done it so many times in the past it should be routine by now. If a scene did not work he would rip at it at once, and then free it—liberate it—from it woeful conclusion. The principle of working theatre is to be a flexible as one can without compromising the entire intent of the playwright.   It is a long entertained principle useful for regulating seemingly weaker passages with little emotional impact, and making them artificially stronger without getting caught.

Hopefully the audience is never wise enough to know that something has been embellished for the sake of a purer form of entertainment.   If done so right it becomes the second possibility that takes its rightful place as number one.   Compare and contrast if you will to the several endings of most major motion pictures.   Each includes one half dozen possible endings, and one is thoughtfully chosen after a battery of prerelease tests. Insiders call this the development of lesser pain.

From two different interpretations Josh deploys a suitable   number   of   contesting   streams   of consciousness. He hopes that this second possibility can transcend the wake state onto the deeper slumber in such a manner as to guide resultant dreams: reducing or inhibiting painful outcomes. From these varying start points he hopes to lead his collective unconscious through trial and error for the emotional benefit of his next waking hour. If it could be done repeatedly he could significantly improve his week. It could be the key to his setting the next iterance of his puppet theatre on the straight and narrow; away from its current gloom and doom.

Tess and Josh are walking toward the arrival desk at the airport. They are being greeted by a finely dressed and very good looking gentleman who appears to be in his seventies. They saw him walking around leaning against the eloquently carved staff as though nothing out of the ordinary was happening, even though his presence was capturing all passing stares from the crowds who hurried by toward friends or taxicabs waiting by the curb outside. There was nothing unusual about his scene outside of the fact that the older man was close to seven feet tall.

When they approached to meet and greet him he was in splendid good cheer and hugs were exchanged all around. Being warmly embraced by someone with such dominating stature was more or less like being engulfed, but in a friendly manner. On closer and more intimate exchange the elder did exclaim that he was very tired from his long and arduous trip, and paired his questioning with the slightest appearance of irritancy and fatigue. But he was never so abrupt to those who greeted him and escorted him and his luggage to the vehicle waiting outside.

For the moment Josh had put his problems aside, and attends as cheerfully to his exotic guest. Yes, the resounding sting of the previous night's dream still haunted his every waking moment, but for this passage of time he was ready and able to suppress it—perhaps even invert it—and push it aside. And when they drove off he was the first to engage in cheerful conversation with this native from another continent.

The arrival of this great giant both literally and with respect to theatre on the far side of the world made the sun seemingly brighter. This whole persona of strange fruit hanging just for the plucking was rendering his world more perfect than ever before. It came with a restorative function to which he plundered as fast, even when he had suggested to Tess that entertaining a vastly different kind of theatre was not only unconventional, but seriously risky. With the cost of bringing this giant of a personality across several oceans into a venue so completely unproven, they just might exhaust every resource they have at their disposal. Both their welfares were at tenuous risk, as well as the people they paid as staff, and the very theatre they struggled to protect.

Was this manner of entertaining a far reaching idea so untenable and less likely obtainable, that they could risk it all? This was the ongoing thought process that they balanced so precariously that friends and business associates told them they were nuts. Strange fruit indeed—this was coming close to an 'all for one or not at all' situation at best. Family extended, and the fanfare from close and distant friends rallied them forward with the utmost of caution. Was this play unattainable? Well walking on the moon must have seemed as unexpected as well.

The restorative function of his new entertainer's presence was beginning to appear and rub off on them both. It was all he could do but contain himself and let this set of sensations and perceptions dominate his waking state as truly infectious. It was a welcome change indeed.

"I am master of this situation."

"What did you just say?"

Tess was looking at him as though he was lacking the subtleties required for etiquette in the present. She intended to pinch his leg hard, but it was though he hardly noticed. Her glare contested his grin.

The vehicle was turning into the path which led to the lobby of the expensive hotel to deposit this honored guest. And when this man was settled in they in turn bid him goodbye, so that he could use the remainder of the day to sleep, and they could be freed to revisit Josh's strange comment along the way.

"We will come by and collect you at eight o'clock. Please have a restful sleep, and dream as you will about this opportunity before us."

The giant is being escorted to his room along with his set of matching luggage by hotel personnel. Josh and Tess are left with the remainder of the day to finalize the assembly and dinner in his honor at their theatre: the two dozen friends and business associates, including one or two reporters who will capture this introduction of a new wave of presence entertainment, from so unlikely a place and as experientially far away.

This thirst of the new is the stream of thought that dominates Josh's waking past the double automatic doors of the hotel. He assumes that he is puppet master of this situation to the degree that his arms and legs are behaving as though he is carrying the weight of the world on his shoulders and heaving it off with straight forward intent. Once master of the immediate situation he works to transpose this feeling of control to his place of business, and hopefully to a more restive set of upcoming dreams. His manner is cartoonish and Tess steps aside to take this all in.

His collective unconsciousness is counting on this manner of change. He hopes to capitalize this sense of freedom with his upcoming night's sleep, and would just as soon skip all of the fanfare of the upcoming events scheduled so far in advance. And when he relays this to an astonished Tess his feeling of euphoria is put into context.

"You could do with an adjustment of professionalism. How could you blurt out such a thing in front of our guest?"

"Asked and answered is all I can say. I have not felt this good in so long a time I found it exhilarating. So what if I called this out. Did you see him? He is so jetlagged he can barely remember how he got from the airport to his hotel. At any rate, all of this can be revisited at tonight's dinner, if at all necessary. He will be so swamped with accolade and acclaim he will hardly remember way was said in the car along the way."

Josh was asserting the right to remain silent for the remainder of the ride back to the theatre. He engaged himself with details of the upcoming dinner and welcoming that he felt all questions and answers at hand were confined to his own counsel. Sensing this communicative stare carefully, Tess concluded that it was a docile and hopeful one. She would let his comment go for the interim, and simply witness his transformation back to the director he needed to be to pull this off.

The professional never takes the back seat of the situation. This matter would rest. She would leave Josh alone for the moment to address all of the open issue which required his interpretations alone. It was a quality she likes about him, even though she knew this had limits.

Perhaps for now she would let him be master until this evening has concluded and they are back in the comfort of their home. And then she would let him have it—the rapid fires of her arsenal for his exclusion of her after all they have been through, to make this night happen at all. He was not off the hook by any sense of the matter: this state of delusion that he was master of anything resembling reality in present tense.

She let him have his way and the time was well spent. When they arrived at the theatre Josh had to submit to the demands of the cast and crew who wished to persuade him to listen to a new plan hatched in his absence, just hours before the new guest producer would arrive. He knew he would be a captured audience when he was escorted into the blush seat mid row, in the front section of the theatre. From this perspective the three stages looked larger than life.

Josh listened to each word of every speaker he heard in their uncontested sequence. He knew each paraphrased entitlement because these were murmurings suggested all along during breaks in past performances. Most of what he heard now was uttered to him in passing backstage as sets were rushed to be broken down and rebuilt on the fly, between the closing and reopening of the enormous curtains on the main stage, and the near sheer partitions of the two side stages. And it was here and now that he took in those words and careful phrases painfully retendered so that they were presented less as ideas and more to the letters of the law.

Whose law indeed; it was all he could think; doing so quietly. He could see Tess remaining on the sidelines and keeping her expressions to herself, hoping not to upset the streams of consciousness of the key and principal target of these projections. He had to submit to them, as he was surrounded, he was inclined to keep absolutely still. The energy of this many people would not be lost to him at all: that instant it was not very angry or hot at all, but rather melodramatic until all of their resources were finally exhausted.

One hour more and he probably would have busted.

The air flowing in and around his placement was more comfortable than he could ever remember. For the moment his thoughts were lost to the few who remained complicit with this recitation and tempered condemnation of what they thought was his intent to sell out. This later mimic was the result of what they had thought was the intent of this new producer. His proposal for resounding change to the venue they believed most appropriate for this theatre was under fire, hours before his scheduled arrival. And for some reason Josh thought this to be invitingly wild.

It was cooler than normal was all he thought for the moment of lore. The next several moments he basked in all of the attention as any other audience would have felt if this improvisational play were about anything at all. He accepted the content and context without demur, and the cost of valuable time necessary to prepare for the arrival of his new guest. Commenting back on this picturesque presentation by the backstage community, supported in full by the talent at hand, he reiterated his final intensions of letting them take the next stage at hand.

"I had intended that you would be as pivotal to the intermixing of this new approach with the old all along. But now that you have all been so forthright I both comment you and offer you this: the show goes on."

It was almost as though he were asking them to use this infectious presentation as a means of discovery. So what if it was not his idea alone. If it is what the others can make of this venue, when they are so inclined to be a driving force, why not let them begin now. This is what he feed them: to rebel and not carry this thing forward would be far more revealing about them.

The air around his placement is really flowing. It is cool to the touch on his exposed skin and he likes being part of the audience rather than the director on stage—backstage for all that it meant. There inputs were duly noted, and his inclination for the time being was to let them roll on. And without further hesitation he stood up and walked out to the sidelines.

"This place's future is as much as in your hands as it is mine. Let's see what you can produce. Our special invitation to this new producer is already in play, so do what you will, but please make our guest comfortable. If he hesitates at all you may lose his financial support to keeping these doors open for the upcoming season."

The planned reception and dinner for the arrival of the producer was an un-halting race against what little time they had left to secure a first class placement. After the first several hours the pace became close to unbearable for some. Things did look somewhat brighter for the others and their hopes spread like wildfire across the brows of the narrow few who showed pre-fatigue. The energy was telegraphed across each section of the little theatre as last minute preparations were made in full anticipation of this man's arrival with a virtual bag of monies to keep this place open for the future to come. Hope lead to experience and many of them were not robbed of a well earned slap of the back for a project done well enough to please even the pickiest donor to this cause.

The traveler was already beckoning at the side door as the vehicle sent to capture him pulled away and turned the adjacent corner and onto the street. Pleasure followed sweat, and anticipation led the way until this rested guest was seated at the head of a very long table.

Josh had relented to their demands, and at the same time his were met, according to his plan.

This welcoming dinner and nonstop presentation was a line crossed in the sand. The food spread out across a sea of eager eaters was sumptuous enough for even a king or queen in equal fashion of artist and patron of the arts. There was enough wine to be poured well into the midnight hour to leave the happy impression that this was more than an occasional affair. After the first course was finished and duly removed, it is sadly realized that Josh had taken a back seat to all of their recitals. It was impossible to let this go on for any longer than fully necessary. This was an obvious oversight.

With less force than a level II gale; since any other type of segue would be deemed appropriate at this time; Josh's proportion at this table was brought into the limelight. There was no reluctance to be found no resistance to what had been done. The transition was noted and with less force in his advance he took the presentation over.

The rejoinder he has paid them all, including this important guest, was agreeable. Josh took the time to bestow the hardships of ongoing live theatre where he lived, in comparison and in contrast to the happy and well fed host. He took time to champion the home of his visitor and the strength of time that was required to secure his thoughts and his visions as to better the relationship between local live and the live that was about to come. His proposition was quickly summarized for all to hear, before his eventful introduction for all eyes and ears to see and hear.

"This well traveled and talented producer has made it his interest to present and seek out our feedback on a proposal well thought out, on my humble opinion. Please welcome our guest of honor and provide him with the necessary attention for the next hour or so. This is a long road to follow; it takes time to reveal it well. Thank you all; please let this begin."

Josh was master of this ceremony after all. The room was hushed for a lingering moment before the guest stood and takes over, long into the night.

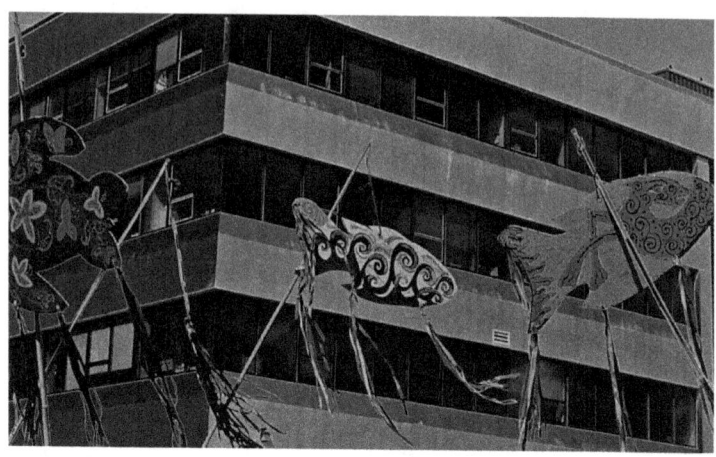

COMMANDING VOICE: *Far be it to say: if this crowd captures your one secret ally, even if under the pretense of being just another face in the crowd, you are still not out of the woods.*

VOICE ONE: *She is but a silhouette hiding out in the recesses beyond access to any crowd. This much is assured. Her movements are not easily captured, and she has an uncommon intellect—most strikingly—that she will find a way to shade her appearance. It will be too late before they know she has this unearthly gift.*

COMMANDING VOICE (irritated): *This sheds little light on whatever dignity you have remaining. Why not resolve to explore other possibilities beyond a secret weapon? The road is less shady and more trodden with respectability in the long run; business acumen shared brilliantly without the unnecessary plumage. Be right and brilliant in equal proportions.*

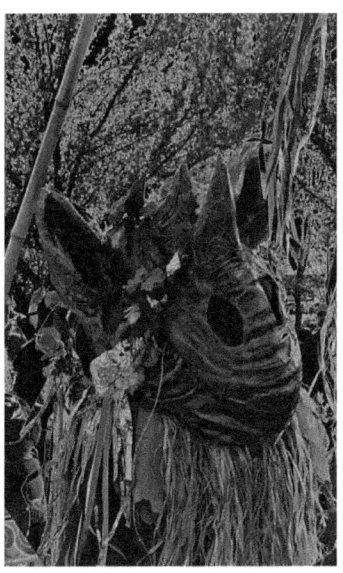

VOICE ONE: *While all eyes are on me now? Am I looking my best?*

COMMANDING VOICE (soothing): *On your way back to the heat of the scene, have trust in the good fortune that will surely come your way with a well thought out plan. The larger the number of contingencies the more perfect it will be for you. A good approach is one that offers the rarest point of view with the most remarkable prize. Suspend all of your anxiety and dazzle them with what you treasure most: a clear insight to the bitter end. Barriers to entry are more often self imposed. Use Tess.*

Perceptive Sensations   Michael O'Connor

Screen Twenty-two

FOR THE CONSIDERATION OF THE PRINCIPLE reader let us consider the smallest expenditure of time and pain to regain the focus of this tale. Hopefully it does have sufficient enough inertia to keep us all going.

The key to the next steps taken by this incredible and talented theatre troupe is not to repress the past in order to embrace the future. Puppet Theater has survived the test of time, as it is a system of undertaking and occupying an idea of the strings that are attached to position author with an audience. It keeps the playwright in check during the painful transfer of an idea from paper to stage; whatever the held position may be there is pain emanating from it.

Whatever draws the playwright's attention to a simple and central theme, it is the audience who gets to provide the only meaningful feedback. If not the artist with pen or type would be abandoning the only virtue they have—separation of intent to what is queued. The picture may not always be neat, and it need not be as far as our incepted Josh is concerned. He had been permitted by all those who surround him to receive the principle amounts of pain as director. But then again this pain is not nearly complete. The producers and all of the money trees that prolong this continuing craft have an equally subtle hand at crafting the pain and the endurance to bear. The cycle is permitted by everyone before the curtains can be parted for an audience to be witness. The first note possible must be started throughout the sound systems, mounted and surround for the memory and all of the senses possible. It is plain or it is complex as the first movement or utterance is revealed and then suspended.

It need not be complete; those constituent parts. That is the purpose of the mind to sew well or to blend well enough, this near perfect adaptation of idea to real time.

There is nothing as strange as good Puppet Theatre. It is a journey proved agreeable against the test of time, thanks in part to those who champion it from behind or on stage, and certainly the audience in front of them. They are in route, less invaded, but where they belong.

Josh feels that he has gone through much hardship in his practice as a contributor to the craft, as well as a theatre owner. This poor man has spent so much time prolonging the dreams and inspiration of others, relating it all to his own life sheltering these stories and releasing them at will when they need to be gone. He has spent so much of his time relating the battles to get stories told by time driven honor to a craft that revitalizes itself every other generation, for nothing more than to see it played out, and perhaps enough to pay rent and to eat. It is those sleepless nights spent with creators of stage design, on hard and dusty grounds that he can best relate to.

People have less and many have had more than this half days journey to prepare, and the after night to break down sets well past the collection of money to pay them as well as one can. But that is certainly not the whole cost and benefit of this ongoing lifelong companion. As told to interested parties all along the path from play to play, there is an interesting enough tale to prolong.

The theatre owner of theatre place avails themselves to the gratitude of an audience. It is an opportunity to hear the claps and cheers and at the same time to understand the prolonged silences. Whatever social etiquette in time and in place that needs to be underwritten; attendance is the best feedback of all; where the artists and the audiences meet after all.

Each attendee officiates, whether seated high or low, in proportion to his or her reaction. If there is any feedback at all it is a sales pitch for more, and it puts Josh right on top of his game.

He is an obedient observer of human nature. This might be the most convenient place to receive a final cheering on from an audience, when his cast and crew come out for a final bow. It is best received from the shadows of a side stage, and a recounting of tickets that let the play go on less hindered for a second season.

The reverence paid to the director and producer is fostered by the contacts who want to be next. They are fostered on by their own set of rules, but guided by the desire and need to be regaled as that follow on practice. If this cycle is ever suspended, or any part of it ever suspected of being a dead end, it might just be necessary to take the life of an associate or friend in one's own hands. To do so is to be obedient to this trade.

Josh lays awake these nights having given the next chapter of his life to the party he alone created. He did so using a language of transference depicted as a train leaving the station at dusk or at dawn. To the traveler on this departure the enactment is considerable, yet he or she does not ponder it to the bitter end. It is simply an introduction to the next stop when every play will depart in as many directions as they began. The director deals with all of the necessary punctuation contrary to expectation. The other parties are simply relieved that they are comfortable while entertained.

Perceptive Sensations   Michael O'Connor

Tess was not so fortunate. She is able to live in the shadows of the theatre but never its means. She in fact is more fortunate. If she is hungry she gets something to eat; if it is dark she turns on a light; if it is raining she can get out of its way and remain dry. With respect to this residency she is a partner to what may or not have been a crime; it was necessary for her to go back for a second look.

"Josh, this is so sad."

She is greeting him at the door with a letter open in her hand. They have entered the kitchen to eat dinner and stay primarily silent until dinner is done. Tess continues to sip her wine and then reopens the letter on top of the cleared table. Josh is washing dishes; it is his time.

By the look on her face he realizes that there is some impending dilemma for which she wants his attention. And then she reveals it with some foresight of protection.

"I am afraid I must prepare you for some bad news. Apparently a rather decayed body was found at the turn of a river, at the base of a mountain you climbed in your youth. It is near the cabin you spent so many years living in."

The train has left the station, and this is a visual only he can see as a chief witness. The departure is not the time he has in mind, and there is no doubt more details of this little departure around the next bend in the tracks.   Tess has selected one paragraph in question and provides details of a necessary degree. The test of time is starting.

This is by no means a trivial amount of detail. Her statements and punctuation is neither hurried nor lost in translation; she continues to read on until the last sentence of this letter is forthcoming. She has actually moved in a manner to accentuate the punch of this last throw, when the scene is revealed as transcribed.

"They have reopened the investigation. It is a strain on the community, according to the Sherriff's spokesperson, besieged by the loss of one of their own. The locals clamoring for closure: observing the rules of engagement of what they term as 'this civilized community so shamed."

Tess has put down the letter and stares for his reaction to the tone and intent of the letter.

"Someone seems to be insinuating that you know more about what is to come out of this investigation."

She is standing now and her hands have dropped to her side.

Josh feels as though he has just enough time to catch up with this train—this scene he thought retired. Without so much as a far more revealing gesture he manages to push the letter to the opposite side of the table without ever picking it up. This duty has landed at his footsteps. He has the choice to address it or step out of its way. No sooner than he has departed with his answer, Tess counters in a manner her own way.

She wants them to visit the location. To hike up that very hill, cross that river, climb to the top ledge of that half dome and look down at that varied view. It is more than a kindly invitation; this is her means of final direction.

"There is no need to repeat myself, Josh. This is what we should do. I do not want you to brush this aside so quickly. I can read it in your face. Why would you not want to do this; he was your closest friend from what I could tell from all of those stories you retold time and time again."

This challenge to meet the future head on was received and rendered as thoughtfully as conceived. He had gone too quickly with his retort. To think that Tess did not address him unkindly; as he would have like to think considering the situation; she was able to secure his by in with little to no resistance even though he knew he would meet his own doom.

"My presence back there would not be met as so likely a return to a memory of my past. They would become so darn suspicious, Tess. Is this really the most appropriate use of time? What is your measure of insistence—to what gain?"

"I simply want to see if this thing can lead to a good story—a play of my own."

There was no need for her to repeat this—describing those extra details was all unnecessary for him to see that she was right. This story deserved to be looked into—it was as welcome as it was received. Josh was soon able to assure his counterpart that she was right to drive home this key and salient point.

"Would you like to direct this project, Tess?"

The look on her face was what he needed to receive. It was even warmer than before, and it had certainly grown friendlier in the absence of his interest to repress the regret that had grown around him.

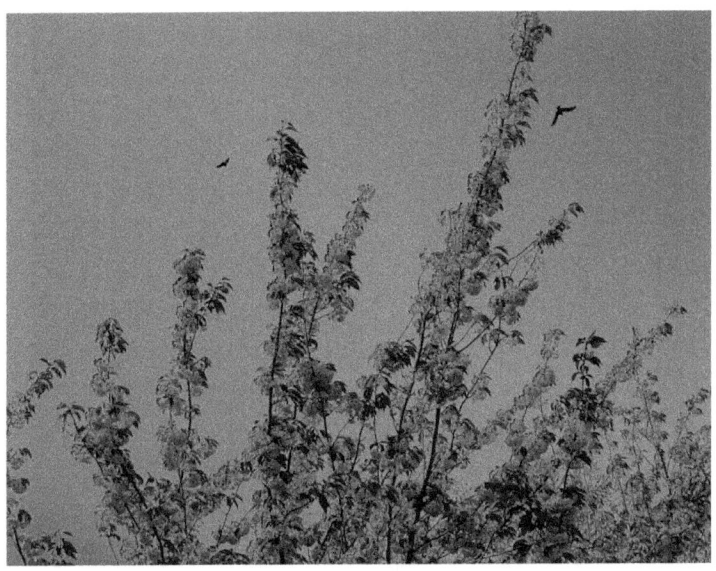

VOICE ONE: *It was always about Tess. Like two birds we are mated for life.*

COMMANDING VOICE (laughing): *Do not look at me that way. I am laughing with excitement; you have found your way. Those barriers you refused to pass are finally out of your way. And if I may add: she is darn charming: you have come to realize.*

VOICE ONE: *At least I do not have to dignify that: I have seen the light. I follow my own example: that day has come and I occupy it.*

Perceptive Sensations   Michael O'Connor

Screen Twenty-three

THAT FATEFUL DAY CAME when Josh was close to his limit of bantering and bartering with this new producer, and his ever engaging Tess who wanted to pursue the fate of a past associate and friend. He and Tess were packing and making ready for a trip to that past location in his life, with equal amounts of dread and fun.

The vehicle was full with baggage to sustain them both as well as an assortment of equipment to document the locale, hollows and plains of his young adult life so far off of the grid. This was an earlier start for both and they moved more in a dream state; she is moving over behind the wheel as she has promised to drive them there and back as part of the cost of entry. They are both in the vehicle but Josh is feeling kind of despondent knowing that there remains another chapter in that part of his life that has not been fully disclosed. He is caught in the crossroads between feeling lonely and being fulfilled by his past and present. What if they would soon collide; the limit of his semi consciousness state prevents him from fully acknowledging or appreciating the prospect of this impending conflict. There is just this vague feeling—a notion— of something that needs to be disclosed along the way. But in which way is not so apparent.

He feels for his true home as she is driving. Most of the departure and early set miles are a combination of silence, grunts and groans, and empty stomachs announcing the need to be cared for with diligence. They have reached a major milestone on this trip and Josh instructs Tess to pull into a known café, and appropriately enough a gas stop. They reach out for both nearly on autopilot. She pumps gas and hardly notices that Josh is already heading into the café to claim a good table with window side seating. He is nearing the limits of his anxious state.

The reception in the café is pleasant enough and it has a home spun feeling of the traditional with the leading edge of wireless network support for visitors, high definition television screens in most corners, and an array of single arm bandits waiting for the next fool to come along. Somewhat dejectedly he chooses to ignore it all after exchanging greetings with the waitress and ordering one coffee and one tea.

One of his more agreeable recollections of this stop was in the opposite of direction. It seemed as though each time he stopped here he was leaving rather than arriving. The directional change made him uneasy.

He was so inclined to simply get up and propose that they seek out another place altogether, but seeing Tess's road weary face makes him clam up and he gestures her to the opposite bench seat. Sliding in across worn and slightly torn material Tess makes all of the necessary adjustments before reaching out for his outstretched arm, and near simultaneously acquiring one of the two menus laying on the Formica tabletop.

This place has the feeling of home, had one spent time living in a café. His heart meant to be in the right place right now, but the grimace on his face was too easy to follow. He knew that she was going to call him on it eventually. His connection with the menu would not be undone by his mood or her intention to adjust it forcefully if she could.

"I wanted this trip to be pleasant for the both of us. When we finish eating I need your commitment to go forward. If not, let's spend the day heading back home and take a longer way to experience some of the local sightings."

She was done and he was done in. It was remarkable how fact she could connect into his world and nudge for the appropriate outcomes. The sight of her face lighting up above the streams of sunlight pouring in and across their table kind of melted his funk away. Soon they were happily talking about the trip and all that they wanted to accomplish: material for her play, and his wanting to simply survive this visit to his dubious past.

His only objection voiced during the meal was the desire for a safe return, considering the outstanding investigation which was still under way. This life lived so far on the outer edge squeezed his vision to a pinpoint sharpness. Would he survive was now master of his scanning ahead of all the possible outcomes. The tension was building considering that a local Sherriff's patrol vehicle was now parked outside and its two occupants were pouring out of either side and heading into this café.

They were hungry, otherwise Josh would most likely have had a heart attack—not so literally though. Consider the likelihood that both tables would simply chew and slurp, pay the bill, and then be on their merry way, respectively.

But then Tess began to flirt.

Tess and Josh have arrived in the center of this very rural town, thinking it was best to check into a motel before heading out to the cabin. She had wanted to widen her total experience with the charming scheme of this place and insisted they take a walk down the merry streets and outskirts of the town. There is this long row of open fence line that attracted her most, given that it was ornate with the cumulative works of local artisans, and it led to a very old barn that was immaculately well maintained and included an open courtyard and veranda covered with potato vines.

As they followed the path of the vines the fragrance of the white potato flowers was overwhelming to the point of a drunken stupor, until they reached out for balance. They had come to the end of the main street. The barn was now in full view and its internal cavity was so enormous that it easily housed two crop duster planes. It was a traveler's delight and Tess reached into her bag and began to document the entire scene with her expensive camera. There was no other way out of this building with the exception of the two large open doors at its front, past the courtyard and veranda. In doing so they had to pass one very large and happy woman who greeted them both as two of her long lost children.

"On gosh it has been so long. Well, I just cannot remember. Josh, how have you been, and who is the lovely princess?"

They had arrived. There was little doubt to the succession of greetings and promises that were being made on this very spot. And Tess stood there completely delighted with the attention and her carefully framed shot.

For Tess this was the start of an ongoing panorama of Josh's past relationships, only now she was being dragged in as well, as though she were always part of the stream of friendships. It was working in stages: a production on the fly directed by this one busy woman who wanted this center of the universe to know that one of their long lost sons had returned to the nest. Within a span of two and one half hours the visiting pair is pulled through a labyrinth of unmarked side streets, paths to seemingly nowhere, and knocks on doors leading to introductions to a sea of people for whom she may never remember one hour from now. Tess became exhausted by it all and Josh just seems to be taking it all in stride.

It is his obvious advantage that he never needs to introduce himself; having had one of those faces which never appears to have changed; all eyes recognize this man immediately.   Only Tess is provided with the requisite introductions.   It is all done in stages—she and the director become one.

At every intersection and crossroads there seems to be an immediate need to eat and drink as well. They are exposed to about as many cuisines as one can manage to work off on the next tug and pull toward the sequential locations and dwelling. None of it is particularly unusual, though Josh and Tess seem indifferent to the actual spreads. They are spurring of the moment: preciously or haphazardly arranged but not in the absence of a trail of leading question: both men and women appear on the scene with fresh picked vegetables and sumptuous fruit which are all regional.

Josh finds himself in someone's bathroom at long last and he is sitting down on a lid covered commode. There is no interest in its actual utility beyond being a comfortable place to hide out for a while. It is assuming on his part that Tess can handle herself in his absence. But then again, it was by her insistence that they are here in the first place. Be this a bathroom or a long and private hall, he enjoys sneaking off for any amount of time possible. To be so noticed and then hardly noticed at all is at the same time perplexing. A cheery and talkative Tess renders this her show as quickly on the mark of the next introduction.

So far no one has bothered to mention the subject of the fondness of a township for the local man gone down by the riverside. The visitors are never burdened with this local but bad news. No one seems particularly eager to yield to a public hearing of opinions or temperament with regard to the open investigation. There are no courtyard debates, as even as Josh crosses paths with several town officials. He has not been subjected to a single inquiry about his last visit.

Perhaps no one really knows for certain, given the trouble he took back then to slip into the outskirts of this town and make way to and from the cabin without notice. The burden is on them to pull these disparate pieces of the puzzle together. He is not inclined to reveal his part in the sequence of events, even though there is still a sense of intimacy between him and some of the residents. He does not want to be in anyone's crosshairs.

After the last interaction the pair is left with the lonesome burden of crossing back across the courtyard of that massive barn, before returning to the particular motel they had chosen to stay for the night. It is their turn to drift past a door that they can close, outside of the eyes and ears of the people on the street either driving or walking. The crisis of the ordeal is finally over at least for the time being. But what about when they trodden off outside: making way to a place to eat and get a suitable drink to calm the sting of overexposure: they must be on their best behavior to mingle again with this very friendly group. It will not suit them to arrive less clad than warranted of the blessed memory of one citizen who can no longer join them. This insight is that apparent.

The knowledge of nonverbal communication helps maintain a balance of how one may wish to be perceived even when not speaking. Josh feels he is courageously prepared for going one more round with the faces who enjoin him as they both walk past the door on entry into a popular eatery and bar. The room seems to acknowledge them both as highly familiar and greetings are called out from all corners of the main room of this rustic country palace. The service is immediate and thoughtful and a bit scary when drinks arrive even without asking. There is something going on but neither Josh nor Tess can put their fingers on it—it is never that charming.

Menus are in route and orders are finally taken after they have finished the first round. In this place in the world there is a strange custom where waitresses call out orders loudly, as though everyone in the bar needs to know what is happening. Interestingly enough this insipid table receives nods from several patrons that they have made the right choice. And then everyone goes back to their own business, respectively.

Josh knows it; he has witnessed this time and time again is this very corner of the bar. The evening will be a performance as much for the prodigal son who has returned with his fair maiden, as it will be for anyone who wants to return those knowing smiles and nods. Everything else is on stage in this performance—having not recognized it for what it was in the longest time Josh finally surrenders. It is a way of saying: "It is coming, just give it time."

Enter regret for the fan who forgets this until it is too late. It is points off for the traveler. This room is bright and the looks of everyone's faces sail across the room like a song that is sung in harmony.

Tess has recovered and has the patient fortitude to allow Josh to sit in silence and eat his meal. She is contented with the friendlier exposure she is receiving and tells Josh that she thinks it is very special. All around them there is this community beauty and the glamour of having been part of it all. After her controlled silence she spells this out for Josh and how she intends to render it for her challenging theatre. The world, she thinks, is giving her a fair turn at the controls of a director. But first she realizes that she has to sort it all out before the real intent of her play can be exposed.

"I do not think that my play will be about you returning to your past at all."

She sighs and then returns to her train of thought. Josh is listening more attentively.

"What I want to do most is portray the familiar, and then contrast it to the rather queer. There is hope in their collective faces, but there is also some underlying dread that I cannot quite put my finger on yet. What do you think, Josh?"

He stops eating, wipes his mouth and then places both hands on the table for emphasis.

"I believe that you were always perceptive. There is another layer, which is for sure. But I cannot tell you what it is—you need to discover this for yourself. It is all part of the process, Tess."

Tess is scribbling something important into her notebook. She has left her laptop in the motel room because she thought it might be rude in so intimate a place; having not wanted to embarrass Josh in front of his friends. And then she looked at him, and those eyes and the pouting suppression she wore on her lips demanded further qualification.

"Just dwell on it, Tess. It will come to you."

For those artisans and those who direct them patience takes the lead. Tess eventually becomes contented with the beauty of living and working in this small town, and the continual excuse to revisit some time period with what every person she crosses paths with so long as they can speak well of Josh. She has become more than an armchair director and takes the personal with the distant and blends them so well she might have lived here once as well.

Those days spent wandering around the river, meadows, and canyons; special treatment is taken in and out of that cabin; she seeks and finds details that even the longest resident pleas surprise. The nights she spends on long benches inside of barns, front and back porches, reveal stories and aspired tellers and at long last she thinks that her play has grown into a book. There is a whole new world in this place: hers is new and his is old, and the crossroads that are passed between them are starting to look whole. What is this world that she sees that Josh cares not to remember in such vivid detail It is the happiest he has seen her and it is no small miracle that his last spectacular moment spent in its past cannot be envisioned. It is still a mystery that the local authorities have not made their move to corner him and sit him down to backtrack on all that he holds to tightly to his chest these days, now marking on several weeks—just shy of one month.

The two of them have spent the last two weeks living in the cabin. What the Puppet Master cares about most now is doing nothing and nothing more. He thinks that the whole of the past affair is well behind him. There is a world beyond this unpleasant relationship with this locale, he thinks about this well out loud. He has already been asking himself if it really matters how much of a role he play in it anymore, but tends to dream of it with pertinent details in full review. He is host to an ongoing battle of the good and the bad during each unconscious moment; the incident that is never far away in the waking hours as well.

Tess does dwell on the mystery, and it does come to her that something is not quite clear. Is there any other effort she can put in it; an explanation in debate is put to the test at the edge of a cliff raising high above the horseshoe canyon she visits today.

"The ascent is harder than it looks, Tess. Are you sure you want to go through with this?"

Tess's feet and outstretched arms are finding sure footholds and cracks in granite as she inches up and above the green tipped tree line. The valley below comes in grand view. Her voice is filling the canyon with happy exclamations covering the river's wind, the golden fields to the west, and how small Josh is looking right now. Her precise wording rises high as she continues to climb, and one could think and be made perfectly clear that she might be horse in the throat if she continues this continuing bellowing.

"Tess, save your strength for the climb. I have been there so often—you do not have to describe it to me in such detail. Think of everyone who is in earshot. They are all locals and they know it intimately too."

He is happy for her; remembering the first instances of his climbs on the same cliff. It also made him happy to recollect, now through her eyes and her descriptions. So what if other were to come by, let her continue so long as it does not take her attention too far away from the task at hand. Tess is not more than half way up to an outcropping that drives Josh nearly to tears. Before other came he bent down to grab a fistful of dry dirt and let it pour between spread fingers. What was he sitting on but the very spot of a fateful impact? If others came by would they watch his nervous pacing or the ascent of a smaller woman reaching out for the flat spot on that cliff?

This was the matter at hand. He continued to watch her and was wishing that she were more of a pro, as she slips and hangs on for her dear life jamming clenched fists into crevasses barely wider than the thickness of her hands. Josh feels the pressure on his own as if he is up there with her now. But instead he is taking up some necessary slack in her safety rope. He had the clear mind and fortitude not to let her attempt the ascent freehand.

Tess screams just short of the outcropping. Her head is turned inward and away from the winding river below, and she can only dimly remember just how far she is above the tips of those green pines. Before this moment nothing could have made her any happier than to have witnessed firsthand a sport that Josh regaled on time and time again. If she could just remember now to stay very calm; such is the advice he has given her and it is recalls as she is hanging on—just shy of a life threatening slip. For the moment she does not resign from the task at hand even after watching the slow trickles of blood that cross both of her forearms.

Like he had said she needs her utmost concentration and strength to make it up above the lip of the outcropping. She is pulling out her fist and grasping air and then sharp granite one hand before another. She is singing, but not in a manner that is noticeable on the ground. Her fear is a steady foe—granite hurts—feet scramble to make haste in pushing her up and over. Tess has risen above it and makes it know to a very nervous Josh on less steady ground at the base of this half dome.

"How are you feeling, Tess?"

Perhaps he too is feeling sorry for her dilemma, in spite of his having to surpass this hurtle a short lifetime ago. The thought occurs to him to praise her now that she is sitting upright and balanced on the top of the ledge. He is disinterested in who is coming up behind him and continues to look up. The thought has never occurred to him that it might be her—the other roommate.

All else fades away from his mind; he will not let his focus train away from the woman above. But then the other voice crack open.

"Is this a joke? Josh you are fucking kidding. Is letting her go up there some kind of bizarre game? I swear I promised myself I would knock you off if you ascended today. Look at me Josh, tell me you won't take the same wonton care you did for him."

Long ago she had mastery of this and held the rope steady for him as he made his way for the first and second time. He had made her promise never to take her eyes off of him until he was completely secure. It dawned on him now that her purpose was to take his focus off the game. The safety rope was taught enough when he let his head tilt away from Tess and over to the woman staring face-to-face. This all mattered as much then as it does now, yet he feels as though he is in exile away from the spot he was required to retain. Moments followed and the gravity of the situation was becoming graver a time went on. Pity Tess: not knowing what was going on.

"I made the same promise to you that I made to him. For a space in time I never let go. But I ask you now: how do you relate to this? You can never know the exact circumstance of that night, can you?"

Tess's fate was in his hands. She did not know how to descend when the time arrives, without his careful directions. And thus he attempted to explain this to the woman but her intent was so far away. From the moment he heard her voice cry out angrily, he knew that she was not going to leave him be.

"Your holding on is not the point at all, Josh. You can look for redemption on your own accord—that is not why I am here. Will you leave her to the fate of the river as well? Why, Josh, don't you shout that up to her and explain it all away. Go ahead, do it in your own words."

Could he ever redeem that promise he made to them both—long past. When he let his eyes divert for them time it took her to say her piece Tess had repositioned herself and was now standing up on the ledge with her back pressed into the granite wall. She was exiled now. He could relate to it all without having to hear it in her trembling voice.

"I will not look away. If it is the last thing I do I will not allow myself to lose focus today. Say what you must— I will not contest it. You were not here to see his fall. You did not listen in to the conversation immediately preceding. It will take time for me to explain everything that had gone so wrong that night—not now; not now least of all."

From this moment on she did not speak of it during his talking Tess off of the outcropping, readying her for the challenging descent. He must use this space in time to try to forget the trauma of his past—the regret of this other woman. Faithful to the woman above and her intent to chronicle everything up to this moment, his forthright commission continues. The rope is loosened and then taut just at the appropriate span of time. Tess is lowering more slowly than he could have imagined. Would this all be worth telling in some act of the play that she insinuated to now be a book? There is a final act or chapter and he is going to let this one be written as a happy one.

For there it is in front of him the answer to his conflict. If the truth is worth telling at all, let it be in the moment of time which matters the most. Until she is down he will spin the tale any which way he wants. And therefore her life is in his hand s and it is moving very slowly.

The nature of being human is best stated by the strings which have been cut ways. It is an aged old story of Puppet Theatre. Never mind that this is the twenty-first century—the past is duly noted as read. And with all the interest one director might have in mind for the perfect production, the plot is never as clear as when the final curtain is parted and the cast and crew step outside of their comfort zone. Read the looks on all of those faces who sat patiently waiting for this theatre to end.

Tess is returned to the ground and all that she can see is the smile across Josh's face. They are alone, the two of them—this interest is their own. She is tired and in pain but tell him that the narrow escape off of the face of half dome was worth it. It is a lesson to be learned, but not in the comfort of home. There is nothing vague at all in his reply. He tells her that he loves her, and is please that she has done this task so well.

"However, that said, if you ever want to do this again I will do everything in my power to talk you out of it. Look at my shirt—it is covered with perspiration—now your blood. Was it all worth it to you?"

Her answer is short but to the point. Indeed her experience will find a suitable closing for whatever she intend to write—this event that has ended well. She gives Josh a brief look into her window of time and has already chronicled several new chapters.

This brief look has been afforded the audience this small test in time.

"What ever happened to your friend no longer matters to me. I do not say this unkindly. If I were to have a glimpse into what happened ahead of my climb I know I would never have made it up there, or down. It certainly does not matter to me now. One day I might ask you to explain. But for now let's go back to the cabin and celebrate. I am dirty, hurting and ecstatic, as you can certainly relate."

Fade out, this sun is setting. The walk across the river is assured; hand in hand the canyon is left empty and the tip of half dome is still peaking out above the tree line for anyone who's still watching. And the sound of this pair's feet crunch the dirt and gravel path that leads them all the way back to the cabin. It is empty when they are arriving, as it is left empty when they leave for this last time.

A curtain has certainly closed. There is a slow and labored response followed by rapture applause. This theatre is done.

Bring out that ghost light.

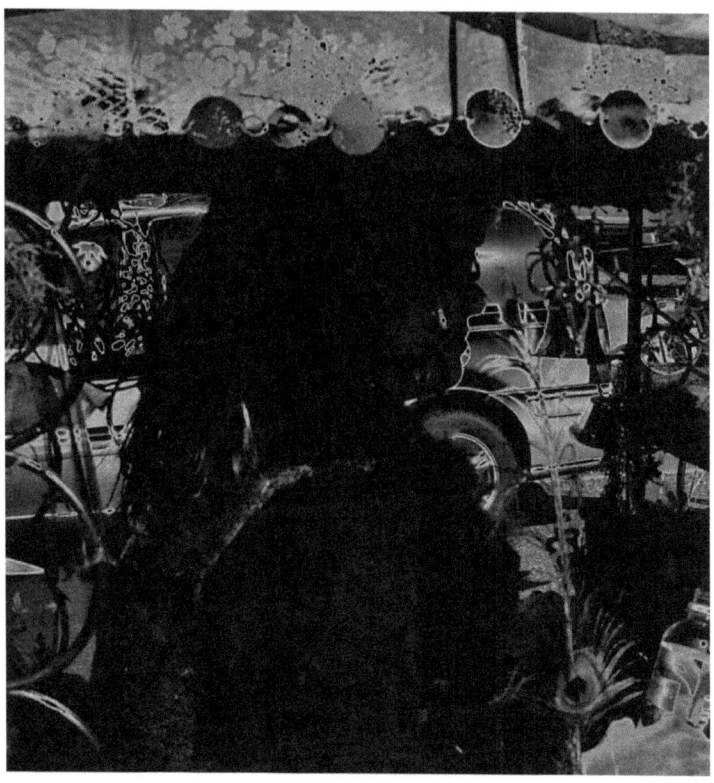

VOICE ONE: *Had I made the time I would have picked her out in this crowd sooner rather than later. The problem is this target keeps on moving. For my own accord I hope that I can maintain a better means of perceptive sensation.*

I have been given another chance to take it all in and retain it if I so desire. I do; I will.

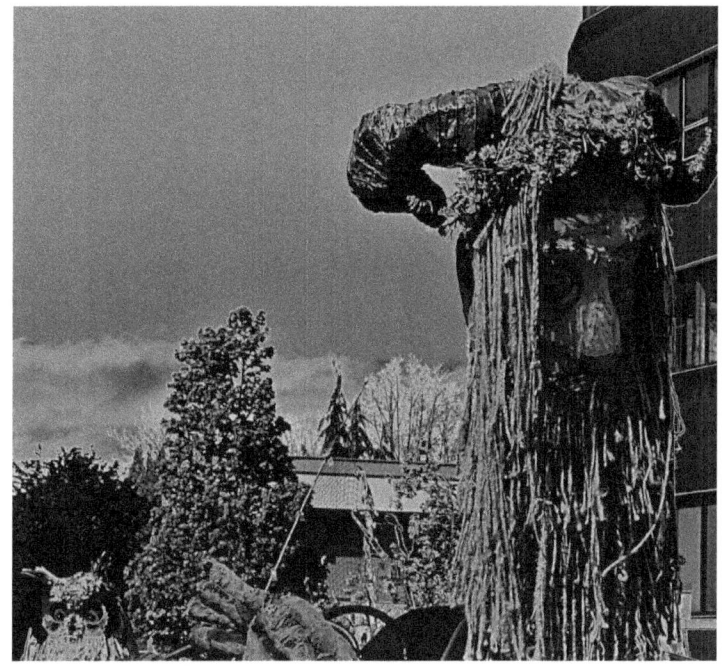

UNSYMPATHETIC VOICE: *Instead of hanging your head on a pole.*

VOICE ONE: *That would not be my first choice—this time.*

Repeat this as often as is necessary.

Exit this Stage

THE NIGHT AFTER THE CURTAINS CLOSED one would swear that the sky became darker at the precise moment the two sides touched. The sky was a slate gray ceiling with little color showing through. Even when the sun appeared close to the westerly horizon one's eye peered for a sliver of orange, red and yellow. In the mind's eye they were there sure enough. But by the time the last glimpse dropped below the line as far as the eyes could see the only glimmer of hope was silver.   What was the consequence of closure?

Night comes bearing a dire warning that it may rain. It is not likely that there will be a reprieve from this set in mood which stayed parallel to the movements just outside of the building.   This presence issues not one warning as much as it presents an enticing point across the parking lot to fix one's eyes upon for something over boredom.   The figure is a dark silhouette against a building; the struggle to stay under its eaves is rough enough against the hard driving rain that finally makes its way to the concrete surface. One step is further from the other; stride gives way to a run. It is just a few degrees short of a record for getting from front door to inside of the only automobile left in this large parking lot. The act is more peculiar to the dive inside and the loud shutting of a metal door to body. It is done in haste should the wind driven rain slide sideways any stronger.

Brisk as it may seem the body inside of the vehicle is seen shaking and then wiping up. The head and shoulders are tilted and a shirt is pulled over revealing a ghost white torso, as if a sail were unfurled from a mast on a sailboat. The shaking and brisk rubbing continue, and perhaps excessively hard but short of violent. Was there really that much damage?

One would think that there is little left to remark about someone getting out of the rain, albeit too late. This scene is accompanied by a sideways sheen of watery spray and one swears it is at ninety degrees. The good news, if there is any at this precise moment of time, is that it is short and it is definitely letting up. How one can see into the night with calm as this in climate change gets underway, all sort of scenarios can be drawn: dress and drive, stay and sort it all out, or draw back the driver's side seat and sleeping it all off. When we are able to see again it will be nearly dawn.

At about four-twenty in the morning the sun cracks open a once darkened sky to the east and it floods the solo car in the parking lot with illumination and warmth. The occupant stirs and is already awake and there is an open mouth that gives up all hope of stifling a giant yawn. Would there have been a flock of morning water birds flying past at this specific time they could have found safe harbor in this parking lot it was that flooded from the previous night's storm. If there were a more precise measurement it would have appeared that it would make at least one fathom of cold water just by appearance alone.

The bottom of this automobile actually gives the appearance of being covered. The reflection is so stilled yet ever surreal.

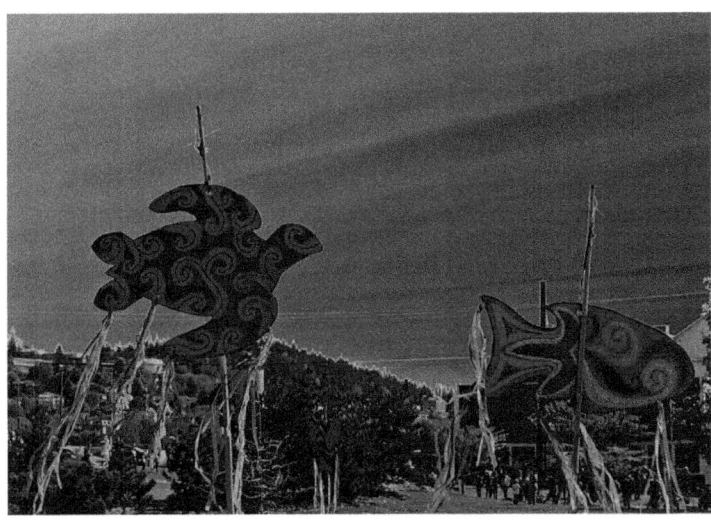

www.ingramcontent.com/pod-product-compliance
Lightning Source LLC
Chambersburg PA
CBHW051438170526
45166CB00001B/37